Warrior in Wel Boots

Cornelius Carr

This title is intended for the enjoyment of adults, and is not recommended for children due to the mature content it contains.

A CIP catalogue record for this book is available from the British Library.
Paperback ISBN: 979-8366525022

Table of Content

Dedication

For

My mam, dad, sister Susan, my two sons Jake and Samuel,
and soul mate Jan

With love

And to the man who helped me find my gift, Marty Turner

About the Author

This book was written by Jan Adkins and Cornelius Carr

Jan Adkins

Jan's background is in theatre, both in performance and management. Jan lives with Cornelius in the Gower Peninsula, near Swansea, Wales. She says Gower is her spiritual home. It's where she was born and spent all of her childhood.

Jan is a creative person and loved working with her partner Cornelius in writing Warrior in Wellington Boots, and she said it was a privilege hearing Cornelius's memoirs for the first time. Jan wanted to capture on paper Cornelius's words as he spoke them, providing readers with the true essence of Cornelius's character.

Jan is a mother to Leanne and Kirsty and has five grandchildren, Sam, Ashleigh, Zac, Max, and Chloe.

Cornelius Carr

Cornelius was born John Carr but changed his name when he became a professional boxer in honour of his late father, whose name was Cornelius Carr. Cornelius began boxing at the age of eleven, turning professional at the age of eighteen.

Cornelius was a professional boxer born in Grangetown, Middlesbrough, England. He won the British Super Middleweight title in 1994 and later won the WBF World Championship Middleweight title in 1999. Cornelius has travelled all over the world during his career and is now settled in North Gower, near Swansea, Wales.

He is a proud father to Jake and Samuel.

Acknowledgment

Thanks to:

Jan Adkins, Marty Turner, Shaun Lacey, Lilian Hogarth, Anne Kennedy, Tyler Ford, Jason Chapman, Ilie Hewitt, Susan Carr, John Nesbitt, Steve Carney and Mark Rogers

Preface

Everyone has a story to tell; some of us have interesting tales about remarkable occurrences that have been life changing. I have never thought that my life was remarkable, but I suppose it has been in many ways. My journey through life has certainly been an interesting one so far; I have relayed my memoirs to share with the world. I am a fatalist; I believe we all have a purpose in life and that our paths are mapped out for us. There are many twists and turns throughout our life journey; some people can take the wrong path, and others take the right path, and there is a fine line between the two paths.

We are also influenced by the people around us: parents, siblings, partners, family members, friends, and our community. Sometimes individuals suffer from bad luck, too, and through no fault of their own, they end up going down the wrong road, or they suffer tragic circumstances. I have learned a great deal of information about the chain of people from my past since researching for this book, and I have unlocked many eye-opening secrets about my family. I understand that the choices we make in our lives (good or bad) can have a great impact on future generations.

Parents play such important roles in our lives; as children, we need guidance, discipline, nurture, support, and love. It's a lottery when it comes to parenting, we can't choose who our parents are or the environment we grow up in. We accept our surroundings as children. It's when we reach a certain age that we assess our lives and question who we are. We begin to compare ourselves with other people, and it could be materially, physically, or emotionally. When I was growing up, I accepted everything that was thrown at me; my childhood was far from 'normal,' and I thought at the time that most kids lived like me.

We all have a life force within us, which we call a personality, a soul, which gives us our own unique character. We are all different, and our character traits can also determine what kind of a life we have in front of us. Some of my characteristics made me who I am: I'm stubborn, determined, ambitious, persistent, impulsive, loyal, and strong-minded. I have negative traits, too, like us all, but it's the good traits that have driven me and have provided me with a fulfilled life. I have also made bad decisions in my life and have had to live with them. I'm no different from anyone else. I'm not afraid to admit that I have made mistakes that had a great impact on my life, particularly during my boxing career.

Everyone has a story to tell; it's strange to think that a large part of my life can be summed up in a book that will take a few hours to read. Writing this book has been an emotional journey. I have opened my soul to the world, and everything I have written is an honest view of my life. A story told is a life lived; this is my story.

Round One – Fighting

I was exhausted and drained both physically and mentally; I felt the lovely cool water running from the top of my head and trickling down my bare back; it was refreshing to feel the coldness of the water on my steaming hot, sweaty skin. I was so hot from the heat of the ring lights, the humidity which emanated from the bodies of the 4,000 spectators in the arena, and of course, from boxing. I had fought solidly for eleven three-minute rounds. I sat on the stool numbly and listened to the words of my trainer Chris, "Keep doing what you are doing! Get some body punches in! Be smart. Don't get reckless, he'll come after you this round because you're in front." All the words he fired at me came loud and fast. I tried to focus. I had one minute to recover before the last round of the fight began. I needed to relax and get as much oxygen into my lungs as possible, breathing slowly and deeply. Then the announcer said, "Seconds out, twelfth and final round." I heard the bell ring signalling for the fight to resume, and bounced up from the stool, the referee brought us fighters together, and we both stood up in the centre of the ring and touched gloves. The noise in the arena was overwhelming. I did my best to blank it out, focusing on the target in front of me. I faced my opponent, and the pace of the fighting was still fast, even though it was the twelfth round.

I realised at that point that I had been in the ring with a highly skilled fighter, he was one of the first boxers that stood in front of me, and I struggled to hit him cleanly. All the years of my dedication and hard work to the sport of boxing will be summed up in this round. I had to win. I wouldn't allow my opponent to dominate any part of the round, and if he threw one punch, I threw two. My opponent came at me like a lion, wanting to finish me off, eager to tear me apart, but I countered well. I didn't want the fight to end with him knocking me out. When I was in the middle of the battle in the ring, I only picked up on certain voices, voices that were important to me, like my trainers' voices; everyone else's voices just became like white noise. I heard Damien shouting from my corner, "Last thirty seconds! Dig in, Corny!" I bit down on my gum shield and dug in as best as I could. The last thirty seconds seemed to drag on forever, but I drew strength from somewhere deep within, I felt powerful energy spurring me on, and I finished the round strongly. The bell rang. I was relieved. The fight was over in more ways than one.

From the moment we are born, there is a fight for survival; it's instinctive. We don't really think about being born, none of us can remember our birth, and no one can tell us what it's like to die. I suppose birth and death are nature's secrets. I read somewhere that some people believe that being born is a traumatic event, but we have no memory of it.

My fight for survival began when I drew my first breath at thirteen minutes past eight in the morning on 9th April

1969, at Middlesbrough General Hospital, and our mam's horrific battle began four years previously when she had a massive stroke giving birth to my sister Susan when she was just thirty-two years old.

Our Sue and I had responsibilities that other kids our age didn't have. We didn't realise it at the time, but we were young carers, and it was a big role for us to play. Although we took our responsibilities in our stride and accepted our commitment to care for our mam, we loved her. We just wanted her to be happy and do whatever was required of us without complaining. I sometimes had to bathe our mam, and seeing her naked became second nature to me; washing her was something that just had to be done. We had a small bath, which we found difficult getting our mam into, and there was a shower of sorts above the bath. The shower was pretty useless, the water pressure was weak, and the water used to splutter out of the nozzle head slowly. It was so frustrating to use on our mam when we tried to wash her with it. Because our Sue was older than me, she had more responsibility as our mam's carer, and it must have made a tremendous impact on her teenage years, especially when she wanted to go out with her friends and had to stay in and care for our mam instead. We looked after our mam because if we didn't do it, who would? We didn't have any support from social services.

As a young kid, I was always toy-fighting with other kids on the street, and it was a way of life. When I was nine years old, there was one boy who was about three years older than me who started picking on me and calling me names. I was mainly bullied because my mam was disabled, and the local kids used to make fun of me; they'd shout at me, "Your mam is a spacker!" I hated it. I could feel the anger burning inside me because of the daily taunting. One day I had enough, and I retaliated; I smashed the older boy's head against a parked car door about four times until some other kids pulled me off him. I was annoyed that they stopped me because I really wanted to finish the job. I wasn't a violent boy at heart, and I think that if I had grown up in a different environment and time, I would have been a completely different person. After that incident, I started to gain respect amongst the other kids, and I liked it. At that young age, I started to get a reputation as a fighter, and I enjoyed the feeling. I wasn't a bully, though. I didn't pick on kids. I was just fearless, not afraid to fight anyone who wanted a go. Violence was normality. I sometimes talk to people about my childhood and tell them about the fights I had from a young age. I was shocked to learn that many people have never had a fight in their lives. I accepted that fighting came with the territory. If you didn't fight the bullies, you became a victim, and your life would become a misery. Life in 1970s Grangetown was tough, I didn't know any different. This was my life, my community, and it really was survival of the fittest. I lived on a big council estate, on the street called Coniston Road. It was a community, though; it was safe to leave your doors open, and no one would steal anything. That's mainly because we had nothing much to steal; we had nothing materially but had one another. Grangetown was my home. It's near Middlesbrough in the North East of England. I get annoyed when people ask me if I'm a Geordie (people from Newcastle), I am a Grangetowner, and my accent is completely different.

My mother, Mildred Carr (Millie Potter), was from South Bank and had two sisters and a brother: my Aunt Nina, Aunt Joan and Uncle Hughie (I have traced the Potters, our mam's ancestors, back to the 18th Century, I looked at the Census records, and discovered they were farmers from Cornwall who must have migrated to Middlesbrough during the industrial revolution looking for work). Many people came to Middlesbrough looking for work, iron ore was discovered in Eston Hills, and this changed the face of the area forever. It made many people wealthy and turned sleepy little hamlets into a landscape of smoking furnaces. We all need money to survive, some people are fortunate and inherit wealth, and some people work hard their entire lives, just keeping their heads above water, and some people are ambitious and risk takers, creating their own wealth. It would be a strange world if all human beings were the same. There will always be the workers and the bosses; it's a way of keeping the cogs turning in our society.

Bolckow, Vaughan & Co were industrialists and had plans to develop Grangetown and build more streets and shops in 1895. Some of the streets in Grangetown were named in honour of Bolckow, Vaughan and associates. My family were one of the first families to move into the exciting new housing development that Heinrich Bolckow planned. Joseph Carr, my great grandfather, opened a butcher's shop on the new street, Whitworth Road. Grangetown became a thriving town due to the industry.

I knew Bolckow Road well. It was a place that would make me into the man I am today. Many times, I had to fight my way down it; all the neighbourhood thugs hung about there, and as a small boy, I often had to run the gauntlet trying to avoid a beating. It's hard to imagine today that a small seven-year-old boy was allowed to go down a dangerous street on his own and get beaten up. It wasn't that long ago, and thankfully times have changed. I never knew the history behind the road or really cared; most of us don't think about road names and how they originated. Later Bolckow Road would become a special road for me, like the Yellow Brick Road in the Wizard of Oz, leading me to special people and to a door that would define my life.

My family was a small unit of four, I did have aunts and cousins on our mam's side who I used to visit now and then, but there were no relatives on our dad's side that I knew of. I've checked the old census records recently and discovered that our dad came from a large family, with a long line of Cornelius's and John Thomas's. I found it strange that there was no connection to our dad's side of the family when I was young. I discovered that my grandfather Cornelius was taken to court by his brother George who wanted a share of the butcher business. George won the court case and was awarded a few thousand pounds when the business was sold. The two brothers didn't speak to one another after the dispute, and that is why I never knew any of the Carr family. The fighting between the two siblings ensured that I had no relationship with any of the Carr family, and I missed out on having an extended family who might have had a positive impact on my life.

I think that our dad was too strict with Susan. If she were five minutes late home, he would take off his belt and whip her with it. I remember being in my bedroom whilst she took a beating one evening, and I tried my best to block out her screams by putting a pillow over my ears, but it didn't work; I could still hear them. After Sue's beating, she would come to my bedroom, and I tried to comfort her. She was about fourteen years old, and I was ten. I said angrily as I hugged her, "When I grow up, I'm going to give him the fucking belt!" I was so angry at him. I wanted to physically hurt him, to punish him for what he had done to my sister. I hated the way he became violent after a session on the booze. Susan and I would cuddle together, crying and eventually fall asleep in one another's arms. The following morning our dad would act as if nothing had happened, whistling whilst he fried his breakfast, and I would look at him in disgust, thinking about what he had done to my sister. I think our dad left emotional scars, which would be revealed later in Susan's life; she was nervous around our dad.

I can also remember feeling the whips of his leather belt on one occasion; it was when I was ten years old. I had 'borrowed' a boy's bike and took it up the hills. The boy went and told our dad that I had taken his bike. When I returned home, I took the bike back to the boy who told me he had reported me to our dad, and I shit myself knowing I was in big trouble. When I arrived home, I thought my luck was in, and I'd gotten away with it because our dad wasn't at home. I sat down to watch TV for a while, and then I heard the front door opening. Our dad appeared in the living room doorway with a look on his face that would scare the crap out of you. He was furious and shouted at me, "You had no right to take that boy's bike!" I was so scared. I knew what was coming. I tried to talk my way out of it, "I gave it back, dad, I gave it back." He just silently unbuckled his belt and gave me three quick swipes of the leather. It didn't really hurt me physically. I was wearing thick clothing, but mentally it has stuck with me. It was the first time I had felt the wrath of my father, and it was the actual act of him taking off his belt and hitting me with it that upset me the most.

He only ever hit me a few times in my life, but when he did, I felt the emotional pain. I never wanted to disappoint our dad and make him feel that he had to punish me physically to keep me in line. I've thought about it over the years. Maybe his mam punished him like that; perhaps it was the only form of discipline he knew. I don't want to make excuses for violence, but I'm trying to understand why he did it. It made me the opposite of my sons. I have been laid back, sometimes too laid back perhaps, never using violence to discipline them, I'm not sure what the answer is when it comes to punishing children, but today I feel there is a lack of respect from children towards parents and authority figures, like teachers and the police. I'm not sure what the solution is, but I feel it's important for kids to understand there are boundaries, maybe that's why boxing worked for me, it gave me the discipline that I needed, and it taught me how to respect others.

My mam worked as a conductress/clippie on the buses for years before she married our dad. I think she met him on a bus whilst she was working. Our dad had never learned to drive, he sometimes took the bus to work, but his main mode of transport was his bike or his horse and cart. In Middlesbrough, there were trolley buses run by electricity. I'm not sure if my mam worked on the electric trolley buses or not. Public transport using electricity was very advanced back in the 1950s, it was ironic that the trolley buses were eco-friendly, but the surrounding industry belched out all kinds of shit.

I'm not sure how long my parents were courting before they got married in April 1964. As I matured, I wanted to discover more about my family. I suppose we all want to know where we came from and the characters who played their part in our existence, our bloodline. I didn't know about the Carr side of the family and wanted to find out about them. I recently spoke to relatives on our dad's side of the family, Ann Kennedy and Lilian Hogan, her sister (who were formerly Metcalfe's) from Grangetown, who informed me about our dad's mam, Lizzie Carr (formerly Metcalfe).

Lilian was at Lizzie's one morning when she heard Lizzie asking our dad, "What do you want for breakfast?" Our dad replied. "I haven't got time for breakfast," Lizzie asked why, and our dad said, "I'm getting married today." My grandmother Lizzie was in shock. She was devastated. She didn't know he was getting married. It seemed a crazy thing to do to her, not to ask your mam to your wedding after everything she had done for him. One of the reasons might have been that Lizzie always thought that there wasn't a woman who was good enough for our dad. Our dad hadn't introduced our mam to his mother or any members of his family, and I'm not sure why he did that. It's as if he wanted to keep our mam a secret.

Our dad was ten years older than our mam. They married later in life, our dad was forty-one, and our mam was thirty-one. There is a photo which was taken on their wedding day with my father looking as if he'd rather be somewhere else. He didn't look happy, considering it was his big day. Our dad was from Grangetown, just a mile from Southbank, where our mam was from. Our dad could spruce himself up to look smart. His hair was thinning, and he started losing it from a young age, but this didn't bother him. He could cover his hair loss with his trademark trilby hat.

Cornelius And Millie Carr On Their Wedding Day - John 'Cornelius' Carr's Parents

Our dad had a responsible and dangerous job which he had been doing since he was a young boy. He had started work at the steelworks at the age of fourteen, which was the age most children left school in the 1940s. He was a big, strong, hard man with a beer belly; he looked a bit like a traveller, always wore a checked shirt, heavy blue jeans with a thick brown leather belt (I knew the belt well because my sister and I were beaten with it, mainly my sister, and I hated him for that), big hob-nailed boots, and a trilby hat with a feather. I wonder if the Carr's had any traveller genes as he loved wheeling and dealing, horses, gambling, drinking (Newcastle Brown Ale and Tetley) and the occasional street fight. Our dad was a tough man in many ways, and he had difficulty showing his emotions, especially towards my sister. He appeared to treat us differently.

Lizzie Carr, my grandmother, was a tiny lady under five feet tall, but she had a huge personality. She tried her best to keep our dad in line. Dad was a big, strong muscular man and a real character. Our dad's first cousin was Lennie Metcalfe. They were like brothers and were renowned in the Grangetown area for drinking and fighting, possibly 'The Krays' of Grangetown. During the late 1940s and early 1950s, the main drinking hole for the duo was Dickie Dye's club, and Lizzie would often go to the club late at night, peer through the window to see if our dad were there, and if she found him, she would go inside, and just signal silently motioning with her thumb for him to go home. No women were allowed in bars during that time, but Lizzie didn't care. If she wanted her son to come home, she went inside any pub or club to get him. Our dad wouldn't argue with her; he'd neck down his pint quickly, put his trilby hat on and then stagger out of the pub and follow Lizzie home like a little lamb. It must have looked funny, a little lady marching ahead followed by a big lump of a man staggering behind her. Sometimes our dad would be so drunk that he would step over the threshold in his terrace house in Bessemer Street, collapse in a heap, and fall onto one of the many sheepskin rugs in the hallway. He was too heavy for little Lizzie to move, so she would call a neighbour to help shift our dad's large body by dragging him on the rug into the front room to sleep off the booze all night.

Apparently, our dad was spoilt. My grandmother Lizzie idolised her son. This isn't surprising that she adored him so much. She had lost a son when he was six years old to Polio (our dad's younger brother John), and she had also lost her husband when she was a young woman. My grandfather died from septicaemia due to stepping on a nail in the garden, and the wound got infected. He died in 1929 when he was fifty-three years old. Our dad was only seven years old when he lost his father. Lizzie was very protective of our dad and was a wealthy woman, inheriting £632 in 1929 after the death of her husband. I'm not exactly sure what happened to the Carr wealth, but I know I didn't see any of it.

We were always skint, the rent man used to call round every week to collect his money, and quite often, we didn't have the cash. He would knock on the door, and we'd quickly turn the telly off, freeze looking at each other wide-eyed, and put our fingers to our mouths. Sometimes he'd shout through the letterbox, "I know you're in there, Mrs

Carr. You'll have to pay double next week." As soon as he'd leave, we'd say, "That was close." Turn the telly back on and resume our positions. The rent man wasn't being nasty; he was just doing his job. I suppose there were many people like us on our estate. His job must have been difficult, dealing with poor families like mine, poor sod.

We were always behind with the rent payments; that was our life, always short of cash, always rummaging around in coat pockets, looking under sofa cushions, and in old purses or handbags scrabbling for a few pence. We had an electric pay-as-you-go meter installed because we couldn't pay our electric bills on a monthly basis. The utility companies decided to install the meters for hard-up families like ours. Each meter needed 50 pence pieces, which were inserted in a slot. Sometimes the electricity would switch off without warning when the meter was out of money, we didn't have any more money to put in the meter, and sometimes we spent days with no electricity until our mam received her disability money and family allowance. Sue and I were both young carers, and we didn't have any financial support like carers have today. I hated being skint, and that poverty feeling was horrible, but perhaps it inspired me to better myself, and even now, I worry about being in that awful position again. At times in desperation, our mam would tell me to go across the road to see Mrs Coxen and ask her if we could borrow 50 pence for the meter. Funnily enough, Mrs Coxen always had a spare 50 pence, I think she was prepared for us to ask for them, and she never ever refused to lend us the money. Mrs Coxen was the first debtor to be repaid when our mam received her social payments, and we were always grateful to Mrs Coxen; she was a lovely lady.

Our mam was a singer, not a professional singer, but someone who just loved to sing, anywhere she had an audience, especially around the pubs in South Bank, she was a real character: loud, happy, funny, a little overweight, and she loved a pint of beer, mainly Tetley (Tetley was one of the largest breweries in the North of England). When she gave birth to me, our mam was disabled; paralysed down one side of her body from her first stroke, which happened during the birth of my sister Susan. Our mam had to stay in hospital for months after she had her first stroke, she nearly died, and the effects of the stroke were life-changing for her. In the 1960s, pregnant women weren't monitored as well as today, I'm not sure if her blood pressure had been checked etc., but if it were today, I'm sure the stroke could have been prevented. Statistics are that 9 out of 10 strokes can be avoided, life is like the flip of a coin; it can change in an instant, and life for our mam became a struggle; she was a fighter, though.

I would have loved to have spoken to our mam about many things, including all the hardships she faced and how she felt about her life, but when you're young, you are not really interested or aware of the sacrifices your parents make or think about their lives from their perspective. It's only when you are mature enough to understand, or you are a parent yourself, that you wonder how the hell they managed to face life's challenges. Having a conversation of any kind was difficult with our mam due to her speech impairment. The numerous strokes had taken their toll on her ability to communicate verbally. She could understand everything I said, but she found it difficult to put her thoughts into words, and she often became frustrated when trying to express herself. She had numerous strokes after the initial big one; therefore, her health was fragile, and she was susceptible to having more strokes, which she had over the years. Strokes have a devastating impact on the person affected and the people around them.

The first time I ever saw live boxing was at The British Legion Club in Grangetown. The Club was close to all the shops, and there would be a gang of us hanging about in that area. Nothing was too hot nor too heavy for us. We would do anything for a buzz, and we weren't stealing or destroying people's property. We were just naughty boys having playful fun. One summer evening, we were all messing about outside the Legion, and Stevie Carney looked through a window in the Legion where there was a small gap in the curtains and noticed that some lads were boxing. We all took turns to have a look through the window, and I was mesmerised. At that point, I didn't have an interest in boxing, but I was fascinated by the way the young boxers were performing and skilfully moving around in the ring.

The lads kept shoving me out of the way because I was taking too long to look at the boxers; we were all jockeying for position at the window to see the boxing action. We were making a noise shouting and swearing at each other whilst we wrestled at the window, and someone saw us from inside the Legion and pulled the curtains together, closing them tightly so that we couldn't see inside and ending the entertainment. We shouted, "Wanker!" and ran off. I didn't know then that it was Marty's lads boxing from Grangetown Boxing Club, the Club that would make me into the person I am today.

Round Two – First Memories

My full name John Thomas Carr is a traditional one that I inherited from previous ancestors, who came originally from Shotton Colliery, Durham, England. My Great Grandfather was Joseph Carr, who moved from Shotton Colliery, Durham, to Grangetown to open his butcher's business. He must have been an ambitious man and a hard worker, building up his business from scratch. He had started life working as a young boy in the colliery and took the leap to open his shop, which was located on 42 Whitworth Road, Grangetown, which is mentioned in the archives in 1890.

Sadly, I only have a handful of photographs of my grandparents and parents; not many people took photographs in those days. Our dad's perception of his mother was that she was a petite lady who was extremely strict. Maybe our dad felt the leather strap too. I think he respected her and feared her, but he didn't talk much about her.

Perhaps she was the reason why he married our mam late in life, he didn't want to leave his mother alone, perhaps he thought she wouldn't survive without him, perhaps that's why he secretly married, he didn't want to upset his mother. There are so many unanswered questions, and the answers have been taken away and buried with the only people who could have answered them.

When I was a child, one of my father's passions was his allotment, he grew all sorts of vegetables and bred pigs, chickens, and other animals to eat and sell. The allotment became my haven as a boy; it was like a little farm with all sorts of animals: Geese, rabbits, chickens, and pigs. We always had dogs, too, mainly to guard the other animals. There was a big steel gate at the entrance to the allotment. Inside the gate, there was lots of wood stacked for fuel for the boiler. There were vegetable plots, animal pens, and a little hut. I can smell that hut now. It was a pleasant smell. It made me feel safe and warm, and the aroma was a mixture of boiling food for the pigs and the smell of wood burning, smoking, and crackling in an old steel drum. I loved poking the fire and watching it flare up and spit out white hot pieces of logs. The heat was sometimes unbearable but also pleasurable. I remember the day my father gave me my first pair of wellington boots. They were black and three sizes too big for me, they came above my knees, and I had to turn the tops down so they wouldn't rub against my legs when I walked. Someone must have given them to him. I loved them and wore them everywhere.

My father had many jobs, but his main role was at British Steel as a manager in the blast furnace, part of his job was overseeing the activities of the blast furnace, including the dirty, labour-intensive job of shovelling scale. He worked shift work there for thirty-six years and took a redundancy package in the late 1970s receiving £6,000, which works out to £166 for every year that he had worked there. British Steel was one of the main employers in Grangetown,

Middlesbrough, and is now known as TATA steel. The miles of industries that overshadow Southbank and Grangetown are like a huge ugly giant with a bad case of halitosis, breathing out filthy bursts of deadly coloured fumes all over the community. The smells in the area hit you like a dirty hammer and changed regularly. The industries pollute and tarnish the once beautiful landscape, but they are like a double-edged sword because they also supply the local people with a wage packet to support their families at the end of every month. I grew up knowing the ugly giant well. The vastness of the industries was a familiar sight to me; a landscape I saw daily, I was used to it, but people who see the oppressive giant for the first time are shocked by its size (over twenty miles long along the coastline) and proximity to the properties.

Everyone who grew up in the area, like me, just accepted the pollution and the industrial overload that surrounded us every day. Fortunately, there are still some natural beauty spots in the area which were my boltholes, like the Eston hills above Grangetown. I also remember playing in the cornfields behind my house on Coniston Road, and it was great fun. My friends and I used our imagination to play games and make dens. We didn't have computer games in the seventies. We would play outside as often as we could, staying out until late, with no fear of being abducted or being preyed upon by weirdos. It was a different world then, almost unrecognizable now. Most parents in my neighbourhood gave their children a lot of freedom. We could roam anywhere we chose to and learn from our mistakes, and we grew up quickly.

I grew up as a Catholic, attending Sunday Mass, and then became an altar boy. My primary school was a Catholic school, St Mary's in Grangetown, and at the school, they encouraged us to participate in Catholic Church customs. I was seven years old when I was selected to be an altar boy at St Anne's Church, and one of my favourite roles in the Catholic Church was ringing the little bell during Holy Communion; the priest would bless the bread, lifting it up above his head dramatically and I'd wait nervously for my cue to shake the small handheld bell.

After a few weeks as an altar boy, my friend and I, Alan Freeman, discovered the cupboard where the priest kept the red wine that he used for Holy Communion. We decided to have a swig of the Holy wine and passed the bottle to each other, gulping it down quickly before anyone caught us. During the last gulp of the Holy wine, the priest, Father Brennan, walked in. He couldn't believe his eyes; he caught us downing the Holy wine. We froze when we saw him and looked at him cheekily with red stained moustaches. The Father was livid and threw us out of the Church by the scruffs of our necks. My role of ringing the little bell as altar boy ended immediately after that. We were just little boys experimenting. My parents didn't find out about the wine-swigging incident, and to be honest, I just brushed it off. I was a fearless kid from a young age, always prepared to push the boundaries.

John 'Cornelius' Carr as an altar boy.

I think our dad's drinking habit started when he was a young man. He drank a lot of beer after work due to the excessive heat whilst working in the furnaces. Most people drank a lot in Grangetown, and the most popular pubs were the King's Head, Bottom House, and Middle House. Those pubs were the closest to the steel works and would be packed with workers when the men finished their shifts; they were the hub of the community. I used to watch our dad in awe as he'd open up his throat, tilting his head back and down a pint of Tetley Bitter in seconds. I'm not sure if there was much enjoyment for him in drinking so fast and not tasting the beer properly; perhaps he should have had a pint of water first to quench his thirst, but I suppose drinking water wasn't the manly thing to do back then.

Our dad suffered from painful boils for years, and they were plastered all over his body, especially on his arse. He found it uncomfortable to sit down because of the sore lumps. His boil problem was getting worse; More and more boils were erupting over his body as he got older, he tried many different methods to get rid of them, but none of them worked. A friend of his told him that he should drink his own urine to cure his skin problem, and our dad thought it was a good idea. Jimmy Spud was a friend of our dad's, and I'm not sure why they called him 'Jimmy Spud;' maybe he grew potatoes. Anyway, Jimmy and our dad got pissed at the allotment one evening. Probably our dad needed a bit of Dutch courage before he drank his own piss, he held a pint glass and peed into it and filled it to the brim, and our dad downed it in one like he did when he drank a pint of Tetley after work. The putrid aftertaste made him cough and splutter, but he managed to keep it down and not spew the piss back up. The piss drinking seemed to be a miracle cure because, within a few weeks, the boils had completely disappeared, and he was cured. I've read about drinking your own urine, and it's something that shouldn't be encouraged, as it has toxins and bacteria, which could be harmful, but it's a fact that drinking his own urine worked for our dad.

I'd often spend time with our dad in the local pubs and sometimes go to the pub with him on school days. When I was ten years old, I remember our dad bringing a bottle of Newcastle Brown Ale home for me. It would be a treat on a Friday night. I'd sit watching television with him, thinking I was a proper man. I'd get a half-pint glass and slowly pour the beautiful amber liquid into it. The smell alone would make my taste buds tingle, and I couldn't wait to take the first sip. I perfected pouring out the ale, making sure the frothy head was the correct size. After I had finished drinking the bottle of ale, I'd feel giddy and warm. I looked forward to a Friday night. Drinking alcohol at ten years old seemed perfectly normal to me.

My father was a well-known character in the area, and he could sweet-talk local farmers to get cheap livestock or animal food. He had 'the gift of the gab;' even local travellers couldn't believe what he'd get away with. Before I was born, he had a horse and a cart. The horse was a stallion named Major. I have been told that Major was a magnificent horse, a huge black horse that raised his front legs high as he trotted, just like a show horse. My father delivered coal and sold various goods, including vegetables, etc. He would sell anything to earn extra cash. My father drank at the Bottom House pub and left Major outside. Major would wait patiently for my father to come out of the pub after he'd had a skin full and then, without any guidance, would take him home half pissed. My father was a man's man; he was illiterate, and he never went to school. Therefore, he had no formal education, but he always knew how to make money though he was street-wise like that. Whenever there was a requirement for him to read, he'd have to ask a friend or a family member to help him, but he wasn't embarrassed about asking for help. Many people of his generation were in the same boat. It was earning money that was a priority instead of receiving an education at school.

I hated school. I would prefer to be at the allotment with the pigs, doing a man's job. My father installed the work ethic into me from a young age, and I've always worked hard; nothing has been handed to me on a plate. I'm always up for a challenge and willing to stretch myself, especially if I think I would be rewarded financially for my effort. My first work experience was at our dad's allotment when I was about five or six, and I lapped it up, feeling important and making our dad proud of me. I'd always seek his approval and help him as much I could, making up the pig swill and feeding the pigs. I was my father's shadow; wherever he went, I followed.

John 'Cornelius' Carr And His Dad At The Allotment

I enjoyed going to the cattle market in Darlington every Monday. My father couldn't drive, so his friend Ray drove our old blue Bedford van. I didn't attend school much, and my parents never encouraged me to go. My education was being around our dad and learning from him. Monday afternoons at the market were exciting days out for me. We would buy and sell pigs, then we'd have fish and chips, washed down with a pint of beer shandy. I was ten years old and felt like a man in my flat cap and wellies.

One of the most memorable days was when our dad asked me to get Ginny the pig into her pen, I went to the area where she was kept, and she wasn't there. Our dad told me to look for her in the field, which was opposite the allotment across a dual carriageway, the Trunk Road. I crossed the busy road, looked over the hedge, and saw Ginny, a huge sow, sniffing a perfect bowling green lawn surrounded by bowling balls. There were bowlers in their whites on one side of the bowling green, looking over a hedge in shock and horror at the huge sow, who was about to demolish the perfectly manicured lawn. They watched Ginny sniffing the grass, preparing to uproot the turf, and they started to panic, asking me whose pig it was. I was just about to say that 'it's our dad's,' when my father appeared and said, "I don't know whose pig it is, but I'll take it off your hands." Coincidently my father had a rope and asked me to tie the rope across Ginny's back leg to control her as we guided her back to the dual carriageway during rush hour, and my father told me to stand in the middle of the road to stop the traffic. I courageously stepped into the road and waved down the rush hour traffic, and then proceeded to guide a huge pig across the road. I then stopped the traffic going in the other direction as Ginny went calmly towards the allotment. I was wary of Ginny, and she had been known to bite and was a huge sow with an attitude problem. When we got Ginny back safely, both of us could see the funny side of the situation, and we laughed until we cried. This was the crazy sort of education that I loved.

Our dad loved meat, particularly braising steak, which he would eat almost daily. Meat was a large part of our dad's diet. We are aware now that eating too much red meat isn't good for you, but years ago, it was the done thing. Our dad would send me to the local butcher with a pocket full of money to buy the braising steak. When I arrived at the butcher's shop, I didn't even have to ask the butcher for the meat. As soon I'd walk into the butcher's shop, he would hand me the steak. He knew our dad and our dad's dad, who was from a long line of butchers. The shop had a strange smell. It's difficult to describe; I suppose it was the smell of raw flesh, the smell of dead animals, there was sawdust on the floor, I didn't know why. Sometimes I'd go to the counter to pay for the meat, and the butcher, more often than not, would refuse to take the money; he'd wave his hand at me in disgust when I offered him the money, and he'd say, "Tell your dad it's ok." I'm not sure why he didn't take the cash. Perhaps it was butcher-on-butcher respect. I used to wonder what would happen if I kept the meat money, but I knew that if our dad ever found out, I'd pay a huge price for the theft. I'd skip home carrying the meat wrapped in greaseproof paper and put the money and the meat on the kitchen table straight away. Our dad would glance at me and mumble, "Good lad." I think he was testing my loyalty and trustworthiness.

My father used to slaughter the animals he bred. One of our dad's friend's sons, John Nesbitt, recently told me the story of the time he watched our dad and five others slaughter a thirty-five-stone pig. John was only five or six at the time and remembered the event well. They cut the pig's throat and held a bucket to its neck to catch the blood, which they then used to make black puddings. John said that the event he witnessed didn't affect him emotionally; it was accepted as being part of the way of life in those days. I think if children witnessed such an event today, they would be in therapy for months for post-traumatic stress disorder. There were no large supermarkets then, selling a vast array of products where you could buy a nicely packaged piece of meat, as we have the privilege of doing nowadays. There were individual shops which sold one product: The Butcher, The Baker, The Sweet Shop, The Grocer, etc. Food was bought freshly years ago, most women were stay-at-home housewives who went food shopping daily, there were no fridges or freezers, or takeaways, apart from the local Chip Shop. I remember we had a pantry and a large cupboard where we kept all the food. Although our pantry was never full, and I often felt hungry, I was a growing boy and needed lots of food.

I've been told that pigs are highly intelligent animals, and slaughtering a pig should be done as quickly as possible so that they are unaware of their fate. Years ago, cutting a pig's throat was the most humane way to kill a pig, as it would die quickly. There were no health and safety rules or animal rights groups back in the day; an animal was killed purely for food in the most appropriate manner. Apparently, after its throat was cut, the huge pig died within seconds, and if the pig didn't stress too much during the slaughter, the meat tasted better. In a roundabout way, our dad was a butcher, slaughtering and butchering animals. It must have been in his Carr genes. His pork was renowned as being the best pork in the Grangetown area. As a young boy, every Christmas time, I remember seeing half a pig's carcass dangling from a hook on the loft hatch. I was scared of going to the toilet in the middle of the night and seeing a large dead animal hanging there in the darkness, and my imagination conjured up all sorts of scary scenarios. I was so frightened that I would wake our Sue up to escort me to the toilet.

Illie Hewett told me a story about our father, which I had never heard before. Illie was a teenager when he experienced an event that had now lodged firmly in his brain. Illie was walking down our street when he heard a faint grunting noise coming from the back of our dad's van, and the van was rocking from side to side as if someone were having passionate sex in the back of the van; he was intrigued and peered in through the back window, hoping to see some saucy action, and instead saw a huge pig rolling around and snorting heavily. Illie knew it was our dad's van and knocked on our dad's front door at 25 Coniston Road to tell our dad about the pig. Our dad answered the door, and Illie said, panicking, "Mr. Carr, there's a big pig rolling around in the back of your van!" Our dad was wearing a checked shirt, faded jeans, and his trademark chunky brown leather belt. He glanced at Illie, walked straight past him, went up to the van, and opened the back doors, and he seemed pissed off. Perhaps he was in the middle of his tea. He climbed inside the van and straddled the pig as it lay half dead on the floor, then he throttled it for a minute or two until it took its last breath. Illie watched as our dad's powerful arm wrapped tightly around the pig's neck. Our dad casually demounted the dead pig, closed the van door, and said, "I thought the pig was dead. I slaughtered it earlier. Thanks, kiddo." He strode towards his front door and walked inside, closing it behind him as if nothing had happened. This was the 1970's, it's shocking to us now.

Our dad would have a fried full English breakfast most mornings. He didn't have a healthy lifestyle: drinking and smoking, with a poor diet, and he was also overweight. He rarely saw a doctor. He was one of the old schools believing that men should be strong and tough, and must persevere, and be the provider, just battle on regardless.

I can remember our dad and me going around cold calling farmers, he knew when it was potato picking season, and he would offer his labour free in return for rotten potatoes, which he'd use for pig food. Some farmers liked us doing this 'Tit for Tat' deal, but other farmers didn't like us on their land and told us gruffly where to go. It was a numbers game. The more farmers he asked, he knew that a few of them would agree to the labour swap. The van would be driven by dad's friend Ray Bircham and stacked high with potatoes that sometimes it was so full it looked like it was doing a wheelie down the road. One day Ray had left the van at the allotment, but our dad didn't want to leave it there overnight. I offered to drive the van home, which was a few miles away, I was eleven years old, and I felt confident that I could drive the van. I had been driving on the farms for a few months, gaining valuable experience. Our dad jumped in the passenger seat, and I sat behind the wheel, arranging the seat to be as close to the pedals as possible. I started the engine up and managed to put the clutch in wearing my wellies, and then pushed the stiff gear stick into first gear. I drove quite smoothly until I came to the first roundabout, which was at the bottom of the 'Mad Mile,' I saw all the traffic and panicked, stalling the van. Our dad said authoritatively, "Switch places, I'll drive." I switched places with our dad, who hadn't driven before, and between the two of us, we managed to get us home in one piece. We never left second gear all the way home to the annoyance of the queue of drivers beeping their horns behind us. I had a lawless life, but it was exciting for a kid. It was a huge learning curve.

One evening before Halloween on Coniston Road, a few of us boys gathered by a lamp post and were talking about Halloween night and how we could find ways to get sweets and money. One of the lads thought it would be a good idea to go to a turnip field, about two miles away, near ICI works, and steal some turnips to sell and use to go trick or treating on Halloween.

Halloween wasn't as commercial as it is now; we didn't have pumpkins, or dress up with fancy costumes, to decorate our homes; we just had turnips (swedes) that we sculpted into scary faces (they weren't scary at all). We'd cut the top off, scoop out the centre of the turnip and carve out two eyes, a nose, and a fanged mouth on the front of the turnip. It was difficult for a kid to do this. We didn't receive any help from our parents, we did most things ourselves back then and made our own fun. After we had made the turnip head, we'd try and place a candle in the middle of the head for the carved-out face to light up; to our frustration, the candle wouldn't stay lit, or it would fall over when you carried it.

It was a dark Halloween evening, but the moon was bright and full. It was a bitterly cold evening at about 6.30 pm. I had my wellies on with my flat cap and anorak when we all arrived at the turnip field. We climbed over a rickety wooden gate, there was light coming from ICI works, and along with the moonlight, we clearly saw the rows of turnips. Immediately we got to work, I pulled up three large turnips. Stevie Carnie had two, and Michael and Alan Jellings had one each. As we were heading towards the gate to make our escape, the farmer appeared at the gate with his torch, shining it in our faces. I squinted at the torchlight, and then one of the boys shouted, "Run!" I was closest to the gate, still holding my three big turnips when the farmer grabbed me by the hood of my anorak. The other three boys ran off across the field out of the farmer's grasp. The farmer said, "You're coming with me, and bring the turnips with you." He took me back to an outbuilding where he rang the police. I was terrified, especially because the farm was close to our dad's allotment, and he probably knew the farmer. Shortly after the phone call, the police arrived in a van and, without a word, shoved me in the back of the van. The interrogation followed; they asked me a lot of questions, and one of the police officers asked me my name and address. I was sharp enough at eight years old to give them the wrong information. I told them my name was John Thomas, and I lived at 45 Coniston Road. Luckily in those days, they couldn't check to see if the details I had given them were correct because there wasn't a computer database back then.

A dim light shone in the back of the police van and highlighted a newspaper page that was strategically placed lying on the van floor, and it read, 'Crime Doesn't Pay.' I think it was placed there on purpose to deter kids like me from getting into trouble with the law. The police gave me a verbal warning and drove me home. Unknowingly to them, it was to the wrong address. We arrived at 45 Coniston Road, which was about twenty houses up from my real address. They took me out of the van and marched me up to the front door. I stood outside someone's house and was dreading someone coming to the door, the police would know I was telling lies, and then I would land myself in deeper trouble.

I tried rehearsing in my head what I was going to say when someone opened the door at 45 Coniston Road, and I was well known on Coniston Road. How would I wriggle out of the situation?

The policeman knocked on the door, and luckily for me, no one was at home. I was quick thinking, "Our dad must be at work. I promise I won't do it again" The policeman probably had better things to do and wanted to leave, he handed me a piece of paper to give to my parents and left. After I was certain the policemen had left, I skipped back to the lamp post near my house, 25 Coniston Road, where I glanced in at my house, the curtains were open, and I could see our mam watching the telly. All the other kids were gathered near a lamp post, including the turnip thieves. I showed them the document that the policeman had given me, which I couldn't read. One of the bigger boys, Charlie Stairs, read it out loud. It was handwritten and said, 'John Thomas of 45 Coniston Road was caught stealing turnips at Wilton Field and has been cautioned by Southbank Police.' I was one of the cool kids that night because I'd been in the back of a cop van. We didn't get any sweets or money that Halloween and my father never discovered that I was a little turnip thief. That was a good thing because I would have definitely had a hiding off him.

My older sister Susan was a massive influence on my life because our mam was disabled. She became like a mother figure to me, even though she was just a kid herself, four years older than me. She protected me, cared for me, and I followed her everywhere. I started nursery school at the age of four, and before school Sue would dress me and give me breakfast, she would find whatever food she could lay her hands on. We didn't always go to school with food in our bellies, and our Sue would then take me to nursery school before heading to junior school herself. I suppose Sue and I were disadvantaged; we had a disabled mother and a father who spent a lot of time at work or in the pub. We just accepted our situation, and it was the only life we knew. We were happy, though, oblivious to our circumstances.

Sue was a pretty girl, like our mam, dark-haired with big brown eyes. She had a great sense of humour and could fight, too. She would sort out anyone who threatened me. When I was about eight years old, I was playing up the hills nearby with a few kids, including my sister Susan. We were playing in a dark wooded area near the SS Castle when we heard, from a distance, some older boys shouting, swearing, and threatening us. We couldn't see them, which made it more frightening; the threats were getting louder, and we didn't know when or from which direction they would attack us. We started running and screaming through the large thick brambles and nettles with our little hearts pounding. We were covered in scrapes and scratches, and we were terrified. There was an opening amongst the trees, and three big boys stood there looking intimidating. Our Sue was at the front of our small gang, and she recognised one of the older boys.

She said, "It's you, you wanker." I had never seen Sue so wild; she was shaking with fear and anger. She was enraged and immediately attacked the boy, punching and kicking him until he was powerless on the floor. She beat the crap out of him as we escaped running as fast as we could to the safety of my house.

My sister had a boyfriend, Barry Kerrison, known locally as Kerro, who was a Middlesbrough Football Club supporter and loved a bit of rough and tumble. He offered to take me with him to Ayresome Park, the home of Middlesbrough FC, in 1980, I was eleven years old. I was excited about going to see my first live football game. I wore my Dr Marten fourteen-hole boots, my jeans rolled up to the top of my black D. M's, my black Fred Perry T-Shirt with braces, and a Middlesbrough FC scarf. To complete the look, I had a skinhead haircut; I thought I looked the business. It was the first time I went see Boro play, and Barry took me to the Holgate part of the ground where all the football hooligans were. We were right in the middle of the action. Everyone was shouting and screaming at the away fans. If the other side scored, all the crowd in the Holgate end would point in unison to the far corner where the away fans were and then shout in an aggressive sing-song way, "You're going to get your fucking head kicked in!" I loved it! It was exciting and thrilling to see all these men behaving in a way I had never seen before. It was like something tribal, and I copied what everyone else was doing. I was part of their gang, and I was gripped by the entire dramatic experience. I felt this is where I belong.

The most memorable time I spent at the football ground with Barry was when Boro played Tottenham at home in 1980. Barry decided to go near the away supporters instead of going to the Holgate end of the ground to watch the match. He wanted to be closer to the away supporters to taunt them, he would shout abuse at them, and they would retaliate by shouting obscenities back. I hardly watched the game that day, and I was more interested in watching the entertainment in the stands. Tottenham had brought a big rowdy crowd with them, and they were up for action. Fans were trying to reach each other for a scrap; they were climbing fences, trying to get on the pitch. It was chaos. Most of the Tottenham supporters weren't there to watch the game, they just wanted to cause havoc, and they were succeeding. Boro beat Tottenham three goals to one, and the away mob weren't happy about the result.

At the end of the game, everyone rushed to leave the ground. Barry and I were in the middle of hundreds of Boro supporters as they pushed and shoved to get out of one of the exits. The police had decided to take the Tottenham supporters out first and separate them from the Boro fans because they knew there would be violence between the warring fans. The police kept our exits closed, and all the people behind us started pushing forward, wanting to get out of the ground. Barry and I were stuck in the middle of the crowd, getting crushed by the surging fans. I was frightened. I fell to my knees, struggling to breathe, and held desperately onto Barry's denim Wrangler jacket. Barry was panicking and started punching and pushing the people around us, shouting, "I've got a kid here! Move back!" Everyone was panicking and shouted out to the grounds staff to open the exits. It seemed like a long period of time before the exits were open, and we were able to breathe again. After the exits were opened and the crowd spilt into the street, I saw people coughing and gasping for air, and some people needed medical attention. The groundsmen were attacked by the angry mob, and this could easily have ended up as a tragedy, like the Hillsborough disaster, which resulted in the deaths of 96 people, with 760 people injured on April 15th, 1989. Even now, I find it stressful to be in enclosed environments surrounded by crowds of people.

One of my first happy memories was the first time I stayed away from home when I went away with the Cubs. I was nine years old when I went to the Lake District on a camping trip with the cubs; it was the furthest I'd ever been from home, and for me, it was a great adventure. I always remembered the food. I loved all the food we had during that trip. At home, I was always hungry. As a growing boy, I needed plenty of food, but our mam struggled to feed us. Because of her disability, she found it difficult to look after me, cook, etc., food was served at indiscriminate times, and there was no routine in our house. Our dad wasn't home much because he worked shift work, or he was down the allotment, in the betting office, or in the pub. The trip away with the Cubs was great, and I had a full English breakfast, lunch every day, and a huge evening meal. I felt like a King. I slept in a bunk bed in a dormitory on a campsite with the other lads, and at night we'd all frighten each other to death, telling ghost stories in the dark, with torches under our chins to make the stories seem even scarier. I felt so happy, feeling part of something special. It was only a few days away from home. I had a wonderful time experiencing the outdoors and learning how to do knots and make fires, but I missed my family, especially the pigs.

When I returned from my trip, everyone was saying how well I looked. I had put a bit of weight on and was looking healthy. A few days after my return home, I started to feel ill, our mam thought it was just a cold or flu, but I was becoming increasingly sick; I became delirious and was hallucinating. I remember telling my parents I saw a man in the corner of the room, and our dad sent me to bed because he thought I was fooling around and making things up. The following day our mam asked a neighbour to phone the doctor because I was so ill; we didn't have a phone in our house. Not many people did back then. Having a phone in your home was a luxury. The doctor came out to see me and said I had a bad cold or flu, but later that evening, my health deteriorated quickly. A neighbour, Mrs Coxen, visited me. When she saw me and how ill I looked, she told our mam to get a second opinion from another doctor. Dr Bandari came and took one look at me, and then I was rushed into intensive care at Middlesbrough General Hospital immediately and was placed in an induced coma.

I had meningitis. I lost most of my memory due to the illness, and I nearly lost my life. Meningitis also affects limbs, sight and speech. I was lucky to survive virtually unscathed, apart from overwhelming tiredness and a scar from an operation on my right arm. I owe my life to Mrs Coxen and Dr Bandari. I was told that if I had been left without medical treatment for another twelve hours, I probably wouldn't be here today. I had been in a coma for over a week; my main memory was coming out of the coma, it was like the scene from Wizard of Oz when Dorothy lands back home in bed, and all her loved ones are surrounding her, looking down at her. I had drips and wires attached to me, I was so scared, but then I saw familiar faces standing over me: Our dad, Billy Griff, and Ray Bircham (two of our dad's friends); their faces made me feel safe. They all smiled at me, I wasn't sure if I was dreaming, but when I felt the fatherly hug from my father, I knew it was real. I was alive. I was in the hospital for months recovering and had lost a lot of weight, and meningitis had taken a toll on my young body.

When I left the hospital, my father tried to fatten me up with goat's milk and eggs. I hated the taste of the goat's milk, he would take me to his friend's allotment who had goats, and they would milk the goats in front of me and hand me the warm frothy milk to drink. He would watch me and make sure that I would drink it all. It was the most revolting drink I'd ever tasted, but it did make me stronger, and I soon gained enough strength to become the young tearaway of Grangetown again.

Our dad came home from the pub one evening and said," I'm taking you to York Races tomorrow." I couldn't sleep that night thinking about it. I'd never been to any event, especially one as big as that, and I didn't know what to expect. We all dressed up; I wore my smartest clothes, with my black school shoes (scuffed at the front but disguised with thick black shoe polish) and my little flat cap. I thought I looked a million dollars. It was one of those rare days when I didn't wear my wellies.

Billy Griff took our dad and me to York Races in his red Citroen CX, and I thought it was a big posh car and the first brand new car I had ever travelled in. Billy Griff was a wheeler-dealer, like our dad, and he kept pigs too at an allotment close to our dad's. He was the Chairman of the Whale Hill Albion Club, a well-known Social Club in the area where my father used to drink. It took us just over an hour to get there, and it was a thrilling shock when I arrived. Seeing thousands of people gathered, milling around, my eyes darted about, trying to take it all in; the most interesting people were the tic-tac men who were standing near the stalls by the racecourse, making strange, animated signs. I was fascinated. It was exciting. Dad said, "Stay close, don't wander off." I followed him everywhere, sticking to him like glue. It was a beautiful sunny day, and everyone was dressed smartly. I smelt the turf and the horses when the first horse race of the day commenced. It was spectacular to be at close range when the horses galloped passed me and hurtled towards the finishing line and has been etched in my memory.

My father wasn't having much luck and lost his money on the first few races, I'm not sure how much money he lost, but for a small boy, it seemed like a fortune. My father never had a wallet; he'd always carry bundles of cash, all rolled up. He'd always bet on favourites, and on the last race, he placed a bet with the remainder of his money, which was over a hundred pounds. I was scared that he would lose that money too, and I tried to deter him from betting, but he didn't listen to me and placed the bet.

Luckily, his horse came in, but he was expressionless. I think he was used to giving and receiving large amounts of money on the horses, he was really cool about the win, and I was jumping up and down, going crazy with happiness. We went up to the same Tic-Tac man who we had dealt with all day, and my father gave him the winning slip. Our dad said to the Tic-Tac man, "Pay him", nodding towards me, and the man counted out three hundred and fifty pounds in notes and handed them to me. To this day, I love counting cash. I think the memory has installed in me a fascination with counting money. I had never seen so much money, but he didn't allow me to hold it for too long to my disappointment. He outstretched his hand and wiggled his fingers as if to say give me the money, and I begrudgingly handed it over to him.

I wanted to travel home in the front seat of Billy's lovely car, and my father said it was ok. Billy was driving and said, "Let's see what this thing can do!" He put his foot on the accelerator, and I watched with a smile on my face as the speedometer climbed up to over one hundred miles per hour. The feeling was exhilarating, and I had never been in a vehicle which travelled that fast before. As we got closer to Middlesbrough, our dad said, "Shall we go and get some food?" He wanted to celebrate his win. Billy said, "Let's go to the Cross Keys." The Cross Keys is a country pub near Guisborough and the first restaurant I have ever visited. We all sat down, it was all very posh to me, and I was surprised to be handed a large shiny menu. The waiters were in smart uniforms, and there were napkins on the table (which I wasn't sure what to do with). I couldn't read, and our dad couldn't read, so Billy read out loud the selection of food on the menu, I was unsure of what meal to pick, but I knew I wanted the best, the most expensive meal on the menu. Billy said, "Why don't we all have steak?" When we placed our order with the waiter, he said, "How would you like your steaks?" I didn't understand this at all, but Billy said, "We all have our steaks medium cooked." When it arrived, and I cut into it, the steak was red in the middle and had the best taste I had ever experienced. I'm now like a heroin addict chasing the dragon, trying to find a similar or better steak that would give me a delicious hit, like the one I ate that time in Guisborough. What a day this had been: dressed up, going in Billy Griff's posh car, going to York Races. Our dad was rich, we travelled over a hundred miles per hour, and I ate a huge, delicious steak.

I pestered our dad for a motorbike. I was ten years old when he gave in and bought me a Suzuki 120 cc, it was blue with one back brake, and it cost him £15. I loved him so much for buying me that bike. It was my reward for helping him with the pigs. All my friends wanted to see my new bike and gathered outside my house to view the machine. Sue came out and said to my friend Geoff Ewart, "That bike was cheap, is it stolen, Geoff?" He looked at Sue with disdain and said, "No, definitely not."

I didn't have the bike long when I went up the Eston hills with a few friends. I didn't really want to go there because the bike only had one brake, and I wasn't that confident riding it. After all, I was only a small boy. Geoff Ewart coaxed me to go up the hills with my new bike, and he said, "You should make the bike look more like a scrambler, and then you can get up the hills easier." Then to my horror, he started to dismantle my lovely road bike to turn it into a scrambler by taking off the mudguards. To get to the hills from where I lived, there were just two ways to get there; you either had to climb Cally Bank or go up the hill we called The Elephant's Arse (but the Arse was far too steep). A few of us drove our motorbikes up Cally Bank, including me on my new scrambler road bike. I had a pillion passenger, Geezer, who said that he would ride my bike back down Cally Bank because I was too scared to ride it due to the sheer drop of the hill. Geoff was a confident kid who led the way to the hills on his motorbike. He said, "Follow me, lads, keep close, and I'll show you the way." Geoff had taken his bike up those hills on many occasions, and we trusted his knowledge.

We headed for The Shale, an area in the hills where kids congregated on their bikes, push bikes and motorbikes. We had only been there for a few minutes, and I was trying to do a bit of scrambling when I found a small, steep hill to ride down, with a dip at the bottom and then an incline up the other side. I went down the hill, but I panicked, tried to brake, but turned the throttle instead, going even faster, I went flying down the ridge like Evil Knievel, and I shot up the ridge at speed and flew into the air, taking off, landing hard and smashing into a brand new Montessa Trail bike belonging to one of the hardest kids in Eston, Jenna! Jenna was about fourteen, and all the younger kids feared him. My scrambler road bike was fine, with no damage, but Jenna's brand-new bike was a right off, with petrol pissing out like a fountain. Jenna took one look at me and then started to pulverise me. One of Jenna's friends pulled him off me, and I jumped on my bike to get away. I found myself facing the steep drop of Cally Bank and stopped, unsure of what to do next. Then Jenna appeared on someone else's bike and rode alongside me and said: "How are you going to pay for the repairs to my bike?"

I said," I'll give you fifty pence a week." Before I finished saying the word "week," I got a punch in the eye. Geezer picked me up and rode my motorbike down Cally Bank with me as a pillion. When I got home, with a big black shiner, my father asked me, "How did you get that?" I said, "I fell off my bike." I think I got away with it, he believed me. However, I did have to go without ice creams for months because Jenna worked on the ice cream vans.

I didn't go back to the hills for a long time after that experience. I stayed in my local area and played a lot on the ICI field, which wasn't far from my house. I was one of those kids who was easily led and was always on the lookout for adventure. There were times when I would look out of my bedroom window and watch the lorries travelling along the 'Mad Mile.' It was called the 'Mad Mile' because drivers could speed, it was a straight piece of road which went from one roundabout to another, and there was no hard shoulder for the police to wait and catch drivers speeding. I used to fantasise that I would be a passenger in a truck, travelling all over the country; from a young age, I wanted to travel and experience visiting new places. Perhaps there was a gypsy within me, and I did have that traveller blood flowing in my veins. When ICI was lit up at night, it was spectacular; it was like Blackpool illuminations, somewhere that looked enticing for a young boy. It looked pure theatre at night, with lights, coloured flames, and plenty of action, from JCBs to articulated lorries moving around, lit up under the spotlight of the works. In the daytime, the cloak and mirrors of the theatre performance I had watched the previous night had vanished to reveal the stark reality of cold steel and grey concrete buildings pumping out pollutant gases and smoke.

We had a lot of freedom as kids, and on this particular day during the summer holidays, a few of us decided to go to Redcar beach, which was about six miles from Grangetown. Stevie Carnie, Michael Jellings, and I walked to the Trunk Road and waited near the roundabout, taking in turns to stick our thumbs out. We were ten years old and hitchhiking. Thinking back to that era, it felt safe for us, and we never encountered any problems, thankfully. I think people would be horrified today to see a few small boys hitchhiking. It was an innocent time before all the technology and the dangers that come with it today. It was a hot day as we stood waiting for a lift. Fortunately, the third car that came along stopped, and we all jumped in, I was in the front, and the two boys were in the back seat. The driver said, "Are you off to Redcar, lads?" We nodded in unison. There was some small talk as we headed to Redcar. We were looking forward to a day at the seaside.

The first thing we did when we arrived was to strip off down to our underpants. We didn't bother with wearing swimming shorts or bringing towels or putting sun-tan lotion on. We left our clothes in piles further up the beach, and I hid my new Dr Marten boots under my clothing before we ran towards the sea. The water was freezing cold, and we shivered as we first entered the North Sea. We always had a competition to see who would immerse themselves fully in the cold water first. I think I was always the bravest, but the other two lads may not agree. After a few minutes, we became accustomed to the cold temperature of the water and enjoyed splashing each other and having swimming races. We played for about an hour in the sea until we felt hungry and went back to the beach to get dry. We'd run around chasing one another in the sunshine until we were ready to get dressed. We were covered in sand after rolling about toy fighting, it was horrible trying to get the sand out of every orifice without a towel, but it was all part of the adventure.

As I started to get dressed, I noticed one of my new Dr Martens was missing. I looked at the boys suspiciously, "Come on, boys. Where's my boot?" We were always playing tricks on one another, and I thought this was another one of their jokes. Both lads were adamant that they hadn't taken it. I didn't believe them; I was cool and calm, believing they had hidden it in the sand and waited for them to own up and give me my right boot back. After a while, I started to get annoyed, but they kept saying they didn't take it. I was starting to get worried, and I knew that our dad had paid a lot of money for the boots, which were only a few days old. If I went home with one boot, I'd get a hiding.

Micky Jellings suggested that we go into Redcar town to see if there was a right Dr Marten boot in black, in size three, on display outside a shop. I was stupid enough to go along with the plan, thinking this was a possibility. There often was one piece of footwear on display outside shops, which would have been easy to steal. However, finding a Dr Marten in my size and the same colour as the one I had would have been like finding a needle in a haystack. I didn't fancy hopping all the way home. We had enough money for chips or bus fare, chips won, and we would hitchhike home. After an hour of hopping around the town with one Dr Marten boot on, I was getting pissed off. There was a display of right-foot shoes in a shoe shop, and I took my chance, the two boys kept a lookout, and I shoved one of the shoes up my jumper. We walked away quickly, laughing and giggling, and in a nearby shop doorway, I took the shoe out from under my jumper and put it on. It was a size six and three sizes too big for me. Micky and Steve couldn't stop laughing, and I must have looked a right sight with one boot and one shoe three sizes too big for me as we walked to the chip shop. I was dreading going home and facing my father. I never told him what had happened; to this day, I still don't know who took my boot. This is an opportunity for the thief to come forward and own up, and I apologise to the shoe shop for taking the shoe.

One of the kids I knew said, "Have you tried sniffing petrol?" I hadn't, but this seemed like a great idea. There were a few kids gathered on the ICI field, and I had my motorbike with a full tank of petrol. We took off the petrol cap and took turns breathing in the petrol fumes. The effects were amazing: The fumes affected me immediately. I became in a dream state, hallucinating. One of the dreams I vividly remember was riding my motorbike topless, wearing just a pair of jeans with no helmet. The feeling I had was peaceful and happy as I rode the bike in the warm breeze. I realise now that from a young age, I had an addictive personality. I sniffed petrol for a few weeks. My addiction came to an end, thankfully, when one of my friends pushed me off the petrol tank because I was losing consciousness. I fell to the floor, shaking and delirious. It took me hours to recover and scared the shit of me. I didn't do it again after that. Addiction to anything can be bad, and I think my addictive personality helped me in my career. I was obsessed with boxing and all the training that came with it. I wanted to become the most famous boxer in Middlesbrough. I wanted to achieve something and make a success of my life.

Round Three – Destiny

When I was eleven and twelve, many life-changing events happened to me. I discovered girls, one of my first sexual experiences was in an old black Morris Minor car which was a neighbour's vehicle parked on a joint driveway with my house. The neighbours left it unlocked as they no longer used it. We would use it, though, to snog girls. One evening my friend Stevie sat in the driver's seat, and Helen and I were in the back seat whilst Stevie pretended to drive. Stevie would say," Where are we going tonight, sir?" And I'd say, "Take us to Redcar." He would go through the motions of driving the stationary car whilst I went to work on Helen in the back seat. She had enormous boobs, and they were the first boobs I'd ever seen in the flesh and the first boobs that I got my hands on. I didn't know what I was doing, and Helen would say, "You're too rough." As I was incompetently getting down to business, a light shone onto the car from the kitchen window of my house, and I could see our dad at the window having a shave. The kitchen window looked directly over the car we were in; we ducked down in the car, not for our dad to see us, especially as Helen had her boobs out and had taken off her jumper. Dad was shaving in front of a mirror that was placed in the window, which overlooked the car. We waited there, half naked, for him to go, and then Helen desperately looked for her top, and I lost the momentum to continue with the groping. These little pretend car journeys often occurred on the driveway, and sometimes I was in the driver's seat, and Stevie was in the back with Helen. These were moments that were a rite of passage, boys being boys.

I was still having the odd scrap here and there and gaining a bit of a reputation in the area as a fighter. It was a Saturday afternoon, and a few of us kids were playing football on the ICI field, one of the Gill brothers, Steve, who was three older than me, started an argument over something, maybe a bad tackle, and we had a bit of scuffle, which was broken up by the other kids. Gill said, "We'll finish this tomorrow." He told me to meet him on the green of Grisedale Crescent the next day at 2 pm.

On Sunday afternoon, I arrived as planned at Grisedale Crescent to meet Gill. I had my favourite football team's shirt on, which was Leeds United. Some of my friends supported Leeds United in the 1970s, and they were a huge football team back then. I remember I had the full strip one Christmas, and I thought I looked the dogs nuts when I wore it. The kit was mainly white, with the number ten on the back. On Christmas day morning, Santa brought me a Leeds United top, shorts and socks, and I couldn't wait to wear them. I thought I would play football on the ICI field on my own. I didn't have any football boots. I had my wellies on. I wanted to be like my idol Tony Currie; he was a magnificent footballer. I had watched Tony do a sliding tackle on TV, and when he got up after the tackle, he had mud all down one side of his strip. I thought that's what real footballers did, and they weren't afraid to get dirty. After about five minutes of entertaining myself kicking the ball on the field, I was bored and decided to do a sliding tackle against an invisible opponent. I went for it, and I was so pleased with the result. My brand-new kit was covered in mud all down one side, exactly like Tony Currie's. I thought I looked like an authentic footballer. I picked the ball up and walked proudly home, believing that I was Tony Currie. I had such a bollocking when I got home for ruining my brand-new kit, but I thought the telling-off was worth it.

I wasn't intimidated by Gill; even though he was older than me, I was fearless, and I wanted to show him that I wasn't afraid of him. My supporters were with me at the fight scene, Shaun Lacey, Stevie Carney and the Jellings brothers and my sister Susan. He had his supporters, including his older brother Michael. We started fighting immediately. There was no warm-up or pleasantries, and punches were thrown straight away. Gill stopped me mid-flow by pulling my Leeds United shirt over my head, and I couldn't see what was going on. Shortly afterwards, someone broke up the fight, and my gang and I started to walk away triumphantly.

As we headed back towards Coniston Road, Gill shouted at me, "I won that." I felt the rage flowing through my veins. I knew he hadn't won that fight, I thought I'd show him who won the fight, and I ran back towards him, kicking, punching and then smashing his head on the concrete floor. His older brother Michael could see that I was winning the fight and came over and kicked me in the face. We were still scuffling and swearing when a man appeared and broke us apart. He grabbed Steve Gill and me by the scruffs of our necks, Steve Gill pulled away, and the man looked at me and said, "I know you, don't I?" I was still seething that the fight had been stopped, and I wanted to punch Gill's lights out, "You don't know me." I said, panting. He said, "I do. I know your dad." I was scared when he said that because I knew if our dad found out about this incident, he would give me a good hiding for fighting. I begged the man, "Please don't tell our dad." The man said, "I'll tell you what. If you come to the Grangetown Amateur Boxing Club tomorrow afternoon after school, I won't tell your dad." What could I do? I was shit scared of our dad. I had to try and stop the man from grassing me up, I said that I would go to keep him happy and quiet, but I didn't intend to go to the boxing club.

I hated school and very rarely attended St Peter's Catholic school. I found it hard to concentrate and rebelled against discipline and conformity. Teachers didn't understand me, apart from one, Mr McNicholas, who was head of my school year. Mr Mac was firm but fair, a big man over six feet tall, and I knew not to mess with him. I respected him. One time I was called into his office, and I thought I was in trouble again. I was often called to his office about something that I had done wrong, but to my surprise, he asked me to look after one of the pupils in my year who was being bullied. I know I was a fighter, but I wasn't a bully. I knew what it felt like to be bullied. From a young age, I was bullied for having a disabled mam, being poor, for having big ears or for any other reasons children could find so that they could batter me. Although I was just a boy myself, I protected the other boy and looked out for him. I made sure no one bullied him again.

The longest continuous attendance I had at school was for three weeks, and on the last Friday of the third week, the whole class applauded me as I walked into the classroom when I turned up for school. The three-week school attendance was short-lived, and school life wasn't for me. The only two things I liked about school were PE and school dinners. I was envious of one of the pupils who always brought a lovely, packed lunch to school. His lunch box was like a gourmet meal to me with perfectly cut crust-free sandwiches, scrumptious pork pies, branded crisps (not the no-frills brand), a selection of fresh fruit, and to finish off; he always had a mars bar. The boy wasn't satisfied with his perfect gourmet meal, and he wanted all the crap the school canteen could offer, greasy chips, sausages, burgers and pizzas. I was kind-hearted and offered to swap with him, I'd have his gourmet delights, and he'd have my greasy school dinner. This was a great partnership that lasted for a while; it was the best scenario for both of us. That's one thing the mean streets of Grangetown taught me, and that was to capitalise on a situation.

Because I rarely attended school, I was in the lowest science group, called L.A.M.P., which I invented stood for Loonies and Mental People. What it really stood for is still a mystery to me. The teacher was Mr Pratt. He looked like a typical teacher. He wore the standard corduroy jacket with leather patches on the elbows of the sleeves. Mr Pratt was an easy target for a kid like me. I sussed him out quickly, realising that I could get away with being silly, and being the joker of the class, my aim was always to make people laugh, poor Mr Pratt, he wasn't laughing. I'd always mess about in class, upsetting Mr Pratt. He often shouted across the room when I was annoying as usual, "Carr out!" and on this day, I replied, "No, Pratt out!" I was always testing the teachers to see how far I could push them. The kids in L.A.M.P. loved my antics, and they had expectations from me. They knew I didn't give a shit about school or science or Mr Pratt. The whole class roared with laughter as Mr Pratt lost his cool and grabbed me, then pushed me out of the classroom door, where I had to wait in the corridor during the entire lesson. I spent the time picking my nose, writing on my hands, and dreaming about the time when I could leave school for good. I understand now how important education is and that teachers have a difficult job to do. I just didn't realise it at the time.

The following day after my fight with Gill, I was helping our dad at the allotment as usual. I had been thinking about the fight the day before, and I was worried the man I had met would tell our dad about the fight I had. I said to our dad, "What do you think about me joining the boxing club?" He surprised me when he said, "Yeah, give it a go." I left the allotment at about 6 pm and headed for the boxing gym. Still wearing my allotment attire, I was nervous because I didn't know what to expect at the club. Boxing wasn't something that interested me at that time. The only boxing experience I had was listening to a Muhammad Ali fight on the radio and peering through the window at The British Legion Club.

I walked down Bolckow Road towards the boxing gym; when I arrived at the gym, I stood at a large blue door and heard shouting and strange slapping noises, which I had never heard before. I hesitated for a minute, wanting to turn around and go home, but then I plucked up the courage to walk in. I stood in the doorway watching the scene for a few minutes, unsure of what to do next, I couldn't see anyone I knew, and I was just about to turn around and walk away when the man shouted. "Oy, come over here!" I walked towards him through the loud, sweaty packed gym, full of young lads training, punching bags, skipping, and shadow boxing. There was a smell of sweat and raw testosterone. I was wearing my flat cap, wellington boots, and stank of pig shit, and I didn't have any training gear; I wouldn't have any money to buy some anyway. The man I met yesterday who broke the fight up turned to me and introduced himself, "I'm Marty Turner. Welcome to the Club. I'm glad you came. Have you got any gear?" I said I didn't have anything to wear, and Marty put me at ease by saying he'd sort out a pair of shorts and a T-shirt for me. I wore someone's old shorts and a T-shirt that evening as Marty put me through the novice paces. I loved it! The Boxing Club was open five nights a week, and I went every night. I couldn't get enough of the training and the comradery, and I felt like I belonged there. They became my family.

After a few months of training at Grangetown ABC, Marty told me I needed to get a medical examination so that I was fit to box. A medical was required from a doctor, and I went on my own to see my G.P. Dr Stein, who said," I don't think you should be boxing, it's not safe for someone who has had an illness like you." Referring to my meningitis, Dr Stein thought I had flu and not meningitis at the time of my illness. I know doctors are human, too and can make mistakes. That mistake could have proved fatal for me. I hold no grudges about the misdiagnosis, but I was lucky that Mrs Coxen was around to save me from death or disability.

I was devasted that Dr Stein wouldn't give me a clean bill of health, but he had his reasons, I suppose. I was upset, thinking that my boxing career had ended before it had even started. I went to the boxing gym that evening and told Marty what Dr Stein had said.

Marty said, "Take no notice. We'll go and see Dr Robson," who had surgery across the road from the boxing gym on Bolckow Road. Marty made an appointment for the following day for us to see Dr Robson, and we both visited the doctor, but we didn't mention that I had previously seen Dr Stein. I had a full medical examination and passed with flying colours. We were both elated and excited that my boxing career could finally begin. I wonder, if I hadn't been granted a licence to box, what would have happened to me? I'm sitting here writing this book and thinking that decisions like that are life-changing. There is a chain of events throughout our lives that map out our future.

My first amateur fight was run by Grangetown Amateur Boxing Club and held at a local venue, The Oakleaf Club in Southbank. I was eleven years old and excited. I wasn't nervous because I didn't know what to expect. I sat in the changing room amongst the other lads, including my friends Shaun and young Marty (Marty Turner's son). Our hands were wrapped and ready for boxing. Our kit was blue with a white stripe with Grangetown ABC boldly printed across the front of my vest. I boxed a lad from Hull named Dave Nicholas. At the weigh-in, my weight was 5 stone and 3 pounds (33 kg). Our dad and all his friends came to support me, and it was the first live boxing match our dad had ever seen. Boxing was not in our blood. I was thrilled that he'd made an effort to be there for me that night. I didn't know what to expect at the fight. How was I going to react to my opponent? Was I going to freeze in fear? Could I remember all the moves Marty had shown me? Everything was rushing through my mind. Marty guided me as I walked to the ring in front of the crowd, trying to stop my little knees from trembling, I glanced over at our dad, who smiled and waved, and his fatherly gestures instantly reassured me. The fight was three rounds which were one and a half minutes long.

As soon as the fight started and the bell rang, all my boxing training came into effect, and I blanked out the noise of the crowd to focus on my fight. At the end of the fight, I returned to Marty at my corner, who was smiling and saying, "You've won!" I was told to stand next to the referee, who grabbed my gloved hand, and the announcer said, "Please put your hands together for these two young boxers who had their debut fight this evening, and the winner is by a unanimous decision Carr in the red corner!" The referee raised my arm in victory, and I raised my other arm in sheer delight like I was a World Champion. I couldn't contain my excitement and jumped in the air. I felt fantastic and couldn't stop smiling. I felt like someone, a winner. I saw our dad's trilby hat amongst the crowd and watched it move as our dad pushed his way to the foot of the boxing ring and he looked up at me proudly whilst clapping loudly.

I received my first trophy, which looked like a mini–FA Cup, and that made me feel even more like a real champion. I carried the heavy trophy proudly to where our dad and his friends were sitting, they all congratulated me, and I put my trophy on the table for them to see it. Our dad picked up a bottle of Newcastle Brown and poured the ale into the trophy, and said, "Get that down you boy." As I drank it with one boxing glove still on, I felt like I had just won a World

Championship match. I knew then that I wanted more. I liked the feeling of winning and lapped up the positive reaction from the crowd, and I soaked up the glory. I felt like somebody, a real sports star, and looked forward to my next fight.

John 'Cornelius' Carr's Fifth Boxing Match

I became a confident boy, training and sparring nearly every day. My reputation was spreading throughout the locality, and there were a few kids who wanted to fight me on the street. There was one kid, Wayne Bryan, who attended a different school, and I heard he wanted to fight me. I was the type of kid who would never say no, especially when my reputation was at stake. A fight was arranged at the Eston community centre one evening. I turned up with two of my friends: Shaun Lacey and David Gill. Wayne Bryan came out with a large gang of boys, about twenty of them. One of his gang came up to me and whispered, "Don't fight him. I think he's got a screwdriver." I ignored him, and the fight started. He stabbed me immediately with the screwdriver, and then to my horror, he put me in a bear hug and bit me in the face. I was in shock; I had never had a fight like this before. The fight was broken up, and the gang quickly dispersed. Shortly afterwards, I felt pain and realised I had been stabbed on the left-hand side of my torso. This wasn't a proper fight for me. I used my fists, and this was a dirty, unnatural fight. I couldn't believe that someone would do this to me. By the time I arrived home, the blood was oozing out of the wound, and I was in severe pain. It didn't seem to be a huge wound, but I wasn't sure how deep the wound was at the time. My sister called an ambulance, which took me to Middlesbrough General Hospital. I wasn't worried too much about the wound and the pain, and I just worried that I would get a beating off our dad if he found out I'd been fighting.

They cleaned up my wound and gave me a tetanus injection. People didn't snitch in our community, and Wayne Bryan had gotten away with it. I couldn't box for weeks after the stabbing; I was gutted about that, but I was happy that my father didn't find out. The result of the bad encounter with Bryan made me realise that I had to stop street fighting. It was too dangerous. My dream was to become a boxing Champion. I had two more successful fights with Grangetown ABC after the match at The Oakleaf Club. My attitude changed towards street fighting, and I found amateur boxing a sport that I loved and something that I was good at.

Round Four – Tragedy

One evening, after dinner, I was watching TV with all the family. My father was asleep on the sofa when he suddenly sat up and grabbed his chest; he was gasping for air and looked frightened, his face was pale, and his eyes were wide open and glassy. He slipped off the sofa and onto the carpet, struggling to breathe. He was taking short deep breaths with his hands clutching his chest. His body was floppy, his legs were open wide, and his head was down; he looked drained, so white and scared. My mam and sister panicked, not knowing what to do. I didn't realise what was happening. I can remember my mam and sister screaming and shouting, "He's going to die." I was just standing over him in shock, silently watching the scene. I felt as if it was an out-of-body experience, and I was frozen in fear. Although my father was far from perfect, I worshipped him and couldn't bear to see him like that. I was just a kid unable to help him. He slowly started to breathe correctly again and sat upright with his back against the sofa, taking his time to regain composure; we were all so relieved when he started breathing normally again. It's strange that I can't remember what happened directly after my father had his fright. It's as if I focused so much on the trauma of the event that my memory of anything afterwards has been blocked, not allowing me to absorb any other details of the day.

The sleeping arrangements in our house were unusual, I suppose, but at the time, I didn't know any different, I used to sleep with my dad, and my sister slept with my mother. We only had two bedrooms in our house, my parents probably thought it would have been improper for me to share a room with my fifteen-year-old sister. Therefore, I slept with my dad. I didn't complain about the sleeping arrangements. I used to love cuddling into his big warm hairy body, and I felt safe. My father never wore pyjamas. He always went to bed in his white Y Fronts underpants. My father kept a piss pot under the bed, and it was white with a blue handle. He used the piss pot even though the toilet was just outside the bedroom door, I think it was an old tradition from when he was young, and toilets were halfway down the garden. That evening I went to bed with my father, he slept next to me as usual, and I wrapped my little arm around his body as tight as I could until we both fell asleep.

For some reason, my family didn't contact the doctor or hospital during the evening of my father's incident, but my father did visit the doctor the following day. The doctor informed him he had probably suffered a heart attack and that he was an incredibly lucky man to survive it. The doctor told him he needed to dramatically change his lifestyle and become a healthier man if he wanted to live a longer life. I think the heart attack frightened my father because he did change his lifestyle for a few months; he stopped drinking and eating unhealthy food, and lost a few stones in weight, too. Unfortunately, the healthy lifestyle didn't last very long, and he soon drifted back to his old unhealthy ways.

A few months later, early one evening, my father was asleep on the sofa. I started play-fighting with my sister when my mam told me to be quiet and not to wake him. My mam said he had been sleeping for most of the afternoon. It wasn't unusual for my dad to be asleep on the sofa. He worked hard, or had been drinking hard, and often had naps during the day. At about 8.30 pm, my dad woke up, and instead of spending some time with the family, which he normally did before going to bed, he said he was tired and went straight upstairs. I watched TV for a while and followed him up to bed around 10.30 pm. I jumped into the warm bed next to my dad, who was sound asleep, snoring as usual. I cuddled into his big warm body and soon drifted off to sleep.

Early the next morning, I was woken by mam. She was shaking me and shouted, "John, John, your dad is dead!" I didn't know where I was, I was still half asleep, but without hesitation, I jumped on top of his large belly and started to pump his hairy chest with my little hands. I didn't know how to do CPR properly, but I copied what I had seen people doing on TV. I really didn't have a clue what to do, I was twelve years old and didn't really understand what was going on, but I knew I had to try something to make him wake up. My mam was distraught; she was wailing and sobbing as I tried my best to resuscitate him. I blanked out her mournful screams. I knew I had a job to do, to save him, he was my dad, and I had to get him back. I remember his face; it was pale and felt cold, his lips were blue, and his eyes were closed as if he were asleep. There was no movement from him, and he didn't make any sounds; there were no signs of life.

I think he had died many hours earlier, so the CPR didn't work, but I kept trying CPR for as long as I physically could. After about fifteen minutes, my arms and hands were sore from hitting his chest. I sat back to see if his eyes would open and listened to his chest for a heartbeat, but there was no movement. He was silent and still, I gave up because there was no response from him. He lay there cold and motionless; my dad was dead. My mam was crying, but strangely I didn't cry. I silently got off his body and walked downstairs in a trance. I opened the front door and wanted to shout out as loud as I could, "My dad is dead!" The sun was shining. It was a beautiful summer day. I saw the world continuing with daily life, kids on their bikes, women pushing prams, and people going about their normal routine, and I couldn't understand why everyone was just carrying on normally as my dad lay lifeless and cold upstairs. I felt numb, and it was like an out-of-body experience again, the way I felt when he had his heart attack a few months earlier. I was in shock, and I couldn't take it in, for I had lost my hero. I never saw him again. As I looked out at the street, I imagined my dad staggering up the road, like he did on many summer evenings.

When I was a kid, most summer evenings were spent playing outside with a gang of friends, shouting and running in the street, there weren't many cars about in the seventies, and we'd play football on the road near my house. My father would be coming home from the pub half cut around 8 pm and shout at me, "I want you in by 9!" I'd nod, acknowledging his words but not really taking much notice of him, I carried on messing about with the kids, but I knew if I wasn't in by 9 pm, there would be trouble. My father would stop and stumble, then put his hands in both pockets, rummaging deeply and rattling all the coins. We all knew what was coming, and waited with anticipation, then he'd pull out piles of loose change and throw the coins high into the air, and we'd wait for the shiny coins to land and bounce all over the road, "There you are, kids." He took pleasure in seeing us all pushing and shoving each other out of the way to scoop up the treasure. I always said, "I want that money." I was annoyed that he'd thrown his money at the other kids. I thought that I should have had all the coins as he was my father, I felt that I was entitled to it, but I suppose it taught me that I had to share. The image faded away, and I stared blankly at the blue sky, wondering where he had gone to.

I can't remember who called the doctor or ambulance when he died. The details of that side of things didn't register in my memory. I know it sounds bizarre now, but that night I slept alone in the bed my dad had died in; the bedding hadn't been changed, and it still held his smell. I didn't cry that night, I felt strange sleeping alone without his warm body next to mine. I wondered where he was. How could someone disappear completely? I didn't understand death and how final it was. I thought that he would come home one day. But one night, I think the realisation set in that he wasn't coming back and that I would never see him, talk to him or hold him again; I curled up in a foetal position alone, hugging a pillow, and sobbed all night uncontrollably.

A decision was made, I don't know who made that decision, but I wasn't allowed to attend my father's funeral. My family somehow must have thought that I was too young to handle the emotional impact of a funeral, but when you think of the traumatic experience which I had suffered finding my dad dead and of the agonising minutes I had spent trying to revive him, that emotional impact was far greater for me than attending my dad's funeral. I struggle with the thought to this day that I wasn't permitted to attend the funeral to say my goodbyes, I should have been there instead of being alone at home whilst everyone attended the funeral. It's very upsetting now to think that I spent that afternoon alone in my bedroom whilst they buried my dad. I didn't know what to do with myself that afternoon. It was torture to wonder what everyone was doing. I loved him so much. I know he was a tough father in many ways, and he made mistakes. He was my hero and still is. I often wonder what would have happened to me if he had lived longer than he did. Which paths would I have taken? I'm certain that he would have been a big influence on my life and the choices I made. Would I have continued with my boxing? My life changed after his death; I lost a role model, a friend, and a father. I missed him, and my heart ached for him. I still miss him, but I believe he watches over me, and I've experienced seeing him, often feeling his reassuring presence when I need him.

After our dad died, my sister and I tried to keep the allotment going, but we were just kids, and after a few months of struggling to look after the animals, we decided to sell everything and let it all go. I was lost for a while, and I wouldn't go to school. I'd stay out all night, up to mischief. I was stealing clothes off people's clotheslines. I'm not sure why I did that. I didn't really want the clothes. It was just doing something naughty, I was chased by irate people a few times, and that added to the thrill. I was shoplifting, all kinds of things, sometimes silly things, like a loaf of bread that I didn't need. My friends were laughing at me because I had stolen a loaf of bread, and I was embarrassed knowing that I shouldn't have taken it; I just threw it in a bin. I think I was searching for attention and trying to see how far I could push the boundaries. My mam didn't have any control over me. I could stay out all night if I wanted to. She couldn't stop me. I even stopped going to the boxing gym. I was wild for a few months; I didn't have the discipline and fear of my dad if I stepped out of line. My mam was disabled, she couldn't chase after me, and I knew that I could run rings around her.

I was at ICI Field when I saw a few lads inhaling glue from a bag. One of them said to me, "Do you want to try it?" They passed me the bag, and I began sniffing the glue, slowly inhaling the intoxicating substance. It affected me instantly, and it made me feel euphoric. I could drift away from the reality of my situation for a short while. At the time, I was sniffing glue, smoking dope, drinking beer and smoking cigarettes, and I was still only twelve years old. I always wanted to try forbidden things. I wanted something to distract me from the realisation that my dad had left me. I didn't realise that sniffing glue was dangerous. I know now that it can prove fatal and can give you long-term health problems. I suppose those issues weren't important at the time, and I just wanted an escape route away from the large empty void my dad had left. I had no one to rein me in, as I was a free spirit, a lost boy who was out of control.

After a few months of being a feral child, I had a visit from my boxing trainer, Marty Turner. I think he had heard that I was losing my way. I hadn't been to the boxing club for weeks, and Marty decided to try and encourage me to go back. I was surprised when Marty entered the living room. I was watching TV. He came up to me and put his arm around me and, in a quiet fatherly voice, said, "Come on, lad, let's get back to training. We're going to the gym now. Get your coat on." I said I didn't want to go and tried ignoring him, focusing on the television set, looking straight ahead, but he wouldn't take no for an answer. I stood up, and he hugged me, the hug felt good, and in a subtle way, he slowly guided me in the direction of the front door. My mam and my sister were encouraging me too. “Come on, our John, get back into the boxing.” To appease them, I said that I’d give it a go. I was just going to go through the motions so that they would all leave me alone. Marty led me to his car, where his wife Pam and son, young Marty (who was my age), sat waiting. Pam was a lovely person; she was attractive, outgoing, and treated me like her son. Pam and young Marty reassured me as I squeezed into the back of Marty’s car. I felt safe with them, but I didn’t know what I wanted or where I was heading; my mind was messed up. They took me to the Boxing Club on Bolckow Road. I didn’t want to be there. I felt uncomfortable, but I didn’t show it. I just wanted to be with the bad boys and up to no good.

For weeks Marty chaperoned me. He’d collect me from my house, take me to the gym, and drop me back home. Marty continued with the routine of chaperoning me to and from the gym; this lasted for weeks until Marty felt I was back on track. It took me a while to get back into boxing, and with Marty’s help, I soon focused again and stayed away from the bad influences of the local naughty boys. I became engrossed in boxing and trained hard. I put all my effort into the sport, and I lost a few fights, but that didn’t deter me; I kept going. With Marty’s constant support and guidance, I soon started to enjoy boxing, and the dream of being a World Champion entered my thoughts again.

The boys at the Club were like my family; they supported and encouraged me, rallying around me whenever I felt down. It was like a youth club, as well as a boxing gym, there was a pool table, darts board and a tuck shop. Marty never asked me for subs, which was 50 pence per week. He knew that I didn't have the money. He even bought me all my boxing gear. I felt a bit uncomfortable wearing the boxing gear Marty had bought me. I thought that I didn't deserve any special treatment. I knew Marty saw through all the bad boy nonsense and believed I had some boxing potential. He became a massive influence on my life. He believed in me from day one and became the father figure that I desperately needed.

John 'Cornelius' Carr Age 12 Receiving Another Boxing Trophy

I was walking to school, late as usual and smoking a cigarette, when I saw one of the senior boxers, who was also a trainer at my gym, Peter Cairns, he walked toward me. As soon as I saw Peter, I quickly hid the cigarette behind my back. He said, “How are you doing, John?” It was just general chit-chat about boxing for a few seconds, and then he headed off in the other direction. I carried on walking, thinking I’d got away with smoking, when Pete turned around and shouted, “John put that cigarette out, or you’ll never become a Champ!” I thought about the words he said all day at school, “You will never become a Champ!” After that moment, I never smoked again. It’s strange how a relatively small exchange would have a great impact on my life. Why do we cherry-pick memories? This memory was etched in my brain. It was so significant, they were just a few words, but they meant so much. Some people we meet on our life’s journey can make us change our route and encourage us to choose a better path, and I don’t think Peter was aware of how his words impacted me that day and how they had a massive effect on my future, especially in my boxing career.

At the age of thirteen, I had many friends in Grangetown; Shaun Lacey was one of my best friends. We both played football for St Peter’s Comprehensive school and Grangetown Boys Club. Shaun always played left-back defence, and I played right-back defence. Shaun was a good boxer, too, he trained with me at Marty’s gym, and we would have sparring bouts. On one occasion, I felt bad because I hurt him with an uppercut. Sometimes I would get carried away in the ring, eager to prove my boxing ability. Eventually, Marty stopped me from sparring with boys my own age and would put me in with the senior squad because I was becoming too sharp and too skilled. Shaun loved all sports. He was also clever in school too, unlike me. I was envious of Shaun's intelligence, and I wished that I had been bright like him.

I became aware at a young age that I had a natural boxing gift. I think that everyone has strength, and we all have natural gifts given to us. I think good boxers are born; they possess a natural instinctive flair, they move well, they have quick reactions and style in the ring, plus they have the right mental attitude. Boxing can be taught to a degree, but there is something a talented boxer is born with; it is in the soul, they have a fire within, and I think a little bit of the devil is required too. Boxing can be a tough and lonely sport; I believe it's important to possess a mixture of many qualities to become a top fighter.

How do you know if you have a gift? If I hadn't found boxing by a fluke incident, I would never have discovered my boxing gift. I could have had other gifts, becoming a rower, a ballet dancer, a rugby player, a tennis player, a musician etc. I have never tried another sport apart from football, and I know I wasn't gifted there. To find a gift, I would have needed to try many activities, but my family was poor, and my mother sometimes didn't have any money to pay for my school dinners, let alone pay for me to have ballet lessons. Opportunities to try new sports didn't exist for kids like me. Could I have been another Billy Elliot? Maybe not, although boxers and ballet dancers have similar tough training regimes and need to have good balance and strength. Money is often required to find your gift, to join a team, club or group, and there are payments required. I watch the Olympic Games and wonder how many entrants are from poor families. Most boxers normally derive from humble beginnings, and it's rare to find an upper-class boy in the boxing ring. Why does being poor make you a good boxer? Could it be the fight to survive, to better yourself, to punch your way out of the shit?

We didn't have access to rowing clubs, archery, fencing, tennis or polo in Grangetown or at St Peter's Comprehensive school. I'll never know if I had a gift to be a dressage horseman. I wasn't born into a wealthy family, to find out. Children with wealthy parents can have many interests in order to find their gift, it's an important factor, especially when you think about the meagre opportunities working-class kids have in comparison. I believe there should be more diverse activities in ordinary schools; successful people should visit schools to inspire young people, to encourage them to find their natural gifts. I believe this should be discussed by decision-makers, and working-class children should have the same access to privileged sports as upper-class individuals have, i.e., rowing, fencing, polo, and skiing. There are many working-class people in the world who will never know they have a gift, and I think that is sad and it needs to change. It's all about the money. No funds, no gift. Meeting the right people also helps. As the saying goes, 'it's not what you know, it's who you know.' I was lucky that Marty found me that day in Grisedale Crescent. If I hadn't met Marty, I'm not sure which path I would have taken. I have a feeling it wouldn't have been the right one. Was it a coincidence that I met Marty, or did fate play a hand?

John 'Cornelius' Carr Age 13 with His Boxing Trophies

It was a Holy Day, on a Thursday, 19th June 1983, and we had a day off school. Holy Days were exciting, it was a chance for us to have fun away from the boring routine of the school day, and we could do something interesting together. All my friends were outside my house discussing where we were going to go that day, and someone suggested swimming at Eston Baths; for some reason, I didn't want to go. This was unusual for me because I loved swimming and diving off the diving boards. Most of the group wanted to go swimming. Therefore a decision was made, and a gang of us walked to the Baths, which was about three miles away. We didn't have enough money to take a bus, pay for swimming and buy a snack afterwards, so we used our feet to walk three miles to the baths.

We were excited when we arrived at the baths. I could smell the chlorine and feel the heat of the pool; as soon as I walked through the doors, my senses were triggered, and I couldn't wait to dive into the water. We paid at reception and had our locker tokens, then changed into our swimwear and raced towards the pool as quickly as we could, racing one another, slipping and sliding on the wet tiled floor. We all wanted to be the first to jump into the water. I hated having the chlorine-filled water in my eyes, it burned my eyes, and I ended up swallowing large amounts of it, too. I couldn't afford swimming goggles like the other kids. The most popular game we played was Tigs (Tag). We dashed, splashed and swam in the warm water, chasing each other in the swimming pool, tagging (touching) one another, and then swimming off. There were three diving boards over the pool, which were at different height levels. The first and second diving boards were springboards with no barriers. The highest board was more solid, like a large platform, with bars at each side. We always went on the diving boards; it was a challenge to see who could be the most daring and brave. We hadn't been at the pool very long when we headed for the diving boards. I saw a few lads on the second diving board, and I was at the top board looking down at them. We were excitable, laughing, and enjoying the fun, taunting each other to see who would be the bravest. The kids on the second diving board jumped off quickly, one after another, including Shaun, but instead of jumping in the pool like the other kids, Shaun dived in head-first. I decided to dive into the pool from the top board shortly after Shaun had dived into the water and swam over to the left-hand side of the pool. After a few minutes, I saw someone getting pulled out of the pool.

I saw a small crowd of people gathered; they were huddled together, looking down, but because there were so many people grouped together, I couldn't see what was going on and why they had gathered there. I climbed out of the pool to see what all the commotion was about, and as I got closer, I saw my friend Shaun lying on the wet tiled floor lifeless; he looked small and limp. I watched helplessly as Shaun went in and out of consciousness. I turned to one of my friends and said, "Oh fuck, that's Shaun. What's happened?" All of us were in shock. We didn't know what had happened to Shaun. I wanted to get close to him to help and be there for him, but one of the pool staff stopped me. A boy who stood near me was rubbing his back, with a look on his face which suggested he was in pain and said, "I think someone landed on me. I've got a bad back."

I wanted to battle my way through the crowd and hold Shaun, showing him that I was there for him, but we weren't allowed to go near him. I was angry and frustrated. We all watched as the lifeguards desperately worked on Shaun, I'm not sure what they were doing to him altogether, but it looked harsh. They were pumping his chest, and then I watched the paramedics arrive and place Shaun on a stretcher carefully, and then they carried him out of the building. I was told that they had rushed Shaun by ambulance to Middlesbrough General Hospital.

After the shocking incident, we all left the baths, and I walked to Shaun's house to tell his mam, Mary, that Shaun had an accident and that he was in the hospital. I stood at the front door, eager to tell her about Shaun. I tried to reassure her that Shaun was ok. I genuinely thought that he was fine. In my twelve-year-old mind, I thought that a trip to the hospital would make him better. I thought that because he was in the hospital, they would look after him and do whatever was necessary to make Shaun well again, I assumed he would be alright, and Shaun would come home that evening. After all, I had made a recovery in the hospital when I had meningitis; why wouldn't Shaun recover? I didn't have a clue about the severity of the accident and how it would affect our lives, and in particular, Shaun's life.

A few days later, I heard that Shaun was still in hospital, but he had been moved to another one. He was taken from Middlesbrough General to Hexham Spinal Unit, where a few of us from the Boxing Club went to see him. Before I saw Shaun, I imagined that I would see the old Shaun sitting up in bed eating chocolates and grapes. The nurse told us that only a few of us could see Shaun at a time. She said that too many visitors would overwhelm him. I didn't like the smells that lingered in that hospital; it was an aroma of a combination of bodily fluids and disinfectant.

I entered his hospital room, where I saw Shaun lying on his back in the hospital bed with a huge round metal ring screwed to both sides of his head, near the temple areas. You could see the screws sticking into his skull. There seemed to be long pieces of steel attached to Shaun's neck and head; it looked like a Meccano set, with bolts and screws and metal pieces all fitted together. I was scared to see Shaun like that. It was shocking, it was alien to me, and I'd never seen anything like it before. I wasn't sure what to do or what to say to Shaun. Shaun couldn't move his head or body but had large mirrors in front of the bed to enable him to see us. Shaun was still Shaun, even though he was trapped in the metal head cage, and he tried to make a joke of the situation, but I couldn't laugh. I was speechless, staring at him.

I discovered that day that Shaun was paralysed from the chest down and that he would never walk again. Everyone was silent as Marty drove us back in the car from the hospital after the visit. We couldn't understand that one silly mistake had changed Shaun's life forever. He would be in a wheelchair for the rest of his life, and he was just thirteen years old. Shaun had many operations and spent months in hospital after the accident. He suffered a lot but smiled through it, taking everything in his stride. The accident could have happened to any one of us that day at the baths, and I wonder how I would have coped if something like that had happened to me.

In all the years I've known Shaun, he's never questioned why it had happened to him. He doesn't complain about anything and remains positive, he is an inspiration to me and many others. He certainly doesn't want anyone to feel sorry for him. His disability has never stopped him from enjoying life: he's travelled all over the world, gained numerous university degrees, skydived, abseiled, and enjoys wheelchair rugby. His accomplishments are endless; he is also a mentor to others who have experienced similar injuries. He's still my best friend, and I love him dearly.

Shaun talks openly about the day that changed his life. He says it was just one of those things, an accident, and no one is to blame. He remembers diving off the board and waking up lying at the bottom of the twelve feet deep pool. When Shaun dived off the diving board, he landed on another boy; it was a freak accident. He must have been concussed, and the spinal damage must have been instantaneous from the bodily impact. Shaun sank to the bottom of the pool. He tried to move his arms and legs, but he was paralysed. He couldn't understand why he couldn't move any part of his body at the time. Shaun says that it seemed like an eternity laying still at the bottom of the pool, but it must have only been just a minute or so. Shaun regained consciousness again at the side of the pool, with everyone standing over him, trying to revive him.

It's a miracle that Shaun survived. The lifeguards weren't at their stations, they were gathered in a different area just outside of the pool. Luckily for Shaun, a young girl who was walking back to the changing rooms saw the accident and ran to find a lifeguard, one of the lifeguards dived into the pool and dragged Shaun out. Many years later, Shaun was in a nightclub when a girl approached him and said, "You don't know who I am, do you?" Shaun thought it was his lucky night. She said, "I was the girl who got the lifeguard who dragged you out of the pool." They both hugged one another and cried. I admire Shaun so much, his daily life is filled with challenges, but you will never see him defeated; he is a fighter too. Shaun lives in Normanby, and we meet up as often as we can, speaking regularly on social media or on the phone.

Round Five – Royalty

At fourteen, I was really into boxing. I was obsessively training six days a week, both with the Junior and Senior squads. I had stopped all the silly stuff by then, but I was struggling to get contests, I'm not sure why. I would always try and be the best, and to be the best boxer in the gym, I needed quality sparring. I would often spar with lads much older than me to stretch my skills, I'd often take a hiding, but I would go back for more the following day. I'd never give up; I was like a dog with a bone. The Boxing Club would travel all over the Northeast on boxing events, and I loved to go with the lads, even though sometimes I wasn't boxing on the show. I'd take my boxing equipment just in case there was an opponent found for me. I was classed as a 'spare.' I'd weigh in and wait around, hoping that an opponent would be found, but it never happened. I still enjoyed the comradery of being around the team.

Our team had a show in Harrogate, and I was a spare yet again, and so was Tony Boyes, who was about five years my senior. Marty managed to find an opponent for Tony, and he was Henry Wharton, who was a young up-and-coming boxing star from Leeds. The boxing event was a dinner show and held at one of the most prestigious venues in Harrogate, The Majestic, which was a large hotel and conference centre where the Queen stayed when she attended the Yorkshire Show. Just before we all got off the minibus at the venue, Marty gave us a lecture, and he said, "Right boys, everyone on their best behaviour, this is a fantastic venue, and I don't want any of you nicking anything, keep your hands in your pockets. Don't let Grangetown down." He specifically turned to me and said, "Especially you, John." Everyone was giggling, and even Marty had a slight smile on his face. The exterior of the hotel was huge, grand, and imposing, and I had never seen a building like it before. I was in awe when I entered the hotel. I was wide-eyed and open-mouthed; it was magnificent. I'd never seen grandeur like it. It had huge windows, floor-to-ceiling velvet drapes, massive sparkling crystal chandeliers everywhere I looked, and the décor oozed sheer luxury. The hotel really was fit for a Queen.

I found out I wasn't boxing, so I went for a wander around the beautiful hotel before the show started. I was an inquisitive young boy, always wanting to see what stood behind closed doors. I was intrigued by the hotel and its opulence. I opened a blue door and saw a large stack of beautiful gold-plated crockery and silver-plated cutlery, and it was mesmerising. The rogue inside me raised his ugly head, and I rushed back to the changing room to get my gym bag. No one noticed me in the changing room because they were busy preparing for the dinner show. I went back to the small room where the crockery and cutlery were stored and filled the bag with whole dinner service for three people, including silver-plated salt and pepper pots. I went back to the changing room and left the haul there, and then went to the large conference room where I enjoyed watching the boxing show. That night was successful for our Club, we had two wins and one loss, and everyone was in a happy mood. It was late when we all left the venue, Marty opened the back door of the minivan, and I put my kit bag on the floor. As the bag went down, there was a huge clink and crash sound. Marty said, "What the hell have you got in there? Open it up!" I reluctantly opened the bag, and everyone crowded around to see what was in my bag. They all sighed when they saw the gleaming haul of gold-plated crockery and silver-plated cutlery stash. Marty wasn't impressed with me. He didn't know what to do, and he couldn't very well take it back to the hotel. I said, "Oh, come on, Mart, that will look good on our table tomorrow. I want to treat our mam." It was wrong to steal, and I detest thieves, but in our home on Coniston Road, we barely had knives and forks, so this small sample of luxury meant a lot to me at the time. When I arrived home, I proudly presented my mam with the shiny treasure, she didn't ask any questions, and I didn't tell her where it came from. We loved looking at it, and it reminded me of the elegant Majestic Hotel. It did look good on our little kitchenette table in our council house. We all ate like royalty for many years. (I'd like to take this opportunity to apologise to the Majestic Hotel for my behaviour in the past).

Marty made a fight for me with a schoolboy champion named Jamie Nicholson. The fight was to take place in Knottingley Workingmen's Club, Knottingley, Yorkshire.

Jamie was the young up-and-coming boxing superstar of his area, unbeknown to me at the time. This was a pivotal fight in my career as a young amateur boxer, my first real test. I'd lost only two of my previous fights before this contest. I was still only fourteen and had fifteen fights in total at this stage, and this contest meant a lot to me. I knew that Jamie had many more fights than me and therefore was more experienced.

When I arrived at the social club, there were posters of Jamie everywhere, even in my dressing room. Marty pointed at a poster and said, "This is the boy you are fighting". I was the underdog, but I wasn't intimidated by this. I felt confident that I had a good chance of winning the fight. Marty had bought me all the boxing equipment, including a white hooded silk robe, white silk shorts, a white vest, and white Title boots; I felt a million dollars, like a true boxing champ. Marty wasn't allowed to go in my corner because he had been banned for six months for shouting at the judges in my previous contest. I had boxed a boy named Jamie Gamblin, and everyone thought that I had won the contest except two of the judges. Marty was fuming because they gave the fight to Jamie when everyone from my Club and the crowd thought that I had unanimously won. Marty was so annoyed.

In amateur boxing, this kind of decision happens frequently, and it deters youngsters from continuing in the art of boxing. For a young amateur boxer to clearly win a fight and for judges to take that victory away is devastating for that youngster. Generally, the hometown boxing star wins the decision whether the boxer deserves to win or not. Bad decisions occur both at low and high levels in boxing matches, and one bad decision that sticks out in my mind at a high level was at the Olympic final in October 1988 in Seoul, South Korea. Roy Jones Junior was fighting Park Si-Hun and was beaten on a 3-2 decision by the judges. Everyone thought that Roy had won that contest. Roy Jones Junior was a superstar of the 1988 Olympic Games, and they robbed him of a Gold Medal. Three years after those Olympics, I had the privilege of sparring Roy Jones Junior in Reno, Nevada, USA. Roy went on to be an outstanding boxer, winning various Title fights.

The Social Club was small and smoky and filled to the rafters with Jamie Nicholson supporters. I had to push my way through the crowds to get to the boxing ring, and as I struggled to move through the sea of people, I thought I saw a big man in a checked shirt with a trilby hat. For a split second, I could have sworn it was my dad. I wanted it to be my dad, but the fleeting image left me. It did, however, give me confidence and a feeling that my dad was around, watching me and supporting me.

I waited in the red corner for Jamie to appear. As he appeared, the crowd went crazy, cheering him as if he was a superstar champion boxer. The sound of the crowd was deafening. The bell rang, the fight commenced, and the noise of the spectators faded away, and the only voice I could hear was Marty's. He was shouting orders at me from ringside, "one-two, move your head, left jab!" This was three rounds of boxing, it was a tough fight, but I felt confident that I had done enough to win the fight. After the contest, we shook hands and stood on either side of the referee, with the referee holding each boxer's gloved hand. It felt like a long time before the announcer received the scorecards, and I closed my eyes, willing the announcer to raise my arm. I was thinking, 'Dad, if you are here, please help me win.' The announcer said, "And the winner is Carr, in the red corner." I searched the audience looking for my dad, but sadly he was nowhere to be seen. The crowd went silent, my small team were elated, Marty was screaming and shouting with excitement, and my sister Susan went berserk, jumping up and down. I didn't see Jamie after the fight, but we did have other amateur encounters later when I won two fights, and he won two fights. As I left the ring, all the spectators were very respectful, slapping me on the back and congratulating me. I was walking on air; it was an incredible feeling. I was lucky that the judges for that fight were honest and fair. As I was leaving the venue with my kit bag over my shoulder, they were announcing who was the best boxer of the evening. Marty said, "Wait, let's see who it is." The announcer said, "The winner is John Carr from Grangetown ABC." I couldn't believe it; the crowd were all standing and applauding as I was presented with a huge trophy which was nearly as big as me.

As a teenager, I didn't have any designer clothes or shoes, but I desired them. I used to envy all the other kids who paraded in their flashy designer wear. The names I coveted were Adidas, Puma, Diodora, Pringle, La Coste etc. There were many cool kids in school who wore designer clothes and shoes, I certainly wasn't one of those kids. One boy picked on me for a few months, making fun of my clothes, saying I had 'Asdadas' four stripe trainers. My shoes were from Asda and made from plastic instead of the real leather product, Adidas three stripe trainers. He was taking the piss out of me. He said, "You think you're hard because you are boxing? I'll fight you anytime." I was wary of him, a little afraid of him, and I kept out of his way. At school, I tried to keep out of trouble because I was committed to my boxing training. I was told your hands are weapons and should only be used in the boxing ring.

I was in the fourth year at St Peter's comprehensive school, and a few of us were playing football in the schoolyard at lunchtime. It was a kickabout between the fourth and fifth-year senior boys. The boy I feared, Pete O'Hara, was playing for the fifth-year side. We both jumped up to head the ball at the same time when he elbowed me in my back viciously. As I turned around, he had a sickly smile on his face and said, grinning, "What are you going to do about it?" I automatically went into a boxing stance and barraged him with multiple punches; he didn't know what had hit him. He didn't have an opportunity to hit me back, and I pummelled him. We were pulled apart, and I shouted to him, "After school!" The other kids in my year were in awe of my fast hands and boxing skills, and within an hour of the fight, I heard that Pete O'Hara didn't want to fight me after school anymore, and he didn't bother me again after that. Boxing was great for me. It gave me confidence and the ability to defend myself.

After my dad died, his loss affected our family both emotionally and financially. My mam didn't go out much, and our Sue suggested that she should go to the British Legion on a Sunday night for a game of bingo and a few drinks with her friends. My mam refused to go. I suppose she was in a bit of a rut. We couldn't understand why she wanted to stay in all the time and not enjoy having a bit of fun with her friends. Our Sue arranged for my mam's friend Betty to call in to try and persuade our mam to go to bingo, and the plan worked when she said she would go. We organised for my mam to attend the Legion with her friends on the following Sunday evening, we helped to dress her in the most glamorous clothes we could find in her wardrobe, and she even put some lippy and mascara on. After her first visit to the Legion, it became a ritual that my mam would go to the Legion every Thursday and Sunday evening. If there was a reason that she couldn't go to the Legion, there would be hell on, she would have a tantrum, get agitated, shout, scream and say in defiance that she would walk there herself if she had to. Well, this was impossible because she couldn't walk very far. She was disabled.

I was a mischievous fourteen-year-old, and I loved winding her up, telling her that I couldn't take her out, and then I'd wait for the sparks to fly. I shouldn't have teased her, but she was an easy target. She would react quickly, firing up, and then have a major tantrum. After she had calmed down, I'd stop teasing her and promised to take her to the Legion, and she'd be dolled up to the nines, sitting in her wheelchair waiting for me to push her there, dead at 7 pm. Sometimes I'd hang around and would watch her from the doorway of the club as she'd play four books of bingo, and that fascinated me, how she marked the books so quickly, keeping up with the speed of the bingo caller. I'll never know how she did it. At the Legion, she could have a few beers, a couple of games of bingo and a singsong, and enjoy having banter with her friends.

It was nice to see my mother getting her life back and not rotting away at home. I'd collect her at 11 o'clock, but she was never on time, always one of the last people to leave the Legion. On the way home, as I pushed her up the road, even though her speech was affected by the strokes, she would try and sing Shirley Bassey songs at the top of her voice. I'd say, "Mam shut up. You'll wake everyone up." But she wouldn't take any notice. She just laughed and carried on singing as loud and as clearly as she could in her own unique way,

"Hey, Big Spender! Duh duh durra. Spend a little time with me!"

One winter's evening, as I wheeled her to the Legion, it had started to snow. I said, "Mam, are you sure you still want to go? You could get snowed in." She looked up at me, didn't say a word and gave me one of her defiant looks. I knew that however bad the weather was going to be, nothing would prevent her from going to bingo that evening. I left the wheelchair at the Legion and walked back home; I kept an eye on the weather that evening and could see it was getting worse; the snow was coming down thick and fast. I spent the rest of the night debating whether I should collect her early or not.

When I returned to the Legion to collect my mam, I was ten minutes early due to the blizzard, and I was worried that I wouldn't get her home. I knew I needed to get there early before the pavements were impassable. The snow was twelve inches deep on the ground in some places, and I could hardly see the road ahead. The snow swept at me in frozen waves as I headed to the Club. I struggled to get to the Legion on my own, let alone pushing our mam in her wheelchair. It was a bitterly cold night, and I was slipping as I crunched my way through the deep snow-covered pavements. I was soaking wet, and my hands and face were frozen. Luckily, I had my wellies on, which protected my feet from the cold, but I wasn't wearing any gloves and wore a thin coat and beanie hat.

When I arrived, I saw my mam sitting amongst her group of friends at a long table. I watched her from the doorway of the Legion. I waved at her to grab her attention, quietly mouthing and pointing at my watch, "Come on, mam, we've got to go. The weather's bad." Children of my age weren't allowed in the Legion. I had to wait outside. She wasn't happy that I was early because she still had half a pint of Tetley left. She was oblivious to the bad weather outside, and she was cocooned by the safety of the happy, warm, smoky club. I repeatedly asked her to leave until she finally made a move to come with me. She managed to stand up with the aid of her walking stick. I used that stick to tease our dog, Rex. It was covered in teeth marks where Rex attacked the stick when I would tease him with it.

With some help from her friends, she slowly walked toward me, swearing and muttering under her breath that I was early. She came to the door and hooked her arm in mine. I led her to a porch area where I had positioned the wheelchair ready for her at the bottom of a small step. The Legion was packed, and everyone was trying to leave at the same time. People were pushing and shoving in their eagerness to get home. I was just focusing on getting my mam down the step, into her chair, and home safely. I struggled to get her in the wheelchair. It was hard work, my mam wasn't a lightweight, and people were pushing past us. I swore at them loudly, "Fucking wait!" As we left the Legion, the snow was so deep the wheels of the chair were partly hidden in the snow. I couldn't see the kerb of the pavement and had to judge where I thought the kerbs were. I was afraid that if I misjudged the path, she'd topple out of the chair. My mam's feet, ankles and shins were lost in the cold snow as I struggled to push her in the wheelchair. She was shivering and silent; being quiet was unusual for my mother, she would always be vocal during our route home. I was worried that she would get pneumonia. I used all my boy strength as a fourteen-year-old to push her heavy body through the drifting snow that night. It seemed as if the journey had taken hours to complete.

Eventually, we arrived home. I was exhausted, stressed and relieved. I helped her take off her wet clothes and warmed her up with a blanket in front of the electric fire. I always feared fires. I was taught not to stand in front of fires from a young age because my grandmother, my mother's mother, had died from the results of her nightie catching fire as she stood before an electric fire to get warm. Apparently, it was a slow, painful death. She had suffered 90% burns and tragically died a few weeks after the accident. She was only in her sixties when she died. I believe that I saw my grandmother's spirit walking down the stairs in the house in Wilton way; she was in her nightdress. I was scared, and my stomach churned over. It was a fleeting glimpse of a ghostly image, and I somehow knew that it was my grandmother. The brief sighting of her has remained a vivid memory. I think I have the ability to connect with spirits. I dressed my mam in her night clothes and put her to bed.

We moved to Wilton Way, Eston, in 1984. It was a three-bedroomed terrace council house, larger than the previous house on Coniston Road. I had a small bedroom of my own, and Sue had her own bedroom, which was larger than mine. I was thrilled that I had my own bedroom. Even though it was only a box room, at least I had some privacy. Our house was always a mess, my mam couldn't clean up due to her disability, and my sister and I were just kids, we just did the best we could, but housework wasn't a priority. It was normal to have piles of dirty clothes scattered everywhere. There was no organisation; it was a chaotic household.

It's a wonder we weren't sparking objects as we walked because we had a massive electricity substation with numerous tall pylons just outside our house, which permanently made a buzzing sound. The substation is still there today near the same properties. We were used to living near it and just accepted that the substation was part of our everyday landscape.

We were always short of money, and my mam had to support the family on a small budget from her disability allowance and family allowance. I used to see all my friends going on holiday and wondered why we couldn't do the same, and I kept asking our mam when we could have a holiday. Our Sue and my mam tried to explain to me that we didn't have the funds to go abroad on holiday. Sue had an idea, "Why don't we sell that old gold chain that our dad had?" The chain was a long heavy chain, which I could wrap around my neck a few times. I think it was an antique pocket watch chain. It could have been my great grandfather's. He had been a wealthy butcher, and there were no other wealthy relatives that I knew of who could have owned it. We didn't know what it was worth or who my dad inherited it from, but we knew it was worth something. I was excited at the thought of going somewhere exotic on holiday from the proceeds of the sale of the chain.

The following day Sue and I visited a pawnbroker in Middlesbrough town centre. The pawnbroker looked at the chain briefly and said, "Oh, very nice, but gold isn't in high demand at the moment, and prices are low." He took the chain into a private room, but we could see him through a small window. He looked at the chain through a magnifying glass, and weighed it, then made a phone call. We couldn't hear what he was saying. He was on the phone for a few minutes, and he came out and said, "The best price I can give you is £300." We were in shock. That was a lot of money back then. We didn't haggle, and we didn't get any other opinion. We took his word for it. Our Sue turned to me and said," What do you think, our John?" I just nodded my head quickly and excitedly, saying, "Yeah, yeah, yeah, yeah." Looking back at this scenario, it was a ridiculous thing to do. We were so naïve that the chain was probably worth three times as much as the money we were offered, but we were young and didn't understand that we were being ripped off. He paid us in cash in £20 notes, and I watched him closely as he counted the £300, slowly placing each £20 note on the counter. I couldn't stop smiling. Spain, here we come! Our Sue quickly shoved the money in her handbag. We went straight to the travel agent, Siesta Travel, and booked a holiday in Salou, Spain. We had enough cash to pay for the holiday for the three of us, our mam, our Sue and me, plus there was enough money left over to use as spending money on holiday.

The package holiday included staying in an apartment complex in Salou, we would travel there by coach and stay there for two weeks. I was so excited, at the age of fourteen I hadn't travelled out of the UK before, the furthest I had travelled to was Leeds. I had seen pictures of Spain, and it seemed like paradise, with palm trees, blue skies, and gorgeous sandy beaches.

This was a huge adventure for me, and I couldn't keep still with excitement as we stood waiting for the coach to arrive. The coach had left Sunderland with passengers, then went on to Middlesbrough, where we were picked up. We put our bags and our mam's wheelchair in the hold of the coach. It was a large modern double-decker coach with all mod cons, including a toilet. Mam and Sue sat downstairs due to mam's disability, and I found a great seat upstairs right in the front with uninterrupted views. I had a double seat all to myself until we got to the next coach station in

Sheffield. I was hoping that no one would sit next to me so that I could stretch out and relax during the thirty-two-hour journey, 1,230 miles from Middlesbrough, to be precise. I put my feet up across the seat and pretended to be asleep, and I could hear all the commotion of the passengers boarding the coach downstairs and kept up the pretence of being asleep upstairs. A man nudged my leg and said in a thick Yorkshire accent, "Eh up lad, anyone sitting here?" I sat up straight and apologetically said, "I'm really sorry. I must have fallen asleep, there's no one sitting there." The bus was full, and there were no spare seats. He settled down next to me and started eating his mint imperials from a small paper bag with a smug look on his face. My plan had failed. Never mind, at least I had someone to talk to. I was a chatty kid.

The coach headed towards Dover. The time went quickly for me as I enjoyed the journey, absorbing every aspect of every new town we passed through, discovering interesting sights along the way, noticing the nice properties, wondering who lived in them, and wishing one day that I would live in a lovely property like that. The next stage of the journey was by ferry from Dover to Calais. I couldn't believe the vast size of the ferry and watched in awe as we sailed away from the white cliffs of Dover toward France. It was a lovely warm sunny evening. The sea was calm, I felt alive as I breathed in the salty sea air as we headed towards France, and I lapped up the new experience.

The coach drove off the ferry with its weary passengers and headed to our destination, the Spanish coast and it had been a long journey to Spain. I must have fallen asleep during some of the coach journey to Salou but surprisingly felt fresh when we arrived in Spain. As we disembarked from the coach, hot air blasted us, and there was an alien, foreign smell in the air that signified we were in a strange new place. I loved the Spanish heat. I loved being a foreigner, and I couldn't wait to unpack my case and go outside to discover Salou. I was so happy. We did everything together on that holiday. We had a great time; I was tanned and thought I was handsome, my hair was blonde, and I was muscular and toned from my boxing training. I used to squeeze lemon juice on my hair as I lay in the sunshine to make it blonder. I had a quiff in the front of my hair, which I sprayed with strong hairspray that I pinched from our Sue, who used to shout at me when I sprayed it generously to keep it high and in place. I wanted to look my best because there might be a Spanish Senorita who was looking for a nice Grangetown lad. One afternoon after lunch, we were at a restaurant bar, my mam was in her wheelchair sipping a cold beer, and our Sue had an exotic-looking cocktail with all the trimmings like Del Boy from Only Fools and Horses, and I had a few shandies whilst playing on the Space Invaders amusement game.

An American businessman, who wore dress shorts, a nice shirt, leather shoes, and a gold watch (which I was fascinated by) walked across the room and sat next to my mam, and they started to have a conversation. He was a good-looking guy who spoiled us, buying us all drinks for the remainder of the evening and bragging about how great America was, and then invited us all to stay with him in Texas. His tales were funny and entertaining and enthused me, and I wanted to go there to see for myself how wonderful America was. He had sold me the dream. By early evening, my mam and Sue were half cut and laughing, giggling and flirting with the American. We all enjoyed his company, especially when he opened his wallet to buy us drinks. We were all having fun talking to the American man when he said, "I have to go now. I'm leaving early tomorrow." He got up from the seat and kissed my mam on the cheek, and I noticed she went bright red, blushing from the kiss.

I pushed my mam back to the apartment, laughing, our Sue and I were making fun of her because she had been flirting and chatted up by the rich American. We said, "Oh, mam, you are going to marry a millionaire, and we'll get out of Grangetown and move to Texas." We carried on laughing and teasing my mam all the way back to our apartment. When we got inside the door of the apartment, we continued to wind up our Mam about the American; we didn't let it drop. Our mam was laughing uncontrollably, and then suddenly, she started shaking and became breathless. She was panicking, struggling to breathe and couldn't gain composure, and her face was turning bright red. It was frightening to watch, and it reminded me of the time my dad had his heart attack. Susan panicked and shouted, "She's going to die." Sue was running around the room in a hysterical state, unsure of how to deal with the situation. I was calm and didn't panic. I bent down to be at eye level with my mam in her chair, I put my face close to hers, held her face in my hands to make sure she was looking at me, and said calmly but firmly, "Look at me, look at me! Breathe, mam, breathe." And I showed her how to breathe. I was very animated, slowly inhaling and exhaling. Luckily, she followed my instructions, watching me, copying me and then, to my relief, she started breathing correctly again. There were no more jokes on that holiday after that. My mam's 'wobbler' scared the shit of my sister and me. We both realised how fragile she had become.

Round Six – Amateur Boxing Association

Marty said, "I had a phone call a few days ago from the Yorkshire squad asking if you wanted to box for Yorkshire against London Select." I had only just returned from holiday, feeling fresh, and I was well up for it. He said, "If you take this contest, you're up against one of the top kids in the country." He was the Schoolboy Boxing Champion, Jamie Robinson from well renowned Repton ABC, the Club was based in the East End of London and had a long tradition of producing Amateur Boxing Champions, and the gym is often filmed for movie locations. The award-winning actor Ray Winston boxed at Repton; it's an iconic club. The fact that he was a good kid from a good club didn't deter me. I think I was selected because of my last fight when I beat Jamie Nicholson. The win against Jamie gave me the confidence and self-belief to face the next fight, and I thought I stood a good chance of winning. I was the only boxer from Middlesbrough to be selected, and the contest was held in Brewster Hall Romford. There were many contests that night, including the young actor from the children's TV drama Grange Hill, Lee Macdonald, known to many as 'Zammo', who was a good amateur boxer.

On the evening of the fight, I was well prepared both mentally and physically, I knew Jamie was the golden boy who was fighting in his hometown, and I was the underdog yet again. He had Jimmy Tibbs in his corner, who later became a famous trainer for professional boxers, and when

Jamie Robinson came out into the ring, I was shocked to see how big, strong, and confident he looked. The room was packed with people, and everyone was cheering for Jamie, but that didn't bother me, I was there to win. They were all strangers to me. I just wanted to prove myself and show them that a boy from Grangetown could be just as good in the boxing ring as any kid from the East end of London.

The first round was close. I remember going back to my corner and Marty saying, "you've got to let your hands go; you've got to get busy." He looked me in the face and said authoritatively, "Let's start backing this kid up; let's do it!" And that's exactly what I did. I went for it. It was a tough contest, but I think I had done enough to win. At the end of the fight, Marty said, "That was your fight. You won that." But I knew that sometimes even though you thought you had won, the judges could give the fight to the hometown boxer. When I was announced the winner, I was surprised and overjoyed. I shook Jamie's hand and his team's hands and said to Jamie, "I'm sure we'll meet in the Championships next year." I had beaten two Schoolboy Champions within a few months of each other, and my dream was to become a Schoolboy Champion and box for England.

The following year was the last opportunity for me to be a Schoolboy Champion, I was fifteen, and my dream to win the Championship had been with me since I started boxing at eleven years old. I participated in the Schoolboy Championships every year and only ever reached the quarter-finals. I knew that this would be my last chance to win. I would be too old to compete in the competition next year. I was 67kg, a welterweight, the heaviest I had been. I had two fights previously to reach the quarter-finals and drew with a boy from Liverpool to fight in the quarter-final, which would be held at Knottingley, the same venue I had boxed against Jamie Nicholson a few months previously.

Two days before the fight, I had a bad head cold; I was coughing and spluttering and feeling like crap. I didn't want to pull out of the fight even though I was feeling rough, Marty suggested that I go to a sauna to try and sweat out the cold, but it didn't work. It was worth a try, though. On the day of the fight, I was feeling awful, I felt weak and lifeless, but I knew I had to gain strength from somewhere and continue with the fight, winning was my dream, and I was so close to fulfilling my ambition. I found out a day before the fight that the boy I was about to box was a Southpaw. I'd always had problems boxing against Southpaws. I'm not sure why. They were just awkward to box, I'd boxed a young Southpaw boxer Tony Penn twice, and he had beaten me twice.

During the fight, my opponent was slippery and difficult to hit. I knew I had lost the first round, I went back to my corner, and Marty was trying to encourage me, saying, "Come on, John, you've got to get yourself together!" I didn't feel strong, and I was weak from the illness. Marty kept shoving Vick's vapour rub up my nose, trying to help me breathe properly as my nose was blocked. During the second round, the lad caught me with a full-on right jab to my face, and it knocked me to my core, unsettling me. My head was spinning. I saw stars just like you in cartoons. I felt lucky to survive the second round and avoid a knockout. Just before the third and last round started, Marty said, "This is your last round. You have to try and stop him!" I was still reeling from the punch in the second round, but I went out in the third round thinking I was not getting caught again. I was being overly cautious in the ring, and then I heard Marty screaming, "Come on, John, let your hands go!" Marty's words triggered something inside me, and I battered the boy, throwing some big shots, but he took it. He wouldn't go down. He was a strong kid and took the beating, and I knew the only way I would win was by a TKO. At the end of the fight, I thought I might have won it, but Marty looked at me, shaking his head, "I don't think it was your fight, John."

The referee brought us together in the middle of the ring, and the announcer said, "And the winner of the 1984 Schoolboy quarter-final at 67 kg is Phillips". I was devastated. I could just about control myself, holding back the tears. I just wanted to sink to my knees and bawl my eyes out. It was traumatic for a young boy to accept that he would never fulfil his dream of becoming a Schoolboy Champion. I'm not sure why I was so gutted. It could have been a combination of things; although I hardly attended school, boxing was a source of recognition, it was a way of being respected by my peers and teachers, and I wanted them to be proud of me, at least I could say I that I was good at something at school.

After the fight, I just wanted to leave the venue and go home to lick my wounds. I walked slowly back to Marty's VW campervan and sat in the back seat because I wanted to be silent and be on my own, but Marty wouldn't have any of it and insisted that I sit next to him in the front. All the way home, we analysed what went wrong in the fight and what I could have done differently. I just had to accept it was over, and my dream was dead. I hated losing. It had a huge effect on me, and I detested going back to school, where people were asking me the same question, "What happened in your fight?" I just wished I could have had a loudspeaker to shout out once and for all, "I lost the fight!" I wanted to bury the loss in a deep grave and move away from that sorrowful date as quickly as I could. A week after the fight, I was feeling fantastic; my cold had disappeared. I thought, why couldn't I fight now? But it was too late. My chance came and went.

I went home and told our Sue that I had lost the fight in the Schoolboy Competition. She hugged me and told me not to worry. I felt that she didn't completely understand how much winning the Championship had meant to me and that it was my last opportunity to win the title of Schoolboy Champion. A few weeks later our Sue asked me to go and see a clairvoyant with her, but I refused. I wasn't into that kind of thing, fortune telling etc. I thought I might have bad news, and I had suffered enough bad news in my life. Sue went to see the clairvoyant on her own, and when she came home, I was interested to hear what the clairvoyant had said. Sue told me that the visit was a waste of time, but she said the clairvoyant had a vision and told Sue, “There is someone close to you who has a big shiny belt on.” It was a strange thing to say, and I didn’t have a clue what it meant. I wondered if she meant my dad’s belt. Sue initially went to the fortune teller to communicate with our dad. She wanted his love. She yearned for his approval and thought that by contacting him in the spirit world, she would find all the answers to her questions and hoped to hear him tell her that he loved her.

A few weeks after I had lost my contest to Phillips, Marty and I went to the Assembly Rooms in Derby to watch the final of The Schoolboy Championships. It was the boy Phillips who had beaten me against Jamie Robinson, who I had beaten a few months previously. For some reason, I felt nervous, and I had the feeling that I was fighting. The venue had a great atmosphere, it was packed out, and the level of boxing was of a high standard, showcasing the best young boxers in the country. Jamie and Phillips had a great fight. It was exciting to watch, and it was one of the best fights of the day; Jamie won on points. This was a pivotal time in my life, I remember it vividly now, I still feel the trauma of losing my fight to this day, as a child it was a massive moment, it was a turning point for me, I just had to find another dream.

Jamie and I met again when we were both professional boxers, training and sparring at the same gym in London. I have met many boxers throughout my career, and whether you win or lose, we always have respect for each other. We are the only people who understand the hard work and commitment that's required to be a boxer. Boxing is a crazy sport; it's a sport which is sometimes hard to defend, knowing that to win a contest, you must hit another person, possibly injuring them badly.

John 'Cornelius' Carr with His Trainer Marty Turner Age 15

I left school at sixteen and enrolled at Middlesbrough College. I was lucky to obtain a place studying for a Diploma in Sport. I was excited at the thought of attending college and becoming a qualified Personal Trainer. I could study during the day and train every evening. I couldn't wait to leave school. I ended up sitting five C.S.E (Certificate in Secondary Education) exams, and these qualifications weren't worth much. I think they were invented to appease kids like me who weren't up to 'O' Level standard. I'm not sure if I passed or failed the exams because I didn't go back to school to find out.

Marty had some good news for me. I had been selected to attend a weekend training with the young England Northeast boxing squad. I knew that all the best boxers in my age group would be there. I spent the weekend training under the supervision of Calvin Travis, one of the head coaches. I was intrigued by some of the more technical training methods for amateur boxing. I learned the new moves quickly and would use them in the future. We finished training early one afternoon and decided to visit the ice rink, which was in Sunderland. We told Calvin that we intended to go ice skating. Calvin said, "I don't mind you going, but remember you are representing the England boxing squad. I don't want any trouble."

None of us could skate on the ice, but we thought it would be a good laugh and it would allow us to unwind after training hard. We all put on our ice skates and entered the packed ice rink, the music was loud, and everyone around us seemed to be enjoying themselves and skating well. One of the lads, Alan Hall, who was a top amateur boxer, was with me as we clung to the sides of the rink, slowly making our way around the edge of the rink, slipping and sliding on the ice. Alan was brave and let go of the side of the rink and tried to stand up without any support. He wasn't upright for long, his legs slipped from under him, and he landed on his arse. I giggled. As Alan lay there on the ice, an older boy, who was expertly skating, saw Alan and slid up to him fast, purposely spraying him with ice from the skid. Alan managed to get up and grabbed the boy, and they were holding on to each other when Alan shouted, "What shall I do, John?" I shouted back, "Give it to him!" Alan barraged the boy with a succession of body shots. The boy went down, holding his stomach. We called all our lads and quickly scarpered off to take our skates back and leave the rink as quickly as we could. As we were waiting to hand our skates in, the skater boy and a group of his friends appeared, trying to look menacing. They were mouthing off, telling us what they were going to do to us. I signalled to them to go outside, and if they wanted trouble, we would gladly oblige. I don't think they realised we were all trained fighters. We were sixteen years old, and the skater lads were about nineteen. I think they thought they had the upper hand in size and age. For a boxer, it doesn't matter what size you are. With the right punch, you are going to go down. As boxers, we are taught not to fight outside the ring, but in a self-defence situation like this, we aren't going to back down.

We all went outside; it was the boxers versus the skater boys, and hardly any words were exchanged between us. I had my target, the skater boy who started all the trouble. He saw the look on my face and started to run. I caught up with him and gave him a right hand, and knocked him out. I wanted to teach him a lesson, perhaps it was wrong, but I was young and would fight anyone if I had to. I know that people can be killed with one punch. It was a dangerous action. I looked down at the boy, and I was afraid that I had really hurt him. He groaned and started to move. My hands were deadly weapons. I regretted punching him and often thought about the incident and what could have happened if I had seriously injured him or even killed him. I walked off and watched him from a distance to see if he was ok, his friends joined him, and they sloped off down the road.

The moral of the story is 'don't judge a book by its cover.' There is another great example of this on YouTube, a group of cage fighters from Swansea are dressed up as women and heading for a nightclub when two bullies try and attack them. The results are hilarious. The bullies are knocked out and later arrested by the police.

Bullies, beware. One day, you'll pick on the wrong person. I was a young trained fighter, and the fight taught me a lesson, too, to keep my fists in the boxing ring. Calvin didn't find out about the brawl, as we all promised never to mention the incident again. I was relieved that Calvin wasn't aware of the fighting as my boxing career with the England squad had just started, and I don't think I would have been selected again if they had known what had happened. In fact, I doubt if anyone of us would have been selected again.

I returned to Salou that September for two weeks; before I went on holiday, I rang the college to let them know that I would be late commencing the course due to the timing of the holiday. The staff at the college said that was fine, and I told them I was looking forward to starting the course.

I attended college four days after the course had started due to my Salou trip. I felt nervous about attending college. I hated school and hoped that college life would be different. I managed to find the classroom within the maze of rooms and corridors, and as I peered into my classroom, I noticed that everyone was seated and excitedly chatting. I stood at the doorway hesitantly when the teacher turned around and looked in my direction and said sarcastically in a loud teacher voice, "Oh, Mr Carr! You've finally decided to join the class, have you?" I explained to him, saying, "I rang the college and told them that I would be late starting the course. What's your problem?" He said, "Calm down, step out of the classroom, and then come back in with a different attitude." I was angry that he was embarrassing me in front of the class and shouted with a clenched fist, "I'll tell you what I'll do. I'll walk out of this fucking class and won't come back." The kids in the classroom were silently watching the drama develop. The teacher knew I meant business and didn't know how to respond. I slammed the classroom door behind me and walked away, thinking I was not taking this shit and walked straight to the bus stop to get a bus home. I was livid as I walked to the bus stop but calmed down by the time the bus came. What the hell was I going to do now? It was just like school. I thought that the teacher would have treated me differently at college, but I was wrong. I couldn't believe I had quit college before I had even started. I was gutted about the situation, maybe I shouldn't have reacted as I did. I'm very impulsive, and sometimes this can be detrimental.

When I arrived back home, I rang Marty and told him what had happened. Marty thought about the situation for a few moments and then said, "What do you want to do, John?" I was adamant, "I'm not going back there." Marty reassured me, "Leave it to me, and I'll see what I can do." That Friday evening, I went to the boxing club to train as usual, and Marty said, "I've got you an interview on Monday morning with GKN Scaffolding." I wasn't sure about working as a scaffolder, but I would earn some cash and keep up with my boxing training.

I had my interview at 9 am and started working at 9.30 am that Monday morning. I was happy to get the job, and my starting wage was £34.50 per week; out of the £34.50 I earned, I gave my Mam £15 'keep' per week; the job would make a man of me. My foreman was Gary James, but we all called him Jamma. He was a nice bloke, and we got on well. It was a very physical job, offloading the wagons and carrying the scaffolding tubes and boards to their relevant areas, but I enjoyed my work. I became strong and felt like a real man. I felt that the heavy lifting in the scaffolding yard contributed to my success as a boxer. It gave me physical strength and being the youngest member of staff, and I also gained mental strength because I had to cope with all the piss-taking from the older men. If I had gone to college, I believe my path may have turned out very differently. I probably would have wanted to go out clubbing and drinking like other boys my age, I was easily led, and I doubt if I would have continued with my boxing training at the same high level.

At seventeen, I really wanted to be a professional boxer. Marty was proud of me and would tell people that I would be a British Boxing Champion, I always felt embarrassed when he did that, but he saw something in me from a young age. He knew I had the potential to be a boxing star. I always wanted to win National Titles as a youth, but for some reason, they always eluded me. I couldn't understand that I could beat youth Champion boxers on Club shows, but at the competition level, I'd always fail. This frustrated me so much I tried to analyse myself; was it the pressure I placed on myself during a competition fight? Was it nerves? Marty always said three-minute rounds are more suitable for me because I took longer to settle into a match. I was desperate to win competition fights, and my aim was to box for my country. That's all I wanted to do at that time. I knew that if you won a competition fight, you had a better chance of being selected to fight for England or Great Britain.

Marty arranged a boxing trip to Esbjerg, Denmark, for one week. It was Northeast Select Boxing Team against Denmark. I arranged to have time off from work to go. John Cosby, my boss, was accommodating. He made allowances for me to attend boxing events. We sailed from Harwich to Esbjerg during the summer of 1986, and there were nine boxers and three trainers on the team travelling to Denmark. Marty, Alan Augiers (Augy), and Peter Cairns, my boxing trainers, were a massive support to me during my amateur boxing career. One of our team was from Ireland, Joe Egan. He is known as one of the 'hardest white men on the planet,' a title bestowed by Mike Tyson when Joe sparred with him in the States. Joe was an Irish International Heavyweight boxer who was vastly experienced and had just returned from America sparring Tyson. Joe told us that Tyson was an up-and-coming young boxer who was going to be the next boxing superstar. At the time, we wondered who Mike Tyson was. Joe is a successful actor and author, and we still keep in touch.

When we arrived at Esbjerg, we were all starving and hungry. The head coach of the Danish Team said that the chef had prepared a spectacular meal, especially for us, their British guests. Our mouths were watering, and I thought it would be a huge steak, like the one I had in the Cross Keys in Guisborough as a little boy. We all met in the large dining room of the team camp. The tables were impressively presented, they placed some crusty bread on my table, and I delved in immediately. After my third slice of bread, Marty told me off. "You won't eat your dinner!" I finished off the last mouthful of bread, and within minutes they brought out the main course. There was a huge dish with a stainless-steel cover, and I couldn't wait to see what the dish was. We all looked at each other bemused when the cover was taken off, and it revealed something we had never seen before. We didn't recognise the food which was placed in front of us. I shouted over to Marty, "What's this?" He said, "Don't be so rude." The head coach appeared and smiled, and said proudly in broken English, "This is a delicacy in Denmark, and we hope you enjoy the raw shark." In Grangetown, we were used to fish and chips. This was fish with a difference. He walked away, and I said, "Do you put salt and pepper on this Mart?" All the boys giggled, and we put on brave faces trying to digest the rubbery pieces of raw shark. I tried to chew it, I was so hungry, but it was like chewing a rubber tyre. I couldn't eat the shark, but fortunately, I'd eaten some bread. We all went to bed hungry that evening, and we couldn't wait for breakfast.

Two fights were arranged for me on this trip, and I knew I would win both of them. I wasn't big-headed about it, I had done all the preparation work, and I was mentally fit too. In the first fight, I won on points quite comfortably. The Danish Head Coach was impressed with my performance and said to Marty, "I have a good boxer who is the same weight as your boy, but he is the Danish Champion. Would you like to make a match in Esbjerg?" Marty told me about the match and asked me if I wanted to take it. I said, "Yes," before he finished his sentence. I was always up for a challenge, and I liked to stretch myself. I wasn't afraid of anyone. In fact, if someone had offered me a fight with the best boxer in the world in my age group, I would have fancied it. The week in Esbjerg was wonderful, I enjoyed the comradery and having a laugh with the lads, but when it came to boxing, I took it seriously.

I felt a little nervous knowing I was facing the Danish Champion, but I knew that I was more than capable of beating him with my boxing ability. On the night of the big fight at Esbjerg, both teams entered the ring, and each boxer was introduced to their opponent and to the crowd. The venue was packed full of people. Around 4,000 people were there, and I'd never boxed in front of an audience that size before. They called my name, and I took one step forward, and everyone politely clapped. When the Danish Champion stepped out, the crowd went crazy, shouting, whistling and applauding loudly. I thought I was in for a tough fight. The boy was tall, lean, muscular and looked confident and strong. I was the underdog yet again, boxing away from home. After our introduction to the crowd, we all had to go to our changing rooms and wait to be called to the ring; my fight didn't start straight away.

We all headed to the changing rooms; my fight was seventh on the list. There were six fights, and then an interval, and then my fight. Everyone has their own rituals before a fight or performance, and mine started around this time. My rituals are visiting the venue, looking at the ring to try and find out which corner I was allocated before the contest so that I could visualise how I would walk in etc. The rituals relaxed me a little bit. I felt more confident, I knew what I was doing, and nothing would be a surprise to throw me off guard. My fight was straight after the interval, and I was more nervous than usual due to the size of the event. I felt more pressure because I was boxing against the Danish Champion in his hometown. I thought I was going to give it my best shot. Marty looked at me, knowing I felt nervous, and said, "Treat this like any other fight. Get out there and get your jab working." Those words eased me, and I thought, yes, this is just another fight, and I've come all this way to win.

I entered the ring with quiet, respectful applause from the Danish audience, and the Danish Champion's entrance was like Elvis was in the building. The crowd reacted with their vocal cords. It was deafening; everyone screamed, shouted and cheered loudly. At the time, I didn't know if he was a South Paw, or an Orthodox fighter, Marty had tried to discover this earlier, but the Danes were secretive and didn't reveal much about the Champion to give me any advantages. (A South Paw boxer is left-handed and leads with his right hand. These boxers are the minority and are sometimes awkward to fight. An orthodox fighter is right-handed and leads with his left hand). In his corner was the head coach of the Danish squad. He looked confident and smug. Both of us boxers met in the middle of the ring before the fight commenced, and the referee told us to touch gloves. As we did so, we eyeballed each other. I noticed that he was taller than me with longer arms, and I assumed he'd be a rangy boxer. He looked confident and strong. We went back to our corners, and the bell rang; he came out in a South Paw stance. I thought, OK, I could handle you. Boxing is like a game of chess; it's tactical, it's thinking a few moves ahead, it's getting your opponent trapped and then attacking him. My last fight in England was against a South Paw, Lee Towers, who had knocked me down twice (the first time I'd ever landed on my arse), but I went on to win that fight, knocking him down four times. The experience of boxing the South Paw, Lee Towers allowed me to gain vital knowledge about fighting South Paws. I knew that I should jab, move off to my left, and bring him onto my right hand. I had this Danish Champion boy all worked out; it was going to be checkmate.

The English Youth Squad Boxing Show in Denmark 1986

The first round was close, but I felt I had hit him with cleaner punches. He was the most technical fighter that I had ever boxed at that stage, but during the second round, I caught him with a right hand, a left hook, and two solid punches to the head. He seemed to lose interest after that, and I gained confidence. Checkmate was coming, and I could hear his team screaming loudly in Danish from his corner. They knew he was in trouble. The audience was getting quieter and quieter as I gained the upper hand, I dominated the third round and thought I'd won the fight, but again he was their star; would they give me a foreigner, the decision? I went back to my corner, and Augy, Peter and Marty were smiling ecstatically and holding their fists up triumphantly. The Danish judges were fair, and I won by a unanimous decision. The crowd gave me a huge cheer, and I had a standing ovation as I walked back to the dressing room. All my team were congratulating me, slapping me on the back. The feeling of success is sweet, it's the taste that we all crave. A few minutes of adoration is worth all the pre-fight nerves and all the blood, sweat and tears that we give in and out of the ring. We work so hard as boxers dedicating our lives to the sport. We live just for moments like this; to feel appreciated, loved, and accepted means so much to us. I shook hands with the Danish team, and the head coach told me, "You did really well, and you will go far."

English Youth Boxing Squad

The Danes were keen on organising a return match with our team, and they came to Middlesbrough six months later. We boxed at The Marton Country Club. The Danish boxing team trained at my gym, Grangetown ABC. Training took place when we weren't there. I was interested to see who the best boxer was on the Danish team, and I asked Peter Cairns, who was there during their training sessions, "Who is the best boxer out of them all?" He replied with a shy look on his face, "Your guy by far. He's here to win." I must have looked disappointed because Peter immediately said, "You'll beat him again. Just box as you did before." I was alright about the fight before I had spoken to Pete. I thought I shouldn't have asked the question, and I started to have a nervous feeling in the pit of my stomach. I hated the feeling of being nervous, but I didn't allow the nerves to control me.

Nerves would give me all negative thoughts, such as outlying the worst-case scenarios in a fight; I could be knocked out by the first punch, I could freeze and forget how to throw a punch, I could lose my reputation, and the crowd would laugh at me. I fought the nerves with positive thoughts and let the nerves work for me and not against me. If I fought on a regular basis, my nerves became less of an issue, nerves became good, and it made me fight harder and more determined to win.

There were twelve fights arranged on a cold winter's evening at The Marton Country Club, and my fight was sixth on the schedule. The Danes were beating us, they had won three fights, and we had won two. Marty was extremely busy that night. He had organised the event. It was a dinner show, and because Marty was tied up ensuring the event was running smoothly, Augy and Peter were looking after us. It was like a large production line of young boxers preparing to fight, and then being ushered to and from the ring.

I would have preferred to be on first or second, get the fight over with, and then sit in the arena to enjoy watching the rest of the fights, but I was on sixth and had to wait my turn. I warmed up, did some shadow boxing, did some pad work with Augy, and I felt that I was ready to face the Dane in the ring. I had done my ring rituals earlier that evening and was confident and happy. I didn't feel anxious at all.

Marty appeared in the changing room just before my fight and said, "I'm doing your corner." I was pleased that he had found the time to be with me, this was a three-two-minute round fight, and I felt reassured with Marty looking after me in my corner. When the Danish Champion entered the ring, I noticed his shorts were covered in badges, emblazed with symbols of boxing competitions, which he had previously won. I looked at all the colourful badges sewn on his shorts and thought I was in for a tough fight this time and he was displaying his credentials, declaring he was a Champion, and I was the underdog. I knew the boy would be seeking revenge after the first fight we had in Denmark when I beat him unanimously, but this was my territory, my hometown, and I was there to win.

He came out in his Southpaw stance but kept switching to an orthodox stance throughout the first round, he was trying to throw me, and I think he succeeded. He won the first round. When I went back to the corner at the end of the round, Marty gave me a good talking to, "You need to win the next two rounds; stamp your authority on the fight. Start backing him up and let your body punches go!" I went back out for the second round with the intention of knocking the boy out. I wanted to show him what I was made of; it didn't matter how many badges he had on his shorts, I'd show him that I was a tough Grangetown lad and would give him a boxing lesson. The last round was my best, I hurt him with a few right-hand left hooks, and he caught me with a few good punches, too. I thought I had done enough to win. Marty was always honest with me at the end of every fight. He would tell me if it was a close fight or if I had lost or won. I liked that honesty, but I didn't like it when he'd say that I had lost. I was a sore loser. That is why I worked so hard in the gym, training and preparing for a fight. I never wanted to lose.

At the end of the fight, I wasn't a hundred per cent sure if I had won. The Dane had done his homework, and he gave me a tougher fight than I had in Denmark. I waited by the side of the referee at the end of the fight, and I was nervous about the result. The announcer said, "By a majority decision, the winner is Carr, in the red corner!" I was thrilled with the result, and to top my evening off, I won 'The Best Boxer of the Evening' award. I was so proud of myself that evening for winning at The Marton Country Club, and the venue would be a prominent place for me with some great things to come.

My next big boxing challenge was against an experienced fighter named Dennis Lowe. He was older than me, this was a Middleweight fight, and I'd only ever boxed at light Middleweight before. At a training session, Marty took me to the changing rooms and said, "I've made a fight with a boxer from Middlesbrough named Dennis Lowe. He's a strong man and a Middleweight." Throughout my career, I've never turned down a fight. Perhaps I've been too brave because there were times when I should have been selective and refused contests. Some of the fights I had accepted were dangerous. Looking back at this fight, it was a big risk for me to take. Dennis was a man, and I was a boy in a man's body. He was much bigger than me, but I feared no one. I trusted Marty’s judgement. The fight was held at a local venue, Philmore's Nightclub in Saltburn.

When I got into the ring, I realised how big and strong Dennis was. I fought to the best of my ability and won the first two rounds. Just before the third and last round started, Marty was reassuring, saying, “Keep doing what you’re doing, John.” I think Dennis knew he had lost the first two rounds, and when the bell rang for round three, he came out like a bull at a gate, and I was shocked at his man-strength and power. He hit me with a right hand and nearly took my head off, and I landed on my arse. I managed to survive the round and won the fight, it was a tough fight, but I fought with tactics and technical ability. Some people said after the fight that they were amazed that I recovered from Dennis’ strong right hand; I was blessed with a strong chin and a thick skull. I think these traits are a must to be a successful boxer.

That fight was a massive learning curve. I realised that it was a rite of passage, I was becoming a man, and that was partly due to the technical work I endured at the gym and the hard physical work in the scaffolding yard. Working at the scaffolding yard, provided a wage, and gave me a workout, but it wasn’t my future. Years ago, there was no backing for young boxing talent: no sponsorship deals, no financial support, no psychological professionals assisting you, etc. Young boxers had to work all day in their day job and find any spare time to train whenever they could, it was tough, it was exhausting. I am persistent, and I'm like a terrier. When I wanted something, and I wanted to be a boxing Champion, I would do whatever it took to get that belt. As a boxer, it can be lonely at times, and although you have the support of your team, when it comes to the crunch you are facing your opponent on your own, there's a tap on your back from your trainer, and off you go. There's no one to fall back on, and it's down to you and you alone when you're facing the battle in the ring. I wasn't from a boxing family, I didn't have a father, and the nearest to being a father figure was Marty. I depended on him a lot.

I've written in a diary since I started boxing as a kid and found it therapeutic. I'd always mark the date of a fight in advance and write in huge letters, 'I WANT TO WIN IN STYLE!' It wasn't just the winning for me; it was how I won. I was my own worst enemy. I'd focus on the bad things instead of giving myself credit for the good things that I did during a contest. When it comes to boxing, I am a perfectionist.

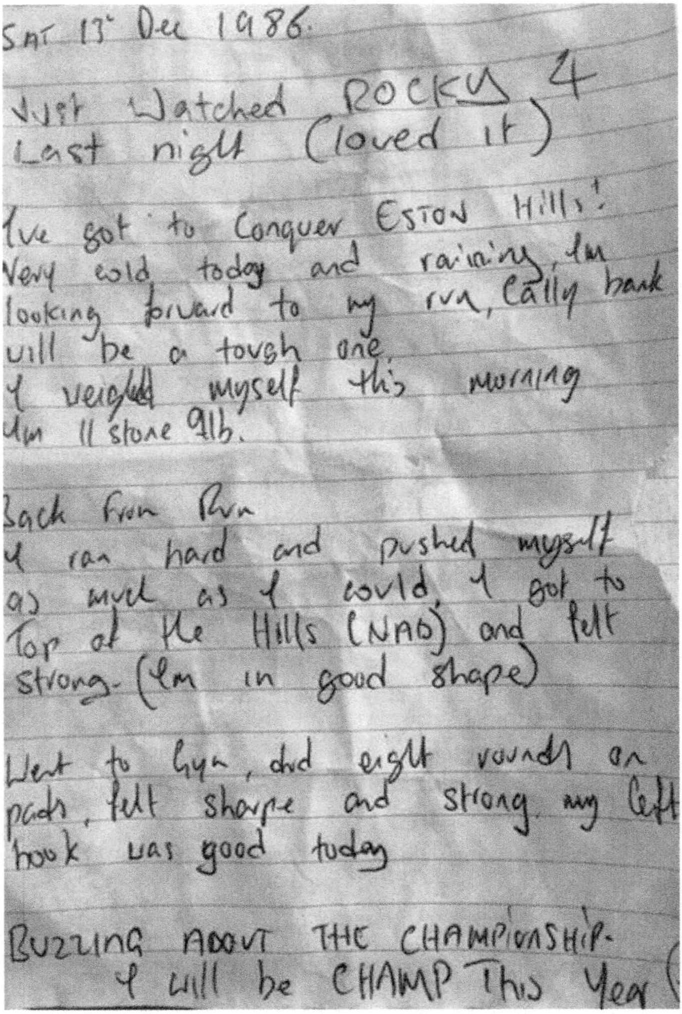

Sat 13th Dec 1986.

Just Watched ROCKY 4
Last night (loved it)

Ive got to Conquer ESTON Hills!
Very cold today and raining, Im
looking forward to my run, Cally bank
will be a tough one.
I weighed myself this morning
Im 11 stone 9lb.

Back from Run
I ran hard and pushed myself
as much as I could, I got to
Top of the Hills (NAB) and felt
strong. (Im in good shape)

Went to Gym, did eight rounds on
pads, felt sharpe and strong. my left
hook was good today

BUZZING ABOUT THE CHAMPIONSHIP.
I will be CHAMP This Year

John 'Cornelius' Carr's Diary

The ABA Championships are an annual competition for all open-class senior amateur boxers. It's the hardest competition for young boxers in the UK. From the age of fifteen, I wanted to be part of the ABA. It was my dream, I'd seen ABA fights previously when I was younger, and I was enthralled by the boxing talent. Two of the fighters I was impressed with were Rod Douglas and Nigel Benn, both in my weight category and came from London, and they were outstanding amateur boxers. Looking back, I only enjoyed watching boxers who were of a similar weight to me, I think the reason for this was that I could visualise myself boxing them, and I always thought that I would be good enough to possibly beat them.

I arrived at Gateshead Leisure Centre on a cold evening in January 1987 to fight in the Northeast ABA Championships. I was seventeen. All my preparation work was done, and I was fit and ready. This was a huge fight for me, I knew the winner of each fight would box in the Northeast final, which was held seven days later at the same venue, and I was there to win.

There were four boxers in the 75kg group, and out of all four boxers, I was the least experienced, I was the youngest, and this was only my third senior fight. In the draw, the four fighters' names go into a bag, and the first two names that are drawn will box each other, and so forth. The draw is done by the ABA officials behind closed doors, and my name was drawn against Paul Salter from the Wellington Boxing Club in Middlesbrough, who was a powerful fighter. He was a man with huge muscles and was a few years older than me, in his early twenties. There is always a competition between amateur clubs to produce the best boxers, and sometimes that creates jealousy between Clubs. I never got involved in Club politics. I just wanted to do my best and always worked hard as a boxer. Again, I wasn't expected to win, I heard rumours that people were saying I was too young and not strong enough to fight Paul, but that made me even more determined.

As an amateur boxer, I'd always done three, two's, which is three rounds lasting two minutes with a minute's rest between each round. This competition in the senior ABA'S was a big jump for me. It was three threes, three rounds lasting three minutes, again with a minute rest between each round. I thought that this was my time to shine and prove that the three threes would be better for me, as it took me longer to settle into a match. I was nervous, but that was a good sign for me. The nerves provided adrenalin, and that natural kick gave me the boost to succeed. It was a love/hate relationship with nerves; I hated the feeling, but I knew it provided positive results. Anyone who says that they don't suffer any form of nervousness before fighting in a boxing match isn't honest. I was nervously confident because I knew I had worked hard preparing for the fight. I sometimes doubted myself that I might not go the distance and tire quickly, but this was just a fleeting thought, and I didn't mention it to anyone. As soon as the first bell rang for the fight to commence, my nerves dissipated.

I won the fight, Paul was immensely powerful, but I was able to outbox him. At the end of the contest, I realised that I had managed to get a small cut above my right eye, and after the fight, Marty and I left the venue quickly to go straight to the hospital to receive attention to the injury.

Luckily, it only required a few butterfly stitches, and they said it would heal quickly. I was worried that the injury would prevent me from performing in the next round. I had left the venue early and didn't know who I would be boxing against the following week.

I was fighting Karl Dukes in the final, who was a few years older than me, and I'd seen him around at some of the boxing shows previously, and he had trained at a young England boxing squad weekend with me. I knew he was a strong puncher, and I expected to have a tough fight. As I was boxing, I realised that all my preparation work at the gym had paid off, I felt sharp and strong, and I loved the three-minute rounds.

My boxing skills flowed, my moves were instinctive, and I didn't have to think about my moves. They all came naturally. The referee stopped the contest during the second round, I was elated. I punched the air with excitement and couldn't stop smiling. I had won the final of the Northeast ABA Championships, and I felt like a Champion. When I returned to the dressing room after the fight, I sat there alone for a few minutes, and then all the emotion inside me came to the surface. I thought about my dad and wished he could have been there to watch me, I wanted to make him proud of me. I cried happy tears, if there was such a thing, winning had brought me so much joy.

The Middlesbrough Gazette always supported me throughout my boxing career. Eric Paylor was a Sports journalist at The Gazette, and he gave me positive write-ups in the newspaper after every fight. This one was no different. The next day my photo and a cover story of the contest were splashed all over the back page of the Gazette, and I still have all my press cuttings from that time, which I love looking at and showing my sons a record of my achievement.

BUILDING a reputation — that's 17-year-old John Carr from Grangetown ABC, who has reached the ABA British boxing semi-finals. After his big win last night, he was back at work with a local scaffolding company today.

John 'Cornelius' Carr Age 17 at the Scaffolding Yard, courtesy of The Gazette

The winner of the Northeast Championships boxes the winner of the Yorkshire Championships. The winner of the Yorkshire Championships that year was a powerful puncher named Henry Wharton, who was older than me and had a reputation as a dangerous fighter. Henry had boxed Tony Boyes from our boxing Club a few years previously, but I couldn't remember him. Young Marty, big Marty's son, had attended the Yorkshire boxing final and had seen Henry fighting.

Two weeks before my fight with Henry, I was at the gym training when I overheard young Marty and a few lads discussing my forthcoming fight with Henry. Young Marty was saying how dangerous Henry was, how he was knocking people down, and how powerful he was. I was eager to know more about Henry Wharton; young Marty was telling everyone how dangerous Henry was, and how he was impressed with his boxing. As young Marty was excitedly describing Henry and how great he was, bigging him up, big Marty appeared and looked at young Marty angrily and said, Shut up you!" Then big Marty took me to one side and said, "Take no notice of what people are saying, don't you worry about him, let him worry about you." I knew then that I would have to be one hundred per cent focused on winning this fight.

The fight was held at Hartlepool Workingmen's Club. It was a small venue which was crammed with people. I'd built up an image of Henry in my head as a man-mountain because I had no idea of his appearance. All boxers like to weigh up their opponents, and I particularly wanted to weigh Henry up because of his reputation. Boxers are required to have a pre-fight medical examination, and as I was queuing to see the doctor, there was a blonde lad in front of me, also waiting to have his medical, and the doctor said, "Henry?" And I knew then that he was Henry Wharton. After I had seen Henry, I thought I could beat this boy, he wasn't as big as I'd thought he'd be, and he wasn't the man mountain I had conjured up in my imagination.

The small venue was jam-packed, and I had some great supporters there that evening. However, most of the supporters were there for Henry. It was hot and smoky; the smell of cigarettes and alcohol was intense as I entered the ring. It was crazy thinking that we were passive smokers who were athletes, we had to breathe in all those tobacco fumes, and we all accepted it at the time. The crowd were gagging to see some brutal action from us youngsters, we were both good boxers, and the supporters knew they were there to witness a good scrap. Henry came out of his corner fast, like a Trojan, heavy-handed and wanted my blood. I could tell by the look on his face that he was there to pummel me, to show me that he was the star of the show. I felt confident and got behind my jab and kept away from his left hook. I was just as determined as Henry. I boxed clever, I was there to win, and I won the fight unanimously. It was a massive achievement for me; Henry had been tipped to win the competition, but I had stolen it, and I felt elated. Henry went on to have a successful professional boxing career. We never met again after that fight, until a few years ago when we met each other at Alexandra Palace in London during a boxing event.

The next round was the quarter-finals of the ABA's, and I boxed Paul Wright, a young England International boxer. It was held in Everton, and I won by a unanimous decision.

It was a tough fight, but my confidence in my boxing abilities grew fast after each win.

It was around four in the morning when I hit my bed in Grangetown after the fight. The nasty sound of the alarm rang out in my bedroom at ten minutes past seven; I only had a few hours of sleep, and I was aching all over, with a thick lip and a shiner from the night before, and I didn't want to leave the warmth and comfort of my cosy nest. My ritual in the mornings was down to fine art: three eggs are beaten in milk (I still couldn't master the Rocky hander egg cracking), then Bran Flakes with sliced bananas, and to finish off I took my vitamin tablets, and then I was out of the door. I had to be at work by 8 am, I wanted to take the day off, but I'd just had two days off for the fight, and knew I'd be pushing my luck asking for more time off work.

All the lads at the scaffolding yard congratulated me about my win as I walked into work. As we were all chatting, we were interrupted by someone shouting across the yard, it was Linda, the secretary, she was holding the phone in the office doorway, "Your sister is on the phone, she says you have your driving test at nine-thirty, she'll pick you up at nine." I looked at my watch, and the time was twenty to nine. I thought, Shit! I didn't know I had my test; my sister had arranged it and had forgotten to tell me. My sister Susan used to manage all my affairs. I started to panic, knowing that I hadn't asked my boss's permission to leave work for the test and I'd just had two days off for the fight. I went to see John

Crosby, my boss and asked him if it was ok to leave work to take my driving test. He wasn't amused but said it was ok, and as I walked to the door of his office to leave, John Crosby shouted, "Well done John, congratulations on your win last night." I turned and smiled at him. I'm not sure how he found out about my win, but I was pleased that he had taken an interest in my boxing.

I waited at the main entrance of the yard for Sue to pick me up and take me to the Driving Test Centre, and she was late as usual. When she arrived, it was nine-fifteen. I was in the right state by the time Sue arrived. She shouted through the open window of her car, "Jump in our John," and took off with me hanging out of the car like a scene from Starsky and Hutch.

Most people prepare to take their driving test; you should be calm and confident that you have done the revision on the Highway Code and know the route of the driving test, well, not in my case. We screeched around the corner into the lane near the Driving Test Centre and then skidded to an emergency stop in the area where all the driving instructors and examiners stood, and then I got out wearing heavy work boots, aching from head to toe, with a thick lip and a shiner to my right eye and mentally and physically exhausted. It was twenty-seven minutes past nine when we arrived at the centre in a whirlwind, and I could just imagine what they were all thinking.

The cold fish of the Tees turned out to be my driving examiner that day. He looked like someone wearing a false nose, glasses and moustache, like the ones you find in a Christmas Cracker. I kept staring at his long, straight nose, and it was a bit of a distraction. I thought I did reasonably well during the driving test, I'd had a lot of experience, mainly because I had been driving illegally since I was eleven. As we neared the end of the test, he asked me to turn into the lane near the Test Centre, and then in a nasal posh voice, he said, "Take your next right." I took the next right, the same right that my sister Sue had taken earlier, and the examiner shouted hysterically, "STOP!" He told me to look left and right, and then said dramatically, "What do those signs mean?" The signs were large, red and circular with a white stripe going through the centre. I looked at them for a second and thought, oh shit. I answered him in a questioning, quiet and slow tone, "No Entry?" He instructed me authoritatively, "Reverse and take the next right." As soon as we entered the Driving Test Centre, the examiner asked me to park the car and then turned to me and said, "I'm sorry, Mr Carr, you have failed, and the main reason for that is that you entered a No Entry area and I also saw you arriving in a vehicle through the 'No Entry' area." I felt like giving him a left jab and saying I boxed an English Champion last night in Everton, travelled back to Grangetown, had a couple of hours sleep, I'm aching all over, I've got a thick lip, a shiner, didn't know I was taking this poxy test today, and you, you Mr Cold Fish, you're a fucking arsehole!

I got out of the examiner's car and walked slowly with my head down towards Sue's car. My face must have said it all. As I got into Sue's car, Sue turned to me and said, smiling at me, "Did you pass then?" I said, "No, I fucking didn't pass." She said, "Why?" I said, "Because I went through a no entry, the one you went through when we skidded into the Centre earlier." The examiner was still in his car, going through some paperwork. Sue started to get out of her car and said defiantly, "I'm going to knock his twatting block off!" I pulled her back into the car and quietly said. "Let's just go." I was gutted about failing and didn't feel like going back to work. Sue decided we should drown our sorrows and have a slap-up brekkie. Sue always supported me, and she was my big sister and surrogate mother. She was always there for me when I needed her.

We laughed about everything, including the arsehole examiner, over our full English breakfast, and she dropped me off back at the yard after breakfast. All the lads at the yard took the piss out of me all day because I had failed my driving test, but it was just banter, and I took it on the chin. Six weeks later, I re-sat my driving test. I was on time, didn't go in the no-entry area, I hadn't boxed the night before, and Mr Cold Fish of the Tees, the examiner, was probably out swimming in the Tees that day, and I passed my driving test.

The next round of the English ABA's was held in Gloucester. Marty had relations who lived in Chard in Gloucester, his sister Bernadette and her husband Luciano, they lived on a farm, and I loved staying there. It was relaxing, and it took me back to the days of my dad's allotment. Marty and I stayed there for three days before the fight. The tranquillity and large open space of the farm were a tonic for me, and it gave me time to prepare myself both mentally and physically.

There were four Champions altogether participating in the first English semi-final. This was going to be a major boxing event. I knew one of the boxers who had won his heats, Rod Douglas, a Commonwealth Games Gold Medallist, an Olympic Bronze Medallist, and he'd won the ABA's three times and was captain of the England boxing team. I knew all about him because I'd seen him box on TV in 1985 final when he won the fight against Gordon Phillips. I thought he was an amazing boxer, and there was a big article about Rod in the Boxing News, but I didn't want to read it because I didn't want media hype or any negativity to creep into my head. I thought it was better for me to have no knowledge about him. Maybe this stems back from the days of the Gladiators, and you don't want to know someone personally who you will face in the arena. It's you or him.

The draws were made for the semi-final, and I drew with a lad named N Redney (this information was taken from my old medical card). I was disappointed that I didn't have to face Rod Douglas. I wanted to fight him to get it over with. My intuition told me that I would be fighting Rod Douglas at some stage, and I felt ready now to face him in the ring. I really wanted to put on a show at the event because I knew Rod Douglas would be watching me. I wanted to show him what I was made of, and I wanted him to know that I was fearless. I was seventeen, and Rod was in his early twenties with years of experience and awards under his belt. I was young and fighting fit, desperate to be the new boy on the block.

I approached the fight on a mission to prove my prowess and stopped my opponent in the first round. As I left the ring feeling overjoyed, Marty said, "Do you want to watch Douglas fight?" I said, "No, you watch it but don't tell me anything." I had to have a clear mind, I couldn't watch the fight, I couldn't allow Douglas to get inside my head. Douglas went out and won his contest; his fight was stopped in the second round.

Two weeks later, I went to Preston for the British ABA Semi-Final. The boxers were: Representing Wales, Nicky Piper, Scotland was represented by Sean Heron, and the English representatives were Rod Douglas and me. Rod drew with Nicky Piper, and I drew with Sean Heron. I won by a majority decision, but I knew it was a very close fight, and Rod also won by a majority decision in his fight. All the boxers in the semi-final had represented their countries apart from me, and I became aware that I was amongst the amateur boxing elite. And I felt proud that I had finally earned my place amongst them. This is what I had strived for since joining Marty's Club at eleven years old. Having Marty as a mentor helped me enormously. He believed in me, and he always supported me along with the other trainers at the Club, Peter and Augy.

When I returned to Middlesbrough, the reaction from everyone was unbelievable. People were coming up and congratulating me, the back page of The Gazette was filled with my success story, and my mam and my sister Susan put on a little celebratory spread. I felt immensely proud of my achievement, and all the sacrifices I had made had finally paid off: running up and down the hills in all weather, training day and night, eating a strict diet, not going out partying with my friends and practically living the life of a monk, and holding down a full-time job. Even though I was in high spirits, I kept thinking I still had one hurdle to go, fighting Rod Douglas. The guy I had watched boxing a few years previously on TV was going to be my opponent in the ring in a few weeks. I prepared myself for the biggest fight that I had ever fought at that point in my life.

A week prior to my fight with Rod Douglas, Marty had arranged some sparring in Sheffield with some professional boxers at The Brendan Ingle Gym. I felt nervous about going to the gym, knowing that some great boxers trained there, including Herol 'Bomber' Graham, Johnny Nelson and Brian Anderson. Later the most famous boxer to come out of Brendan's gym was Naseem Hamid. Brendan put me at ease immediately; he was impressed with my boxing and followed me in the competition. A few years previously, I had boxed one of Brendan's boys, Lee Towers, we had a tremendous contest, knocking each other down, and both of us putting up a good fight, and I won that contest on unanimous points. Brendan remembered me from that fight and told me that he had tipped Towers to beat me.

When I sparred the first boxer at Brendan's gym, I felt confident and thought that I had done well, then a tall, rangy boxer named Johnny Nelson got in the ring with me, and I soon realised the guy was behaving like an arsehole, he was trying to kick my legs away from under me, and doing fancy tricks, holding me etc., showing off in front of everyone in the gym. I thought I hadn't come all the way to Sheffield to be treated like this. He showed me a complete lack of respect, knowing that I was a few days away from the biggest fight of my life thus far. Brendan told him to stop and replaced him with Brian Anderson, who was a British Light Middleweight Champion. Before we started sparring, Brian came over to me and whispered in my ear, "Let's just have a good sparring session, kid," he put me at ease, and we had a good sparring bout. I learned a lot from Brian. We are still friends today and meet annually at The Boxing Writers' Dinner, held at The Savoy in London at Freddy Burcombe's table. Freddy is a lovely man who was a sports correspondent. His work was published in many newspapers and magazines, he supported me throughout my boxing career, and I am grateful for all his support.

The Final of the ABA's was held at Wembley Arena on 1st May 1987. The excitement before the ABA Final was amazing; there were many Middlesbrough fans who had travelled to London to support me. Throughout my career, the people of Middlesbrough have rallied around and supported me, and I was and am immensely grateful for that backing. My dad's friend, John Nesbitt, brought my mam and sister to Wembley in his camper van. It must have been such a difficult journey; London is a ten-hour round trip, and my mam was disabled in a wheelchair.

Augy and Peter had travelled to London separately and then joined us in central London. We travelled in Marty's car with Vinnie, Marty's brother, into central London the evening before the fight. It was the first time I had experienced being in the historical capital city. All the way there, Marty allowed me to play loud Soul Funk music on his cassette player. I loved that music. It helped me relax and put me in a good mood. I was shocked at the large number of people and traffic that were pushing their way slowly through Trafalgar Square. We walked under The Arch towards Buckingham Palace and down The Mall; I would have liked to have seen the Queen, but it must have been her day off. I think the Queen would have spotted me. I was the only person shadow boxing and limbering up outside her house, near her front gates. We all thought it was funny. The walk did me good; I chatted with Marty and Augy about the upcoming contest, and they told me how well I had done to get this far. I always take everything in my stride. I'm a very laid-back person when I'm not in the ring, and I try not to allow any negativity to get in my way.

It was late afternoon the following day, and I could see Wembley Arena getting closer as we drove towards the venue. It looked huge, and I could feel the nerves in my belly expanding by the minute. I like to complete a ritual before a fight, and I've done this since my fights in Denmark: I walk around the venue on my own, look at the ring, feel the ambience before the spectators arrive, weigh in, and then visit the doctor. I only wanted to see the arena once. I never went back into an arena before a fight, it could have been superstition, but I completed these rituals throughout my boxing career. On my way back from seeing the doctor for my pre-boxing medical, I was looking for the changing rooms, I hadn't seen them yet, and I wasn't sure of which one I had been allocated. I asked a steward who pointed in the direction of a changing room. I walked into a large dressing room expecting to see my kit bag and Marty and Augie waiting for me, but I couldn't see any sign of my team, so I sat on a bench and waited for a few minutes. In the room, there were a couple of boxers warming up, and I glanced towards some lockers, and lying on the floor, spread out, with his eyes closed, was Rod Douglas. I knew it was him immediately because of his shiny, bald head. I wasn't sure what to do, obviously, I was in Rod Douglas's dressing room. I stood up and said loudly. "I think I'm in the wrong changing room." Rod said, "Yes, mate, I think you are." We smiled at each other and had a little chuckle which lightened the mood. I eventually found my changing room where Marty and Augy were waiting, I told them where I had been, and they saw the funny side of it.

I always like doing my own hand wraps for training and contests. I've done this since I was young. I like them to feel comfortable on my hands. Putting your wraps on properly is so important. Your hands are your tools and your weapons and need to be protected. I was ready for the fight! I felt like a gladiator limbering up with my white silk hooded gown on, and as I entered the arena, the noise of the crowd was deafening, and I felt strong and confident. As the fight commenced, I realised how powerful Rod was, and he was five years my senior and a top-level amateur boxer. It was like trying to push a solid brick wall back. I couldn't move him. I thought I had won the first two rounds, and the third was close. At the end of the contest, Marty thought I had won, but I wasn't sure. As I stood next to the referee who was holding my gloved hand, I had a flashback to when I boxed Jamie Nicholson. I stood there praying for my name to be announced. The announcer said, "The 1987 ABA Champion at 75 kilos is …" To my utter disappointment, he shouted, "Douglas!" As Rod and I went to shake hands after the contest, Rod said, "You're a good fighter. You'll go far."

When I returned to my changing room, everyone congratulated me. Some said I had won, some said it was awfully close, and I was sad that I lost but pleased with my overall performance. I watched the fight again on YouTube recently and thought it was a close fight, and I was proud of my eighteen-year-old self. Rod Douglas was a huge star at the time, and I did alright for a boy from Grangetown.

Two weeks later, I had the huge privilege of training with the young English squad at Crystal Palace, London. At the first training session, there was the youth (under 19's) and senior teams trained together in different sections of the hall, and the head coach of the senior team was Kevin Hickey. I knew most of the lads in the senior squad because we'd been boxing together in the ABA's. Guess who part of the senior squad was? Rod Douglas. I kept glancing over to watch the senior squad and Rod Douglas training and kept thinking how much I wanted to train with them. I felt gutted that I couldn't be a part of their team, as I had just achieved becoming second to one of their top boxers, and I felt I was part of the boxing elite in the UK. I belonged with them, I didn't know any of the youth boxers, and I felt that I deserved a place amongst the big boys. I thought it was a come down to be in the youth squad after my recent achievement in the ABA's.

Later that evening, the youth squad and trainers were having supper and discussing boxing. A few of the youth boxers were saying that they had been chosen to box for England in the World Youth Championships in Cuba. I was shocked because I hadn't been chosen, I didn't say a word to the boys, but I was angry that I hadn't been selected. I got up and walked over to one of the head trainers and said, "Can I have a quiet word, please?" I asked him why I hadn't been picked to go to Cuba. He said, "You haven't got any international boxing experience." I replied, "Didn't you see how close I took your number one boxer in the ABA Final two weeks ago? He's ranked at number three in the world?" He then threw a spanner in the mix and said, "You've been chosen to box for England Youth in Sardinia in the Multi-Nations Championships in a few weeks." I was pleased, surprised, and disappointed all at the same time, and said, "But I wanted to be part of the Youth World Championships too." He put his arm around me and pulled me closer, saying, "Don't worry, your time will come."

The following morning everyone was training, and Kevin Hickey, the senior head coach of England, approached one of my coaches and asked if Rod Douglas could spar with me. I agreed to spar with Rod and started walking toward the ring. Kevin Hickey told me, "This is just sparring, mind. It's not a fight." I got into the ring, and within thirty seconds of sparring, I could see that Rod meant business. His style was heavy-handed, coming forward and throwing strong punches. He was powerful and aggressive, I thought I'd just boxed him two weeks ago, and now he's trying to dominate me in a sparring bout in front of the whole England squad. I thought I might only be eighteen, but I was not being bullied by anyone, so I fought back and caught him with a few good shots. Everyone in the gym stopped training and watched us go toe to toe. Kevin Hickey stopped the sparring and said, "Come on, boys, you are just sparring. This is not a fight!" Looking back, this scenario should never have happened. We had recently fought a big contest, which in my head I thought I had won, but everything was still raw for both of us. We started back sparring gently, but within a minute, we were hard at it again, trying to knock each other's blocks off. Kevin Hickey stopped the sparring again and told me to get out of the ring as if it was my fault. I never saw Rod Douglas again after that. I respected him as a boxer and was sad to hear about his brain injury during a title fight with Errol 'Bomber' Graham in 1989.

Two weeks later, I went to Sardinia, Italy, with the English youth squad. I was excited and nervous because I'd never flown in an aeroplane before; this was a big deal for me. We arrived in Sardinia, which was a lovely island, the people were friendly, it wasn't a tourist destination, it was unspoilt, we were based in the North of the island, in a town called Santa Teresa Gallur, you could see another smaller island of Corsica from where we were staying.

There were four fighters in my weight category, but one of them failed his medical. Therefore three names were drawn, and one boxer would have a bye (which meant one of us could go straight to the final). The draw took place, the East German boxer and the Bulgarian boxer would fight each other, and I had a bye to the final. The East German boxer was the favourite to win due to all his boxing experience. The Bulgarian knocked the East German out in the first round, which surprised the trainers. It was a good win for the Bulgarian fighter. I knew I would have to prepare mentally to beat the Bulgarian boxer, and he looked like a tough cookie.

A trip was planned to take all the boxers from the various nations on a boat trip to Corsica. The sun was shining, and all the lads were in high spirits. As I sat down on the boat, I saw the Bulgarian boxer staring at me. He was the boy I was due to fight tomorrow. I pretended I didn't see him, but he walked over to me and introduced himself. He looked hard-faced and didn't smile. We both knew that we would face each other in the ring within twenty-four hours. I just sat there with my arms and legs spread out in a relaxed mode. As he walked away, he turned around and said in broken English, "I hope you lose tomorrow." I used all my self-control not to chase after him and start the fight early. Before a fight, I would prepare myself mentally, and I would concentrate on my rituals, sometimes adding a new ritual, like touching the ropes with my back on both sides of the corners. That night I lay in my bed reminiscing, rewinding back to previous fights, thinking I've had a successful year, that Gold Medal is mine, and I'm going to beat that hard-faced Bulgarian bastard.

I met my opponent in the ring the next day. The Bulgarian was fearsome and mean-looking. His eyes were steel blue and icy cold, glaring at me. I wasn't afraid of him. He could eyeball me as much as he wanted. I couldn't wait to get my fists in his face. I was ready. This boy was nowhere near as good as some of my previous opponents, but he thought he was the dog's nuts. I annihilated him within two minutes, and the referee stopped the fight. I won. I didn't receive the right decision in the final of the ABA's, and now this was my moment of glory, winning a gold medal for England. My dream as a kid was always to box for my country, and I had achieved that. And when I appeared on the podium as the medal was placed over my head and the national anthem played, I cried happy tears.

I sat next to one of the older and more experienced England coaches on the return flight from Sardinia. We had a great conversation and got on well, he told me I had a massive future ahead of me, and there would be a lot of promoters chasing me, trying to make me turn professional as I was the new young English boxing star. He said, "Don't turn pro. You're only eighteen, get more amateur experience at the top international level. Wait a few years." His words always play back in my mind.

Round Seven – Turning Professional

My sister had booked a holiday for the two of us to go to Benidorm. We had arranged a carer for our mam. I was really looking forward to a week off work and spending some time away from training at the gym. Our Sue feared flying, it was for the first time she had flown, and it was only my second time. I tried to distract her on the aeroplane, by having a few drinks and making her laugh.

The apartment block we stayed in was nothing special; it was cheap, and we didn't have much money, but we had each other and could enjoy a change of scenery together. The atmosphere was lively, full of Brits abroad making the most of the sunshine and cheap beer.

One evening a guy approached us in a club, we had a conversation, and then he asked me, "Is Sue your girlfriend?" I laughed, saying, "No, she's my sister!" Sue and the guy got up and danced, and I watched them from the bar as I queued for another pint of cheap Spanish lager. I started chatting with a pretty young girl. She told me her name was Tracy, she was eighteen and was from Rotherham, we ended up having a dance and a laugh, and enjoyed each other's company. I walked her back to her apartment, kissed her goodnight, and arranged to meet her the next day. I had two days left of my holiday, we spent the following day sunbathing and doing things that eighteen-year-olds do. I planned on taking Tracy back to our apartment that evening, but Sue said she wanted to take her new boyfriend there. I asked Tracy if I could stay in her room and sleep on the sofa bed. She agreed, but I didn't use the sofa bed! Tracy and I kept in touch when we returned home, and the relationship blossomed.

The words of the England coach were true, there were promoters chasing me, but I was very naïve about the boxing industry, I didn't have a clue how the business worked. On my return from the holiday, I heard that Mike Barratt, a promoter, and trainer Bobby Neil from London, were coming to Middlesbrough to see me discuss my career and talk about me turning professional. I'd previously spoken to Gus Robinson, who was a local promoter based in Hartlepool, but I wasn't interested in his proposals, the fees that Gus offered me were laughable, and he was a small promoter, I knew that I wouldn't have had the right opportunities under his management.

Mike Barratt worked with Micky Duff, they were well-known in the boxing industry, and I was excited about meeting them, thinking this was my big break. I was just a kid with dreams, all I thought about was boxing at a high level, and I didn't think about the business side of things, I didn't have a plan, and I didn't have anyone managing me. If only my fifty-three-year-old self could have time travelled to this period of my life and told me that turning professional wasn't the right thing to do at this stage, I know my career would have been completely different in a positive way. I would have said to the younger me, "You've only had thirteen senior fights, you are a novice in the world of boxing, and you are talented, but there is plenty of time for you to develop, stay amateur, and keep learning, win more competitions, and by the time you are twenty-one you will be a man, and you will understand how the boxing business works." Unfortunately, there is no such thing as time travel, and I did what I did at the time, thinking it was the right thing to do. After the meeting with Mike Barratt and Bobby Neil, Marty and I sat in his car discussing the deal offered to me, I said, "I don't think it's good enough, Mart." Marty agreed, and I thought ok, I'm staying as an amateur.

I wanted to earn more money and asked my boss at the scaffolding yard if I could be moved to site work, it was shift work, and that meant my wage would be trebled. John Crosby agreed to move me to the ICI plant in Wilton (as a kid, ICI was an iconic place to me). I was to start work there the following day. Just before I left John's office, I told him that I was appreciative of all the support he'd given me by allowing days off for my boxing, etc. He wanted to know if I was turning professional, and I told him that I hadn't decided yet. I did one week of day shifts at ICI, I didn't like working on site, I didn't know anyone, and I felt uncomfortable working amongst a massive team of people; it was much different from working in the small yard where I knew everyone. The following week I had to work the night shift, and that was unbearable, I hated it, it was boring, and I didn't go to work the following week, I wasn't happy.

Marty called me and told me that someone from Frank Warren's office had contacted him and wanted to arrange a meeting with me in London. Frank Warren was the new up-and-coming boxing promoter. He had some talented young boxers on his books: Terry Marsh, Light Welterweight Champion of the World, Georgie Collins, Welterweight, Nigel Benn, Middleweight, and many more. I had watched Georgie Collins on national TV, and Warren's team was promoting him, and he was receiving massive exposure. I thought that's what I wanted.

I met with Frank Warren, along with Marty and Augy, at his grand office in London to discuss his proposals; we also met Ernie Fossie, who was Frank Warren's right-hand man in the boxing world, my first impression of Ernie was a cockney geezer, streetwise, and opinionated. When I first saw Frank Warren, he was sitting behind his large shiny desk, as soon as I walked in, he stood up with his hand outstretched to shake my hand, I shook his hand and was surprised at how limp and smooth it was, I expected a strong manly handshake showing me who's boss. Terry Marsh had watched me in the ABA's and had reported back to Frank that I was a potential young prospect and that Warren should sign me to his team. Frank congratulated me on my boxing successes and promised me an amazing deal, and included in that deal was an apartment for me to stay in London with another young boxer. I was swayed by the package offered, I would be a full-time boxer: I would receive a signing upfront fee, all my bills paid, an apartment in London, national TV coverage, and was guaranteed ten fights in the first year.

It surprised me when Marty suggested in Frank Warren's office that he thought it would be a good idea to change my name and rebrand myself now that I was a professional boxer; he suggested I should take on my dad's name, Cornelius. I loved the idea, and I know my dad would have been proud of me for taking his name. I did find it a bit strange that Marty had never mentioned this before, but I'm so glad that he suggested it. The whole deal sounded like a dream come true, and I thought I was on my way up the boxing ladder; I had arrived in the big smoke. I asked Warren for ten minutes alone so that I could speak to Marty and Augy outside to have their advice. They both agreed that it would be a fantastic opportunity to move to London and sign with Frank Warren. I signed the contract.

I planned to move to London at the end of August when the boxing season started back, then the boxing season was from September to May, like the football season. Now professional boxing is a year-round sport, but amateur boxing continues to have a season, from September to May. I always preferred training in the summer, I didn't like getting up at 5am on an icy cold morning to go for a run, and I always ran before breakfast. I always wondered why boxers got up so early to go running when most boxing events are held in the evening. I understand that going for a morning run is a great way to burn off fat, it forces your body into a catabolic state, simply put, it's a good way to lose weight and keep fit.

When I returned home to Middlesbrough after the meeting with Frank Warren, there was a lot of excitement, and the press covered my story both locally and nationally. I was becoming a boxing star in Middlesbrough, and I loved it. I handed in my notice to the scaffolding company and thanked them for all their help and support; I was relieved that I didn't have to work at ICI anymore. I looked forward to a few months off before the real hard work of being a professional boxer began.

Tracy and I were getting on well; we had a long-distance relationship, and I was travelling back and forth to Rotherham on a regular basis. I had a few girlfriends previously when I was young, but the feelings I had for Tracy were different. We became best friends and lovers. We had a great summer together, and life was good.

I asked Shaun if he'd like to come to Rotherham with me, as I would be moving to London to live in a few weeks, and I wanted to spend some time with him before I went. I was nervous about the thought of living in London, not knowing anyone, and leaving all my family and friends behind in Middlesbrough.

Tracy's parents had gone away for the weekend, she lived in a small two-bedroom terraced house with a steep staircase, I hadn't really thought it through about Shaun's sleeping arrangements and hadn't considered his disability. That evening the three of us, Shaun, Tracy and I went to a few local bars and ended up in the local nightclub, I loved the music of the 1980s, in fact, I have a wide range of music which I enjoy, ranging from Punk Rock to Soul, some of the sounds of the eighties were a bit cheesy, but most of it was good. This would be my last night of drinking, I was a professional athlete now, and I knew that when I moved to London and started training again, drinking alcohol would strictly be off the agenda.

When we arrived at the night club, I noticed a few steps at the front entrance and thought, how the hell am I going to get Shaun up those steps in his wheelchair. I said to the bouncer, "Are we alright to go in?" The bouncer didn't even look at me and dismissively said, "If you can get him in, go in." Most bouncers in other clubs helped with the wheelchair, but this knob could not be bothered; he was huge, he appeared to be full of steroids, and he was bright red and angry looking. I wanted to say something to him about his attitude, but I knew that if I did, we wouldn't get in, and our night out would be over. I tried to lift the wheelchair reversing Shaun up each step slowly, Tracy tried to help too, but it needed the strength of another guy to get him up the steps.

After a few minutes of struggling with the wheelchair, we managed to get Shaun into the night club. We were smashed drunk that night and had a great time dancing and drinking. In Middlesbrough, it's common for most people to enjoy drinking; it's a culture that has happened for generations. Is it a working-class culture to drink excessively? I don't know. We had to lift Shaun down the steps on the way out, luckily, two lads helped me lift the wheelchair as the red-faced steroid head looked on. I kept my mouth shut. I didn't want any trouble, and I didn't want to lose my boxing licence before I got it.

When we returned to Tracy's house, we were hammered. It was time for bed, and then it dawned on me that I had to get Shaun up a steep, narrow staircase. I couldn't carry him in my arms in front of me because I would have hit his legs and head against the walls. The stairs were very restrictive. In my pissed state, I considered other methods to get Shaun upstairs. I suggested to Shaun that I give him a fireman's lift and that I throw him over my shoulder. We were all giggling, the alcohol had taken its toll on our brains, then Shaun muttered, "Get me up those stairs, Fireman Sam."

Before we attempted the hurdle of getting Shaun up the stairs, I looked him directly in the face and tried to be serious for a minute, saying, "Please don't make me laugh." I bent down towards Shaun's belly, preparing myself to pick him up, and as I did, a loud fart escaped. I had to abort the lift due to the smell and the laughter. Unfortunately, Shaun was stuck in the stench for a while. He was a sitting duck, but eventually, we gained composure and tried again to lift him, and with one big heave, I threw him over my shoulder and out of his chair.

I was at the bottom of the stairs with one hand holding on to the banister for support and the other hand holding Shaun's legs tightly as he lay across my shoulder. I started the task slowly, taking one step at a time. Shaun was heavy, a dead weight, we were both doing well, and we were just two steps from the top of the stairs when Shaun shouted, "I think my arm's fell off." When you're drunk, everything is exaggerated, and the slightest daft actions or words would have you in hysterics. I nearly collapsed laughing, and slightly fell backwards and almost dropped Shaun; if I had dropped him, this would have been disastrous for us both. However, with one big push, I used all my strength, and I tossed him up in the air, and he fell onto the landing area. We both lay down on the landing laughing and repeating, "My arm's fell off." Tracy didn't see the funny side of our antics; she was worried and told us to calm down. After a few minutes, the laughter died down, and I struggled to pick him up again and somehow managed to throw him onto the bed.

Over the years, Shaun and I have had some memorable nights out, and this evening was one of them. We didn't stop laughing. Shaun was flat out on the bed, and I undressed him to discover that he had a new urine device fitted called a conveen. The conveen was attached to his penis, then a tube was attached from the conveen and went into a urine bag; the bag was Velcro strapped to Shaun's leg. I hadn't seen this type of device before and wasn't sure what to do. Luckily, Shaun, even though he was drunk, was able to give me instructions on how to change the conveen. Shaun told me I had to remove the old conveen, spray the shaft of his penis with clear spray glue to keep the conveen in place, and then roll the new conveen over the head of his penis, like putting on a condom. Shaun needed to have an erection for the conveen to fit properly.

Shaun was giving me instructions, and the task was like competing in the Krypton Factor, I couldn't fathom it out in my alcohol-drenched brain. I asked Shaun to explain again. I would have done this job perfectly if I had been sober, but in my drunken state, my aim and dexterity weren't great, and the glue ended up all over my and Shaun's body and all over the bedding. My fingers were sticking together. It was a strong glue, like superglue. I eventually managed to pull down the condom like conveen over Shaun's penis. There was so much glue, the conveen was solid, and so was Shaun's penis. Shaun had a hard-on for me to put the conveen on, and we did see the funny side of the situation. We weren't embarrassed about Shaun's hard-on. In fact, I was a bit envious that he could get a hard-on even though he was pissed, and he also had a huge cock too. We giggled about it all until we fell asleep. Nights like that were memorable; Shaun has a great sense of humour, he's one of those guys who is always smiling, he's never been short of attention from the opposite sex, women love him, I can understand why, he is an amazing person, funny and always positive, full of life.

Ernie Fossie arranged to meet Marty and me at Kings Cross Railway Station in London, and it was Monday, 24th August 1987. I was feeling nervous and excited; Marty reassured me this was a huge deal for me. I was now a professional boxer, paid to fight at the age of eighteen, with just thirteen senior contests under my belt. I knew that Ernie had been chosen to be my coach. I was a bit wary of him because I was used to Marty's style of training, I had never trained with another boxing coach full-time before, and I didn't know what to expect.

Ernie picked us up at Kings Cross Railway Station in his mini. We all crammed in as he took us to St. Pancras Boxing Club, Kentish Town. On the way to the gym, Ernie drove like a bat out of hell, and he always did drive like a lunatic. He knew all the rat runs of London. It excited me, though, this new fast pace of city life. As I went into the gym, I felt like I was entering the arena for a fight. I had butterflies in my stomach, and I couldn't believe how nervous I was. Jimmy Tibbs was training some boxers, I recognised them because I'd seen some of them on TV: Erol Christie, Tony Wilson, Pat Clinton, Tommy Shields, and Roy Rowlands. Ernie shouted across the gym to a young dark-haired lad who was punching away at a bag, he came over, and Ernie introduced us, "This is Damien Denny from Northern

Ireland. He'll be sharing a flat with you." Damien stuck his glove out, and I tapped it, then he went back to resume his training. Ernie told me I could do some training at the gym before going to see the flat, and I didn't train much. I was in awe of the other boxers and couldn't take my eyes off them.

The flat was based in Whetstone, North London, about ten miles from the gym. On the way back to the flat, Ernie informed me that I had my first fight on 25th September at York Hall, Bethnal Green. There wasn't room for Damien in the mini. He had taken the tube back to the flat. As I went to get out of Ernie's car at Whetstone, Ernie handed me the key to the flat, dropped Marty and me off in the car park, said, "It's number two. See you tomorrow." and sped off. Marty and I went into the small flat and waited for Damien to arrive. It was a small, basic one-bedroom flat with a double and single bed in the one bedroom, Damien had the double, as he was there first, and I had the single bed. It wasn't long before Damien came crashing through the door with his large kit bag. He was smiling and chatty, and he welcomed me. I think he was glad to have some company. I instantly liked him. Damien had won numerous titles as an amateur boxer; he'd had a few professional fights in London at that time and had won them all. Marty stayed the night, ensuring I was safe and settled before returning home to Middlesbrough the following day.

After a few weeks of living with Damien, he and I became good friends. Damien had a girlfriend in

Leytonstone, and he'd often stay there at weekends, and I would have the flat to myself. Tracy came to see me in London on the first weekend of my move. It was an exciting time visiting all the major London landmarks, I felt like I was on holiday for a while, but I knew that hard work was required very soon because my fight was in four weeks' time.

As an amateur boxer, I competed at 75 kilos (11 stone 8 pounds) and felt strong in the middleweight category, but after a few weeks of training in London, I was unintentionally losing weight. I weighed 11 stone 4 pounds. I think the weight loss was due to a change of diet, fending for myself, and being homesick. Also, I wasn't working in a physical job anymore, and it was a complete change of way of life for me. Weight is so important for a boxer: Making the weight at a fight is always on a boxer's mind. If you don't make the weight that the fight is stipulated at, there are consequences, there could be financial penalties, or the fight could be cancelled. A boxer needs to fight in their correct weight category so that he feels strong; if you are overweight at the weigh-in, you will have to lose the excess weight to be able to fight. The fighter has the responsibility to make the correct weight; losing weight on the day of the fight is not good, and wearing sweat suits to make weight before a fight can be dangerous because you are dehydrating your body. Ernie suggested that I became a light middleweight boxer who should weigh around 11 stone.

I was preparing for my first professional fight at light middleweight, and I was feeling good. Damien and I would train every day, running first thing in the morning and training at St Pancras gym in the afternoon. It was a bit of a trek getting to the gym each day. We didn't have a car; we'd catch a bus to Arnos Grove Underground Station, and then a train would take us to Kings Cross, then onto Chalk Farm, and we'd walk ten minutes to the gym. It was about an hour travelling time each way. I hated it at first, it was a chore, but I did get used to it eventually. In the beginning, when I first started travelling on the tube, I used to say hello to people and try and have a chat, like we do in Middlesbrough, but everyone appeared to be in their own bubble, and ignored me, they'd look at me as if I was an escaped lunatic. The strange thing was that I became just like them after a few months, I never spoke to anyone on the tube and became lost in my own little bubble.

My first professional fight was at the famous York Hall in Bethnal Green, London. My opponent was Paul Burton, who came out of the Brendan Ingle camp, and Brendan was in Paul's corner. The fight was televised on Seconds Out, which was a London production Company that promoted young up-and-coming boxing prospects. I was a little nervous and had completed my usual rituals before the contest providing me with much-needed comfort and confidence. I weighed 11 stone 1 pound, which was one pound lighter than I should have been, but I felt strong. I didn't like anyone else wrapping my hands, as an amateur, I had always prepared my own hands ready for a fight, but now my trainer wrapped them, and I never got used to it. It was the first time I had boxed without my vest on, it seemed alien to me to be topless, but when the bell rang for the fight to commence, I forgot all about it. The fight was six three-minute rounds, and it was stopped in round five by the referee. I had won my first pro fight, but I didn't feel elated, I felt as if I had lost some power and hadn't fought to my full potential. I was homesick and met the crowd of Boro fans after the fight, including my old trainers Marty, Peter, and Augy, who had made an effort to travel all the way to London to support me, it was heart-warming to see those friendly faces, and I wanted to go back home to Middlesbrough with them there and then.

Life as a professional boxer wasn't a bed of roses, I'd moved to London on my own at the age of eighteen, I'd changed to a different weight category, everything was alien to me, and I was alone and lonely. I had determination and persistence, I am a stubborn person by nature, and I thought that I couldn't lose face by returning to Middlesbrough, and if I left London, I wouldn't achieve my goal of being a British Boxing Champion. I had to be positive, I was lucky that I had Damien as a support, he was older and more experienced than me, and when I felt down, he would pull me up.

Damien had a cousin who owned an old - fashioned Irish pub in Holloway Road, North London, his cousin Ollie was a real character; a big strong Northern Irish man with huge hands, he was like a bear, hard as nails, a street fighter, with always an elaborate tale to tell. Sometimes Damien and I would go to the pub for something to do and escape the confines of the small flat for a while, the pub was a change of scenery which was filled with various characters who entertained us. London can be a lonely place for a young boxer or for anyone who is on their own in a big city, I wasn't used to city life and always wanted to go back home to a place where I belonged. Luckily, Damien had relatives living in London whom he would often visit and get that valuable support that family can give, I didn't have anyone apart from Damien.

One evening Damien and I were drinking orange juice, as usual, sitting at the bar chatting, when a stocky stranger appeared in the pub doorway. He was a big lump of a man and shouted to everyone in the pub in a broad Southern Irish accent, "I'm the hardest man in Holloway Road, if any man wants to take me on, come outside." Damien and I looked at each other, and with raised eyebrows, I said. "What the fuck?" Ollie was behind the bar wiping a glass. He didn't respond to the man, he put the glass down and rolled up his sleeves, then silently lifted the bar hatch and walked towards the doorway to where the big lump of an Irishman stood. Ollie looked the man directly in the eyes and told the man in a deep Northern Irish twang, "I'll take the challenge." Damien and I moved quickly towards the door along with some other customers who were eager to see the outcome of the fighting talk. Damien and I looked on in anticipation and wondered what would happen next as they both went outside, we quickly followed them to see how the drama would unfold. There must have been about twenty people gathered on the pavement to watch the entertainment, the strange thing was that there was no shouting or words of encouragement coming from the crowd, there was just an ominous silence.

Both Irishmen took the boxing stances of 1920's fighters, very upright with clenched fists held out straight; it was all very gentleman-like. Ollie threw the first punch with his big fists, and the stranger countered with some jabs, missing Ollie altogether. There was a nasty sound of fists on flesh and bone-crunching noises; the tit-for-tat punching continued until the fight ended when Ollie blasted the stranger with a right cross, which Frank Bruno would have been proud of. The stranger fell to the floor and was on his hands and knees on all fours, covered in blood, when Ollie said. "Are you finished?" The stranger looked up at Ollie with a bloody nose and cuts and bruises on his face. Ollie repeated himself, "Have you had enough?" and the stranger slowly nodded his head in defeat. Ollie put out his bloody hand to the stranger and helped him up, saying, "Right, come and have a drink now." The street fight lasted no more than four minutes, and both men were exhausted. Fighting is stressful, it's a male primitive animalistic act, all male animals fight for mating rights or to be the most dominant male, it doesn't matter who you are; fighting someone is unnerving. We think that twenty-first-century men are sophisticated, and we have moved on since the dark ages, but we are all just mammals who have primal instincts, and I think that our testosterone-fuelled nature will never change throughout the centuries. Ollie guided the broken stranger into the pub, cleaned him up, then poured him a pint of Guinness, wagging his finger at him and saying, "No more Shenanigans." Damien and I couldn't believe the drama we had just witnessed and returned to the bar to carry on sipping our orange juices.

As an athlete, I had to sacrifice many things which other young eighteen-year-olds take for granted: drinking alcohol, late nights, and clubbing. I didn't really miss partying, I accepted my commitment to the sport of boxing, but every now and again, it was nice to behave like an average teenager. I was looking forward to going back to Grangetown for the Christmas Holidays in 1987. It would be great to see everyone again because it had been four months since I had moved away, and this was the longest time that I had ever been away from home. I was so happy to be back amongst the people I loved, my family and friends. I had arranged a big night out that weekend with all the lads, I hadn't had a drink for four months, and I couldn't wait to let my hair down. Christmas time in Middlesbrough is one big party! A day before I was due to go out with my friends, I had a phone call from Ernie Fossie informing me that I would be fighting in Cardiff on 12th January. I was devastated, I just wanted to enjoy my time at home, having fun, drinking, and partying with my friends. Instead, I had to be teetotal and train in preparation for my upcoming fight.

I did go out locally with my friends but sat in the corner sipping my orange juice, thinking about my fight, which was in two weeks' time. That Christmas, I trained every day, including Christmas Day, and didn't drink any alcohol, it was a working holiday. Marty opened the gym for me to do some training, I loved being back at the old gym, it still had its unique smell, and it brought back great memories. On Boxing Day, I went to see Tracy in Rotherham for a few days before returning to London.

1988 was a good year for my boxing career, I had seven fights and seven wins, I was happy about the progress of my career, I was having excellent sparring bouts, and my boxing skills were improving, but I wasn't happy living in London. If it weren't for Damien, I would have returned home to Middlesbrough in the summer of 1988, but Damien told me to persevere and stay in London, and I was glad that he did, I trusted Damien; he became like a big brother to me.

Our team moved to a gym in St Paul's that year, which was right in the middle of the city, and we trained there between 12 noon and 2pm. As we left the gym each day after training, there would be a queue of yuppies in their designer suits waiting to get into the gym. Looking back, we missed a prime opportunity to make money, we should have trained them one to one, I know they would have loved to have been coached by professional boxers, and in those days one to, one boxing coaching would cost around £40 per hour in London, it was the time of Maggie Thatcher's YUPPIE (Young Upwardly Mobile Professional) era, many Londoners had money to burn.

Damien and I were struggling financially. We weren't skint but we were living off the low wages of the fighting purse. It wasn't a huge amount of money. We had plenty of time on our hands; after training, we would just go back to the small flat and watch TV. We were both bored, if we had trained others, we would have gained financially, and we would have enjoyed meeting people; it would have also been a great opportunity to promote ourselves to sell contest tickets. Damien and I weren't Londoners, and we found it difficult selling tickets for our shows, not that we were under pressure to do this because the TV coverage paid for our shows. I guess being with a big promoter had its advantages. Being with a small promoter can out pressure on young up-and-coming boxers. They are often required to sell show tickets to cover their purse. The last thing a young boxer needs before a fight is this kind of pressure, selling tickets and collecting the money, but we must accept that it is part of the business, putting bums on seats. I've seen popular six-round fighters sell around £6,000 worth of tickets and receive just £1500 for the fight, taking away deductions of 25% for the manager and 10% for the trainer, plus paying income tax leaves him with £780. Most young boxers often struggle financially and emotionally. They need as much support as possible in the early days of their career, and having a mentor is so important to them.

My last fight of 1988 was on 20th December at Swansea Leisure Centre when I boxed Kevin Hayde, a strong Welsh boxer. The crowd at Swansea didn't like me because I was English. There has always been a rivalry between the English and Welsh people. It dates back hundreds of years. I don't think Welsh people have forgotten historic invasions by the English. They shouldn't blame me; I had nothing to do with it. The ironic twist is that I now live in Swansea with my Welsh partner. The crowd shouted obscenities at me and told me to go home. After each round, I returned to my corner, and some of the spectators took advantage of my proximity to them so that they could hurl abuse at me. I retaliated, putting my hands on the ropes, standing up, and hurling abuse back. Ernie told me to sit down and ignore them. I was cocky and wouldn't take crap off anyone. I hadn't experienced this behaviour before at a boxing contest and was surprised at the nastiness of the crowd. I thought ok, I'll play the baddy. They were acting like the spectators of a wrestling match instead of a boxing contest. I won the contest, and at the end of the fight, Kevin and I shook hands.

I returned to my corner, where I saw a group of lads standing up and shouting more abuse at me. They were calling me a wanker and making the wanking hand gesture. I laughed at them, making them even more irate. I left the ring with security guys surrounding me, not that I needed them. I was up for it.

There were other fights that evening at Swansea leisure centre, including Tony Collins vs Russell Mitchell. Both boxers were in the same category as me, light middleweight, and Tony was one of my sparring partners at the gym. Tony was one of Frank Warren's young prospects. We were shocked to see him beaten that night. He lost by a TKO (technical knock out). I was in the changing room after the fight, and I started chatting to Russell Mitchell, whom I discovered was an American from California. He'd watched my fight earlier that evening with his trainer, and they said they were impressed with my performance and told me that I would do well in the States. I have always loved American boxing and admired the boxing legends who came from the USA. Russell's words had planted a seed in the back of my head.

I'm a funny bugger, if I don't like someone, I can't hide it, and I didn't particularly like Ernie, my trainer. One of the main reasons for this was his two-facedness, he would tell boxers they were the best thing since sliced bread to their face, and as soon as they walked out of the room, he would slag them off. I hated that. I knew he was doing the same to me, but I was stuck with Ernie. I had signed the contract with

Frank Warren. I didn't hate Ernie, but there were things that he did that went against the grain. When you spend a lot of time with him, as I did, you see the real Ernie. He spoke about boxers detrimentally. I'm a loyal person, and if someone is good to me, I'm good to them. I know boxing is a business, and I was part of that business, but it dawned on me from a young age that boxing can be a cut-throat game, and I was just fodder. I'm a straight person and have never been able to lick arse, and many people don't like the fact that I'm direct and to the point and not gushing with flowery shit. I knew many arse lickers who rimmed the anuses of many arseholes in the boxing world and became successful from it. The most shocking example of successful arse rimming was an autograph hunter who stood outside boxing gyms and became a leading matchmaker for one of the biggest promoters in Britain at the time. It just shows that arse-licking pays sometimes.

After the Kevin Hayde fight, I returned to Middlesbrough. The homesickness never left me. I'd go home at every opportunity I could. Middlesbrough was a big pull for me, and I needed my friends and family around me, people I trusted. I was young and immature and had a lot to learn. I didn't have life skills. The streets of London certainly weren't paved in gold, and the streets were ruthless and lonely. I thought of ways how to leave London but still box under the Frank Warren banner. I came up with an idea, I rang Marty and asked him if he would train me in

Grangetown, and he agreed. I informed Frank Warren that I would be training in Middlesbrough and no longer in London. His office accepted the new arrangements. I found it strange that during the fourteen months since signing with Frank Warren, I had no contact with him. He was my manager, but obviously, he had bigger fish to fry, and I felt neglected. I could never speak to him on the phone. It would always be his secretary saying, "Frank is in a meeting. Can I take a message?" I knew he wasn't in a meeting, but what could I do? I just wish there were more honesty and straightness in the boxing business, but it's a game to the big boys, and if you don't play ball, you will lose every time.

When I signed the contract with Frank Warren, he guaranteed twenty fights in two years and six to eight fights in the third year, one of the fights being a Championship title fight. Many choices I made showed that I was immature, and I had no one to guide me in the right direction, no one with the skills and experience in the professional boxing world to stop me from damaging my career. I paid the penalty for moving back to Middlesbrough. I lost my first fight after the move to Bocco George, a tall, lean African boxer. I was devasted by the loss, but it was my own fault. I boxed like a novice. I'm not sure why. It could have been several things that affected me. I struggled to get good sparring partners; I was sparring with amateurs. I trained hard, running up the hills every day and training day and night in the gym. I don't blame anyone, it was my decision to go home, and it wasn't the right move at that time.

After the Bocco George fight, I took stock of the situation. I had a rest from boxing for a few weeks and told Marty that I had to return to London. I knew it was for the best. Marty always supported me in whatever decisions I made. It was difficult to gain composure after that fight. It knocked my confidence for a while, and I felt that I was being punished for returning to Middlesbrough. I was only given one fight that year which was against a strong Welsh man, Carlo Colarusso, which I won when the referee stopped the contest. I had three more contests after winning the Colarusso fight under Frank Warren. In fact, I fought Carlo a second time when he gave me a much harder fight. I beat him on points when we went toe to toe in Darlington. We went to war that night. It was my hardest professional fight to date. It was a real warrior humdinger of a fight. After they gave me the decision, the announcer asked everyone to give a big round of applause to Carlo, but instead, everyone gave him a standing ovation for his gallantry, it was a good tough battle, and he deserved to be recognised for his boxing skills and bravery. I live near Carlo now, and we have met up a few times recently. He's a lovely guy. He told me a secret that only a few people knew about but is now willing to share publicly. After our war, he was afraid to go to sleep that night, worried that he may not wake up because of the punches he received to his head. As boxers, we don't talk about these issues. It comes with the territory, punches to the head, head butts, and elbows to the head. They are just part of the job description. It's a dangerous business and a side of boxing that spectators don't think about when two warriors are pummelling one another in the ring. Thankfully we are now both fit and healthy former professional boxers.

My relationship with Tracy fizzled out, and there were arguments constantly. It was difficult having a long-distance relationship. I really didn't have time to travel to Rotherham. I was based in London and working hard there.

In November 1989, there was a boxing show at the Broadway Theatre, Barking, where Frank Warren was promoting his show. A masked gunman appeared out of the crowd and shot Frank twice in the chest, he survived, and a boxer who had nominated me to Frank when I was an amateur was charged with attempted murder. Terry Marsh spent ten months on remand and was released after being acquitted at trial. At the time, there were many rumours regarding the incident, and the reason behind the shooting was never disclosed, but everyone had their own theories. Frank recovered from his wounds and continues to work as a boxing promoter.

Damien asked me if I wanted to stay with his family in Lisbon, Northern Ireland, for a week just before Christmas 1989. I'd never been to Northern Ireland before. I obviously knew about the 'Troubles' because of the TV coverage and the stories Damien had told me, but I wasn't concerned about going there even though I was English, and it could be a dangerous place for me. I didn't know what to expect and how everyone there would react to an Englishman, but I trusted Damien. I was looking forward to a nice break away from London. Just like Wales, there's a historic rivalry dating back to the twelfth century when England invaded Ireland. I'm not a historian, but the bitter taste of English oppression has remained with Irish people, and in many ways, I can understand why they resent English people and particularly those with political power.

We flew from London and landed in Belfast on a drizzly winter's night. Damien's family was really welcoming and put on a spread for us. Damien's family were all Catholics like me, not that religion was ever discussed or mattered. He had three brothers and one sister. Damien's parents were lovely, genuine working-class people and easy to get on with. The following day we borrowed a car and drove towards Belfast city centre; after driving a short while, we could see an army roadblock ahead with two Land Rovers blocking part of the road where four soldiers stood with guns, and they flagged us down. I was frightened. I'd never seen this before; Damien didn't look worried. He smiled and reassured me, saying, "Let me do the talking." We stopped as directed by the soldiers, one of the soldiers told Damien to wind the car window down whilst another soldier peered inside the car at us. He looked in the back seats. I remember his eyes, and they were popping out of his head. He looked wired, ready for action. I think he was scared, too. He was just a young British lad. There were many car bombs and attacks on British soldiers by various Irish factions. The soldiers were wary of everyone. The enemy wasn't clearly visible. It could be any civilian who wanted to murder them. The British soldiers had a bad reputation for being brutal when they occupied Northern Ireland, but it was a tense time for everyone concerned, and many of the soldiers were young boys. I can sympathise with everybody who was put in such a volatile situation. A few of the soldiers checked around the vehicle and asked Damien a few questions, "Where are you going? Where have you come from?" My heart was racing, and I wasn't sure what would happen next. Luckily, the soldiers just waved us on, and we were free to go. Damien was used to these roadblocks and the possible threat of violence. For him, it was a way of life.

As we entered the city, on the outskirts of Belfast, there were huge murals of various images relating to the 'Troubles' painted on the pine end of terrace houses and walls, with huge, coloured flags waving from properties. I didn't understand what all these symbols represented.

That evening we went on a night out, we visited a typical Irish bar, and because I was in Ireland, I thought I'd order an iconic Irish drink, a pint of Guinness. I asked the barman for a pint of Guinness with a lemonade top, I always had lemonade tops in my beer, but the barman looked at me in shock and horror and refused to serve me the drink. Damien told the barman, "For God's sake, serve him whatever he wants. He's paying for it!" I said, "It doesn't matter if it helps. Give me a pint of Guinness and a dash of lemonade in a separate glass." He served me the drinks. For him serving a Guinness with a lemon top was sacrilege.

That evening I got the taste for Guinness but couldn't drink more than a few pints. It was filling. After drinking at the Irish bar, we went to a few more bars and then to a nightclub. After fifteen minutes at the club, I lost Damien. I was leaning against a wall drinking my pint when a pretty young girl came over and asked me a few questions, "Where are you from? What are you doing here?" I thought my luck was in when out of nowhere, a huge burly man pushed her out of the way and spoke in a broad Northern Irish accent and intimidatingly asked me similar questions to the girl, "Where are you from?" I said, "England." Then he interrogated me more, "What are you doing here?" I said, "I'm with my mate," he said, "Who's that?" I said, "Damien Denny." His reaction changed, "Damien Denny, the boxer?" Most people in Belfast knew Damien. He was famous there for his superb boxing skills. The burly man looked at me and smiled, and offered me a drink. I accepted it and had a double Jack Daniels and coke; we spoke for a few minutes about boxing. I think he owned the club. When I found Damien, I told him about the encounter. He told me they must have been checking me out, thinking that I was a soldier. I suppose I did resemble a soldier; I had short-cropped hair and was fit and lean. I can't imagine what would have happened if I'd been there alone and hadn't given them the correct answers. It was the realisation of where I was at that time in history.

Cornelius with Damien Denny

Frank Warren moved all the boxers to a new venue which was based at The London Arena, near Millwall, the venue, known as London Docklands Arena, was demolished in 2006 to make way for a housing development. The new gym was in a part of London which was difficult to travel to from Whetstone, it would be a three-hour round-trip train journey, and we needed to change stations frequently, as it was in the Docklands area. I had one fight at the London Arena, which I won against Peter Gorny; it was the heaviest I had been as a professional boxer. My weight was 11 stone 12 pounds, and I was in the Super Middleweight division. My next fight was in Sunderland against Frankie Moro, and I beat him on points.

My contract with Frank Warren was coming to an end, and I was feeling a little uncertain about my future. A few months prior to the end of my contract, there were no discussions with Frank Warren to extend my contract, and there was no communication with Frank at all. I had never built a rapport with Frank Warren. I was just another pleb in his books. I tried to speak to Frank on numerous occasions but to no avail. I was ready to leave after three years with Frank. I had only thirteen professional fights under Frank, having just one loss. I was only twenty-one years old, and I was disillusioned with boxing. I nearly walked away from the profession, but that dream and passion to be a Champ lingered, and I persevered.

Round Eight – Deep South

I went home to Middlesbrough to regroup. I wanted to think long and hard about my career and which direction I was going to take. I believe that I had turned professional too young. I wasn't mature enough mentally to handle the pressures of being a professional boxer. I should have stayed amateur for longer, gaining vital experience and life skills, staying in Grangetown with the support of my family and friends. I had felt lonely in London; I didn't belong there, and city life wasn't for me. I had constantly been boxing for ten years, rarely taking time out of the gym. Training and fighting had been my life, and now I was lost. I was waking up each day without a purpose.

A good friend who lived a few doors down from me, Stevie Carney (one of the turnip thieves), suggested that we both travel to Corfu for a few weeks and that I forget about boxing for a while. I thought it was just what the doctor ordered. Stevie was a self-taught musician and didn't have the opportunities to perform in front of audiences in Middlesbrough, and he thought that he could get some work as a musician in Corfu. The first week in Corfu, we went mad, drinking, partying, and having one-night stands. I was quite shy in those days and found it difficult to chat girls up, Stevie would sing them some love songs, and the girls would be like bees around a honey pot, looking doe-eyed at him. Even though I was shy, I still managed to have some girlfriends. Girls would approach me, and I enjoyed having female company, I was used to being around testosterone-fuelled males all the time. Girls smelled nice and were easy on the eye.

In Corfu, Stevie got a job as a DJ in the bar which was below our apartment, and we'd spend our evenings at the bar drinking and chatting up girls. I felt good. I was tanned and relaxed, my body and mind had time to rest, and I didn't have to worry about training or boxing. After two weeks of partying, I was due to fly back home, but Stevie persuaded me to stay in Corfu for a little longer, which I did. After the third week in Corfu, I was sick of partying and started to think about my boxing again. I had met a Cypriot girl, but her parents didn't approve of our relationship, they weren't happy that I was English, she worked as a holiday Rep and didn't like partying, unlike me, she was a nice decent Cypriot girl.

One evening I was at the bar with Stevie when two girls came in; Amanda and a friend came. They went straight to the DJ booth and asked for a record to be played. Stevie had his eye on her friend and was more his type, blonde and tall. They ended up seeing each other for a while, and Stevie persuaded the girls stayed an extra week in Corfu. Amanda and I got on very well, but it wasn't a romantic relationship because I was with another girl. I was due to leave soon, and Amanda and I swapped contact details before I left.

After my trip to Corfu, I went home to Middlesbrough to decide which path I was going to take now that my contract with Frank Warren was over. My relationship with the Cypriot girl had ended, and we both went our separate ways. One evening I went with Marty to one of his amateur boxing shows at the Marton Country Club in Middlesbrough, where I met Bobby Thompson. I knew him from when I worked at the scaffolding yard. He introduced me to an American named Beau Williford, who was a former heavyweight boxer, trainer, and manager. We had a long conversation, and he suggested that I go to the States to do a bit of boxing training and meet some of his boxers. He gave me his number and said we should keep in touch. I wondered why Beau had asked me to go to the States. I wasn't sure what his intentions were at the time.

That night in bed, I made my decision to go to America and contacted Beau the following day. Within a week, I had booked my flight to Lafayette, Louisiana, in the deep south. At the time, I didn't know where Lafayette was situated in America. I had no idea of the vastness of the USA, and I wanted to learn more about America and learn from American boxers. There was no such thing as Google back then to check it out.

I'd always remembered the night I met Russell Mitchell in Swansea Leisure Centre when he told me that I should go to the States because I would do well there, and I also thought about the Texan in Salou who sold me 'The American Dream'. Now I would see America at last and gain valuable knowledge and perhaps meet some of my boxing idols and have some top sparring and maybe a few fights. This could be a great opportunity for me. I was twenty-one years old with my life in front of me. What did I have to lose by travelling to the States? I paid for the flights myself, I've always been good with money, I'm a saver, I always ensured there was always enough money in the bank so that I could support myself, I hated experiencing poverty, I never wanted to be in that situation again.

I couldn't fly directly to Lafayette. I had to fly three times from three different airports to reach New Orleans. The first flight was with Air India. As soon as I got onto the aircraft, the strong stench of stale curry hit me. I love curry, but the smell was putrid and stomach-churning, the aircraft was old and rickety, but I tried to ignore my surroundings and looked forward to going to the place where my boxing heroes came from. The flight was scary, there was severe turbulence, and the seat belt signs regularly flicked on; during a turbulent time, I was desperate for a crap, and it was painful holding it in. As soon as the seat belt signs pinged off, I scarpered to the toilet with clenched butt cheeks, and I made it just in time. As soon as my arse hit the toilet seat, my bowels exploded. The curry served earlier had made a great impact on my body. As I sat on the toilet, they announced that there would be more turbulence and that everyone should return to their seats, but I couldn't leave the toilet. The curry was still at work. When the turbulence hit again, I thought the plane was going down. It was shaking rapidly and dropping down suddenly and uncontrollably, like being on a runaway roller coaster. I gripped my feet and hands to the side walls of the tiny toilet cubicle, trying to stabilise myself as the plane rocked violently. At one stage, when the aircraft dropped dramatically, my arse left the toilet pan, and I floated in mid-air for a few seconds, I kept thinking about what way to go, I was scared stiff, but luckily for me, my time wasn't up, and the turbulence subsided.

After an eighteen-hour journey, I arrived in New Orleans, I love warm climate countries, and being there reminded me of my first trip to Spain when I experienced, for the first time, the warm air blasting me like opening an oven door. The humidity in that part of the States is indescribable. I come from the North of England, and I wasn't used to that kind of heat. I was kitted out for Northern winters and soon undressed to be more comfortable as I sweltered in the humid climate of Louisiana. Beau met me at the airport and led me to his Cadillac, which was metallic blue and the size of a tank. As we drove along the Freeway, I opened the window of the car, and Beau said, "What are you doing?" I replied, "I'm letting some air in." He said, "I've got the air conditioning on, man, don't do that." In Louisiana, no one drives with their car windows open due to the overwhelming, intense heat.

I stayed in Beau's home for a week. It was a large bungalow in suburbia with all mod cons; Beau and his wife made me feel welcome, but I still felt a little uncomfortable staying at Beau's house. I didn't really know him, and I was a young lad of twenty-one, I needed my own space. Beau had a word with his neighbour Bill, who had a workshop that had a loft bedroom, the building was about two miles away, and it was decided that I stay there.

I went to the workshop and saw the loft room for the first time, I was a bit shocked, my house in Grangetown wasn't a palace, but this place was dismal and gloomy. It was a long dark attic room with no windows and had one single bed and a bathtub, the toilet was located downstairs in the workshop area, it would be a bit different staying in the loft room in comparison to the luxury I'd experienced living in Beau's bungalow. The long room had an old blue carpet with no furniture apart from the bed, there were no pictures on the walls, and it had a shade-less light bulb dimly lit in the centre of the ceiling, it was basic, but it was free; thanks to Bill. The room had a musty smell. It smelt old, it hadn't been used for a long time, and it had a stale odour. The first night I stayed there it gave me the creeps, I was a bit nervous being on my own, and the light switch for the loft room was situated down the steep stairs in the workshop. At night this meant that I had to switch the light off in the workshop, clamber up the stairs and find my bed as fast as I could in the pitch blackness. The workshop building was cladded with steel, and at night and as I lay in my bed in the loft room, you could hear the steel expanding and contracting, making all kinds of weird noises which echoed throughout the room. My imagination played tricks on me. I was conjuring up all sorts of surreal thoughts in the complete darkness, and I had many sleepless nights there. One night I lay in bed in the darkness, it was deathly silent, and I was settling down, getting comfortable, and looking forward to a good night's sleep after a hard day's training. I heard a small scratching noise near my left ear, and then something brushed past my face in the blackness of the room, I screamed out loud and dived quickly out of bed, I couldn't see a thing, I wondered what the hell had touched me. I ran downstairs and switched the light on in the loft room, I slowly went back upstairs to investigate the mysterious, touching incident, I looked at the bed and saw on the pillow the biggest, ugliest brown cockroach I had ever seen. Looking at it sent shivers down my spine, I didn't want to kill it, I threw a towel over the pillow and the cockroach and took it downstairs into the workshop and shook the towel, setting it free. I was wary about cockroaches in my bed after that and checked everywhere, ensuring it was roach-free before I got into bed.

The gym Beau trained at was a big shed of a building with a few bags and a boxing ring; the gym was owned by Kenny Vice, a super lightweight American boxer. I trained in the gym every day, and sparred with a few of the boxers there, including Kenny, he sparred hard, he was tall, lean, and muscular and had a punch like a mule. We respected each other, I admired Kenny's boxing skills, he was a gentleman outside the ring, but inside the ring, he was a nasty piece of work. He lived near the gym in a trailer with a hoard of kids, I'm not sure how many there were altogether, but there wasn't much of an age-gap between all of them.

Beau arranged for me to fight six three-minute rounds in New Orleans against a fighter named John Marlborough, I won the fight in the first round, and Beau handed me two hundred dollars, about £120. Fees weren't discussed with Beau; I wasn't sure how much I would get paid for the fight, but it wasn't about the money, I wanted to get experience, but two hundred dollars was much less than I was used to getting paid. I was never forthright when it came to business, I was young and lacked confidence in that department, I was unskilled in negotiation, and I felt uncomfortable discussing fees.

I had been training hard and was eager to get more sparring with different fighters, and Beau surprised me when he said we were going to meet some inmates at Angola Prison, which is the largest maximum-security prison in the United States. He said, "You'll get a few rounds of sparring in with these guys. They're hard bastards." Beau had a good relationship with the prison personnel, he often took boxers there to spar with the inmates, I didn't know what to expect, but I was up for the challenge.

There were six people in our party who went to the prison, security was tight, and when we reached the jail entrance, there were huge metal gates surrounding the compound with armed guards everywhere. They checked us over thoroughly, checking inside and outside the van we had travelled in, searching our bags, patting us down and making us empty our pockets, the security checks took a while to complete. The prison guards were concerned about the clothing that one of our boxers wore, and he wore light faded jeans and a white T-shirt. Unfortunately, his attire was the same as the uniform of the inmates. He had to take off his clothes and wear his boxing gear not to be mistaken for an inmate. It was a scary thought to be lost amongst the prison population, who knows what might have happened.

Angola prison is renowned for its violence, it regularly sees inmates attack and kill each other, and 90% of prison inmates will never leave Angola Prison alive. They had an electric chair at Angola known as 'Gruesome Gertie,' and the last person to be executed by Gertie was Andrew Lee Jones on 22nd July 1991. Gertie killed 87 people and now sits at the Louisiana Prison Museum in Angola. Angola's inmates enjoyed any form of distraction, such as sparring with outsiders, this would break up the monotony of prison life. When I visited the prison, I was unaware of Angola's deadly reputation, I just thought sparring there would be a great experience.

We all entered the prison, and the smell of stale sweat and bleach immediately hit my nose. There were heavy doors, large keys, and armed guards protecting us from the prisoners. Even though we were protected, I still felt vulnerable. The armed prison guards told us to stay closely together and warned us not to wander off away from them, and we were allocated three guards to look after us who stuck to us like glue. We were guided into a large hall where there were inmates weighing in, which I thought was strange because I was told we were just there for sparring sessions, I was then asked to jump on the scales. I looked at Beau with a questioning look, and he started laughing, saying, "Get on then." I did what I was told, and my weight was 11 stone 10 pounds, one of the prison guards shouted, "He weighs 164 pounds." As soon as the guard shouted my weight out to the crowd of inmates, I heard a big deep southern voice shout out, "I want him! I'm going knock your white ass out!" I turned to Beau. I'd probably gone even whiter by then and said, "It looks like I've got an opponent." He replied, "You certainly have, boy!" My new opponent was called 'The Alley Cat'; he'd had 90 fights and had only lost four of them. I was told I had two opponents and I would be boxing three lots of three-minute rounds with each fighter.

The first fight was against Leroy 'Hurricane' Johnson, and the second fight was against 'The Alley Cat'. I did my rituals before the fights and asked one of the guards to escort me to the ring. He didn't understand why I wanted to see the ring and the venue before my fights; I tried to explain that I had done this before all my contests. It was one of my customs. When I entered the venue to do my rituals, I was taken aback by the smell, the noise, and the size of the audience; the smell of testosterone filled the air, and the noise they made was ear-popping. They were excited and showed it. For them, boxing was a welcome release from the confinement of their cages and the dull routine of prison life. It was the first time I had seen people wearing jeans so low that you could see their underpants. They walked slowly, dragging their legs to look cool, and were intimidating, eyeballing me. They had tattoos all over them, even on their faces. As I warmed up for the fights, Beau said, "These guys are serious, and they want to knock your ass out." I knew that, all right.

I thought, my God, I had woken up that morning looking forward to going on a jolly, excited at experiencing something new, and not training at the gym for the day, and now I'm 110 miles away from Lafayette in the largest maximum-security prison in America, and about to fight two of its caged monsters. I'm just a boy from Grangetown. I was 4,500 miles away from home and thought, what the hell am I doing here?

I was at the doorway of the venue waiting to go into the ring for the fights when I heard the announcer say, "Introducing all the way from England, Cornelius Carr!" All I could hear were loud boos, hisses, and whistles coming from the inmates. I'm not afraid to say I was nervous; I was blonde, white, and from England. It felt as if everything was against me. Most of the inmates were black and Hispanic and were intent on seeing my lily-white ass being knocked out.

I was in the ring waiting to see my opponent for the first time. They announced Leroy 'Hurricane' Johnson, and the crowd went berserk, screaming, clapping, and whooping as he entered the ring. I wish someone could have filmed the look on my face as he appeared. He was a black, stocky, muscular Mohican-haired inmate with thick chains around his neck and body and was controlled on a leash by his trainer. He behaved like a wild animal, growling at me. The leash holder was struggling to keep control of the Hurricane. He was showing his teeth and snarling at me. He pulled hard, tearing at the chunky chains wrapped around his neck and body. He seemed desperate to be free from the shackles to rip me apart. He looked as though he wanted to kill me. His black eyes were huge and filled with hatred, he was strong, and his huge muscular frame glowed with sweat. The crowd went mad, waving their bandanas and handkerchiefs, making as much noise as possible, this was a theatrical performance to scare the shit out of me, and it worked.

When the bell rang, Leroy came out swinging, wanting to knock my head off, throwing big punches, but I made him miss his target, and after the first round, I could see that he was breathing quite heavily. He might have looked the part, but he was struggling to box me. Beau advised me to carry on and, when he would charge at me, to step back and bang a right-hand left hook. Halfway through the second round, I followed Beau's advice, and I caught him with a clean combination. It was one of the best powerful shots I'd thrown in my life at that point. He fell to the floor. The referee pointed for me to go to the neutral corner and then started to count to ten. When the referee got to 9, Leroy tried to get up. He was wobbly, the crowd went silent, and then the referee stopped the fight. I walked towards Beau, saying, "What's happening now?" Before he could answer me, the crowd began to stamp their feet and chanted loudly, "All-ey Cat, All-ey Cat, All-ey Cat!"

Leroy left the ring, and within a minute, the announcer said, "Our next fighter needs no introduction. Please welcome 'The Alley Cat!" The crowd was out of control, shouting, screaming, and waving at any piece of clothing they could find. The Alley Cat was a tall, slim black guy, and he was rangy with dreadlocks and a gleaming smile of golden teeth. Beau knew he was a Southpaw and a slick mover and told me to get close to him and aim at him with body punches. The first round was difficult. I was trying to close him down, but he was skilful and cocky, with his hands down low, not really wanting to engage with me. I think his jabs won him the first round, I went back to the corner to face Beau, who shouted at me to get close to him and close him down and not to give him any leeway. During the second round, I was getting frustrated with his jab and move and the way he teased me with his gleaming gold smile, he was sneering and taunting me. I rarely lose my temper, especially in a fight. Boxing promotes self-control and discipline, but this guy really wound me up, and I put my hands to my sides and shouted as loud as I could, "Fight me, you black Mother Fucker!" The crowd loved it, they wanted a show, and I wanted to give it to them. I thought I had won the second round when I returned to my corner. Beau told me off for saying 'black motherfucker', he said, "Do you want a prison riot?" I didn't listen to him; I was focused on beating the shit out of the Alley Cat.

In the third round, I caught him with a stinging right hand to the head and a left hook to the body. He winced, I thought I'd got you now, and you're going down. The crowd was going mad because I was beating up their golden boy. There were just thirty seconds left of round three when I had him on the ropes, I could hear Beau shouting, "Keep punching, keep him on the ropes!" And I did keep punching him until the final bell rang. The crowd loved the fights, there were no winners or losers in prison boxing, but I knew I had won, and so did the Alley Cat.

The audience gave us a standing ovation for our performance, which I thought was a nice touch; after I changed into my casual gear, the security guards took us back into the arena to watch the remaining fights. The guards were scanning the crowd carefully. A situation like this could turn into a mass brawl or prison riot. Most of the inmates congratulated me, the Alley Cat was sitting in a ringside seat, and he waved me over. With a guard's approval, I went over to him, and he gave me a special gangster handshake, but I wasn't sure how to respond to it and awkwardly copied what he was doing. He flashed his golden smile at me and said, “You’re a good fighter, man! Do you want to come back to my cell tonight?” I laughed nervously, smiled, and said, “Not tonight, mate.” I think he really did want my lily-white ass, literally. I discovered that the Alley Cat was incarcerated for murder when I met him in 1990, and he was due for release in 2016. I don’t know what became of him, but I respected his boxing skills.

I had been in America for eight weeks. I was corresponding with Amanda, the girl I had met in Corfu; writing letters to her cheered me up a bit because I was lonely with no real friends or family around, and there was no TV in the loft room. Someone had left a bible in the loft room, and out of boredom one evening, I picked it up and tried to read it, although I couldn’t understand the way it was written. Every evening I would pick it up and try to comprehend the text, it was difficult to read, but I kept trying. One evening I was sitting on my bed. I had been reading the bible when I started thinking about my dad and all the memories I had of him. I put the bible down and closed my eyes with my head resting on a pillow. I reminisced about those precious times we had spent together and how he was taken from me too soon; it had been over eight years ago since I had lost him.

Something inexplicable happened to me that evening. I had a spiritual encounter that I’ve never experienced before or since. It felt like I had been overwhelmed by something good, the feeling throughout my body was euphoria and happiness. I thought it was the spirit of my dad visiting me. I had seen and felt his presence before, but this experience was intense. It was beyond words and magical. This was a beautiful, serene encounter that enveloped every organ, muscle, and vein in my body. It possessed me for about two minutes. I felt deeply emotional and started crying happy tears. There was something beautiful inside me, which was calming, blissful and good, it swept over my body, and I didn't want the ecstatic feeling to leave me. But slowly, the beautiful feeling was fading away and leaving me, and I was getting upset and shouted out, "Please don't go! Please don't leave me!" But it drifted away until it had completely gone, and I got on my knees and started praying for it to return. To my sadness, the calmness and peace which was given to me moments earlier had now vanished forever, and its departure had left me devasted. I sobbed and grieved for something lost, it was something precious, I believed that it was my father who had shown himself to me, but it wasn't in a visible way like the ways I had seen him briefly previously, this was something much more intense, this was mind-blowing, a visit from him which was soul to soul. It was an experience that affected me deeply, I'll always remember the heavenly feeling that overwhelmed my body. I don't know what had happened to me, whether it was my dad trying to communicate with me or if it was some force of a higher spiritual level that was out of this world. I hadn't been drinking or taking any medication or doing anything which would have affected my mental state. I was stone-cold sober and felt blessed that whatever or whoever it was, had chosen me to visit, and I felt blessed that I had this remarkable experience.

Although I was raised as a Catholic, I hadn't been a practicing Catholic since I was a child, but I always prayed in certain situations for good things to happen; for example, for me to win a fight and for nobody I cared about to come to any harm. That night after the beautiful encounter I didn't sleep much. I was reliving the extraordinary experience and trying to make sense of it. I heard the shutters of the workshop downstairs open around 7.30am and rushed downstairs to see Bill standing by the entrance. Bill was six feet tall and weighed about twenty stone (280 pounds), he was a nice man, always ready for a chat and keen to help anyone. He was a former American Footballer. I asked Bill if I could speak to him, I was dying to tell someone about the spiritual experience I had a few hours earlier, and I wanted to talk to him about my dad. Bill was a good listener, and I told him in detail about the experience: I discussed with him that I thought that my dad had visited me, and how I had an overwhelming euphoric feeling last night, and how it had a great emotional effect on me.

After I had finished telling Bill about the whole experience, Bill concluded that it wasn't my dad who had visited me last night, he put his big hand on my shoulder firmly and said, "Son, you're born again, Jesus Christ is in your life." Bill told me that he had placed the bible in my room, he hadn't spoken to me before about religion and his beliefs, so I was shocked to discover that he was such a God-Fearing man. I told Bill that I found the bible difficult to understand, and later that day he bought me an expensive simplified leather-bound version of the bible.

I was becoming engrossed in the bible, I was reading it every day, I did my best to understand the bible's messages and the meaning of its stories. I was spending a lot of time on my own, I had no TV or radio, I was in a strange, unfamiliar place, and the Bible was the only form of company at the time. I even went to the local church every Sunday, it was like attending a West End show, the entertainment was fabulous, everyone was singing and dancing, jumping around in a trance-like state, the atmosphere was electric, and everyone made an effort to dress up and wear their finest colourful clothes and hats. There were plenty of girls there too, I missed female company. The preacher introduced me to the congregation, "Today, we have with us a young professional boxer who comes all the way from England, and please give a warm Southern welcome to Cornelius Carr!" Everyone flocked towards me, wanting to shake my hand and hugged and kissed me. These were welcoming gestures, I was lonely, I embraced the closeness of this pious community, I enjoyed spending time amongst these flamboyant religiously friendly people. The preacher approached me at the end of the service and invited me to his house for a small party which would be held in a few weeks' time.

This was my twelfth week in America, and I was comfortable in my surroundings, I was getting along with everybody, training and sparring at the local gym, but I missed female company, I was young and needed a loving young lady to wrap me up in her arms. I had another fight in Greenville, Mississippi, I won the fight in the first round as a TKO and earned another $200. On my return from Mississippi, I went to the preacher's house to attend the small party I had been invited to, I was amazed at the size of his mansion. It was a massive, beautiful property with vaulted ceilings which had huge wooden beams everywhere, a bit different to the basic loft room I was staying in, and the council houses I had lived in, in Grangetown. The preacher proudly escorted me around his mansion, and I was speechless at its magnificence, I'd never been to a property like it before, it blew my mind.

The preacher had two children, a boy of nineteen and a girl of seventeen. I was twenty-one and thought these children were fortunate to have such a privileged lifestyle, I wondered how the preacher could afford such luxurious surroundings. The preacher's children asked me to go to one of their bedrooms to have a chat about the UK and my boxing career, I think they wanted to talk to me privately without their parents listening; they seemed very straight, old-fashioned, innocent, and sheltered from the outside world. They were fascinated with the experiences I had and the stories I told them about life as a boxer in London. I asked the boy what he did for a living, and he said he wasn't working but was training to be a preacher. I said, "Is there any money in preaching then?" He laughed and told me, "I'll be making $30,000 from spreading the word of the Lord in Mexico." I was shocked at the amount of money he would earn.

When we returned to the party downstairs, there was a huge buffet waiting for us. No expense was spared, the food looked delicious, and it was perfectly presented. People at the party approached me, shaking my hand, and with their left hand, they grabbed my shoulder, saying, "Jesus has touched you, Cornelius. God is with you." I was young and lonely and soon became embroiled in the world of religion, I was a believer, I felt happy and content amongst these people. They welcomed me with open arms. I felt that I had known them all my life.

The preacher approached me and told me they were all going to pray for me. I was wondering why they wanted to pray for me. I felt fine, I was confused, but I went along with it. There were around twenty people who stood up, including me, and formed a circle holding hands. They all closed their eyes. I didn't close my eyes at first. I looked around at everyone, and they were all silent. Then the preacher said, "We are all here to pray for Cornelius." And to my surprise, the preacher started talking gibberish, and it was made-up language. It sounded bizarre. The person to the right of the preacher began speaking gibberish too, and it was followed by the next person to his right and so on until eventually, it was the turn of the person holding my hand next to me to talk gibberish. At the time, I thought that the euphoric encounter that I had enjoyed a few weeks previously would engulf me again and I would be able to show them, but I didn't feel anything. I just felt embarrassed. The person next to me started talking gibberish, then stopped. He squeezed my hand, indicating to me that it was my turn to talk gibberish. I was so confused. I was waiting to be absorbed by the heavenly feeling again, but there was nothing. He pressed my hand again, but still nothing. I really wanted to feel something spiritual again, and it seemed a long time that I stood there silently with my eyes shut, desperately wondering what to do. I didn't want to pretend and talk gibberish. I felt foolish, it had no meaning to me, and then a girl on the other side of me started talking gibberish. It was farcical.

This was a bizarre experience; I didn't know what this ritual stood for until I asked the preacher afterwards. He told me it was 'talking in tongues,' it's when a spirit enters your body, and words are released through you via the spirit. They all reassured me that I would be able to 'talk in tongues' on another occasion. That night in bed in the loft room I thought about the last few hours and how crazy and shocking the experience had been for me. I still didn't understand it. I stopped going to church after that because it had affected me in a negative way, I was disillusioned by the whole setup, but for some reason, I still carried on reading the Bible.

Beau had a phone call from Roy Jones Junior's team asking if I wanted to spend two weeks at their sparring camp in Reno, Nevada. Roy Jones Junior had a fight coming up against Art Stewart, it was a contest on the undercard of Ray 'Boom' Mancini vs Greg Haugen, and he needed sparring partners as part of his boxing preparations. I had watched Roy Jones Junior in the 1988 Olympics when I saw his awesome boxing skills for the first time, I felt that he had been robbed in the final; he was probably the classiest fighter in the Olympic boxing team, and he outshone everyone, he was the star of the show. However, the judges awarded Park Si-Hun, a South Korean boxer, the winner, and it was a 3-2 decision by the judges. His record as a professional boxer in 1992 was16 wins and no losses. He was a talented fighter, and I admired him. This would be a great opportunity for me to meet him and experience sparring with one of the best up-and-coming boxers in the world. I hadn't witnessed him boxing at a professional level, and perhaps it's because he wasn't represented by big well-known promoters such as Don King or Bob Arum.

I took a Greyhound bus from Lafayette to Pensacola, where Roy lived; at Pensacola, I met one of Roy Jones' team. It had taken me eight hours by bus to reach Pensacola, Florida, where Mike, Roy's friend, was waiting for me at the bus depot. Mike was a huge thick-set black guy who looked me up and down and kept giving me strange glances, and then in a southern drawl, he said, "Man are you here to spar Roy Jones?" I wasn't big in stature, and I wasn't tall, in fact, I had shorter limbs than the average boxer, and I didn't have the physique of a typical boxer. I think Mike thought I was crazy to get in the ring with Roy, he thought Roy would hurt me, he went on to say, "He knocked out two heavyweights last night!" I replied, "I'm looking forward to sparring, Roy." He smirked and remained silent for the rest of the journey whilst he drove me to an airport near Pensacola. At the airport I met all the boxing team, including Roy. I couldn't believe how big Roy looked, he was much taller and broader than me, and he was muscular, with a thick, strong neck.

When I arrived in Reno, I had an opportunity to speak to Roy Jones' dad, and we had a conversation about my career, and he told me he had seen me boxing in Italy. I was on the undercard of Darren Van Horn vs Lindell Holmes. I was surprised that he had seen my boxing and that he had remembered me. Reno was like a mini-Vegas. It's glitzy, glamorous, full of life, and of course, has plenty of casinos. Reno is renowned for the 'Battle of the Century' when the fight between two heavyweight legends fought in 1910, and they were Jack Johnson and James Jeffries. At the time, it sparked riots nationwide when Jack Johnson won, and he was the first African American boxing Champion who held the title until 1915.

I shared a room with a young American fighter named John Scully, and we got on like a house on fire. I felt as if I had known him for years. He had great boxing knowledge and had some top sparring with famous world-class fighters, including Roy. John told me that Roy is one of the best boxers he had sparred with, and just before we went to sleep later that night, I asked John, "What is the best way to spar, Roy?" John replied, "Haven't you seen him boxing?" I told John, "I haven't watched him as a professional. I saw him at the 1988 Olympics." John continued to say, "If he hits you with one shot, you know that five or six more will follow. Good Night." I couldn't sleep a wink, knowing I'd be facing Roy in the ring the following day. John and I had so much fun together. We were both young and full of life, he was great company, and we are still friends today.

In the morning, we had a knock at our bedroom door at 6am, and it was time for us to start the day with a run. We normally ran for a few miles every morning. Every time I sparred, I prepared as if I was training for a fight: running, training at the gym, sticking to a healthy diet, and not partying or drinking, etc., I was very dedicated to my boxing, I took it seriously, for me I felt like I wasn't just a sparring partner, I was there to take something away from the session and to learn from the experience. Whatever you do in life, you need passion, determination, persistence, and commitment to be successful. Self believe is also important, I always wanted to be the best I could be. Boxing can be a lonely sport, and sometimes you doubt yourself, I didn't have a team around me to boost my ego and help me through any negativity, I faced many challenges alone.

I loved being part of Roy's team. That afternoon I entered the ring with Roy for the first sparring session, I was nervous and felt that he was in a completely different league to me, but I put up a good performance. Roy was slick, fast, and difficult to hit. For me, those are the key factors of being a successful boxer. Roy's father kept encouraging me during the sparring, saying, "Keep it up, keep it going." He was a good influence on me, and I got on well with Roy Jones Senior. I wrote in my diary that night about all the things which I had done correctly, and I highlighted my mistakes. I like to analyse myself. I am my worse critic. Roy Jones Junior and I were in the lift on one occasion, and I couldn't believe how big Roy was, and I said to him. "How the hell do you make middleweight?" He looked at me and tapped the side of his nose as if to say it's none of your business.

After two weeks of sparring with Roy Jones Junior, in preparation for his fight, I asked Roy Jones Senior if he could get me on the same bill as Roy, he tried, but he couldn't find me an opponent. I was disappointed as it would have been an amazing experience for me. Roy Jones Junior won his fight. It was a TKO, a devasting knockout against Art Stewart. Roy Jones Junior went on to win many World Titles and was one of the best boxers of the 1990s. I received $1,000 for sparring with Roy in Reno, which was gratefully received, and I also took away with me precious knowledge which I used throughout my boxing career.

On my home to Lafayette on the Greyhound bus, I started to question what I was doing in Lafayette; it wasn't the boxing mecca that I thought it was going to be. When I returned to my little dark loft space after staying in a five-star hotel in Reno, I felt a bit depressed. I had been staying in luxury in Reno, I had been part of a team, and now I was back to reality, living in the sparsely furnished lonely loft room, and I was homesick. I thought about the team at Reno returning home to their loving family and friends, and I was returning to loneliness. I trained every day with the uncertainty of my future on my shoulders, I had no fights lined up, and Beau kept pressuring me to sign a contract with him. I had read the contract, I wasn't a businessman, but I knew that the deal was not favourable to me. Boxers are the warriors at the front line, they are the ones putting their lives at risk, and they should be rewarded financially for their bravery. There have been so many fighters ripped off financially over the years by managers and promoters, and fighters have been severely injured or died for their sport. I wasn't business-minded, but I knew that signing up with Beau wasn't a good move.

One night after a training session at the gym, I called in to see Beau at his home. I knocked on the door, but there was no answer, so I opened the door and shouted, "Anyone at home?" Beau came into the hallway in his dressing gown. He seemed agitated about something, I'm not sure if he had been arguing with his wife, but he was angry. He said nastily, "What do you want?" As soon as he shouted at me, he lunged at me and tried to slap my face. I looked at him in shock at his actions and said, "You Twat!" I couldn't believe that he'd treat me like that. I hadn't done anything to deserve it. I picked up my training bag and walked out, and started walking back along the country road to my loft room, which was a few miles away. A few minutes later, Beau appeared in his car and drove alongside me as I marched along the road. He wound his window down and couldn't stop apologising for his behaviour, but it was too late. I had lost respect for him. I couldn't trust him; his behaviour was unpredictable.

I packed my bags in the loft room and visited Bill to say goodbye and thank him for helping me, and I liked Bill; he was one of the good guys. I was relieved when I landed at Heathrow Airport a few days later and smelt the cool, fresh English air again after spending months in the humid air of Louisiana.

Round Nine – Promoters

I returned to Middlesbrough to start afresh after my American adventure, I worked with Marty again, and my first fight was against Frank Eubanks (no relation to Chris Eubank), who was a tough fighter from Moss Side, Manchester. Frank's trainer was Phil Martin. He was an exceptional northern trainer who had coached many champions and was a former light heavyweight boxer. I was fortunate to have a financial backer who sponsored me for about six months and didn't want anything in return. He just wanted to help me. His name was Eric Neil, and he was a lovely guy who had his own construction business in Middlesbrough, PRS Construction. I wasn't earning much money at the time when Eric sponsored me, and I was very thankful for his help. If he hadn't backed me, I probably would have been unable to continue as a professional boxer. Boxing is a hard game. If you were not up there with the high earners and were a fringe fighter like me, life was tough; journeymen were making more money than I was, and most people who weren't as persistent as me would have thrown in the towel a long time ago.

John Spencely and Cedric Kushner were the joint promoters of the boxing show. It was a sell-out at Thornaby Pavilion. I was excited to fight in my hometown of Middlesbrough. It was my sixteenth professional fight, but my first contest on home soil as a professional boxer. The atmosphere was amazing, and the crowd gave me their loudest support when I entered the boxing ring. I stopped Frank in round five. It was a good win for me. After the fight, Phil Martin approached me and told me I'd be a Champion one day, I didn't see Phil again, but I never forgot his prophecy. Henry Cooper commented on my fight for Sky TV. He was the first boxer to knock down Cassius Clay, who later became Muhammad Ali, in June 1963 at Wembley Stadium. He complimented my boxing skills by saying, "The boy has a good left hook and has a promising future." I was thrilled with Henry's comments and praise. I had always admired his boxing skills, particularly his left hook, known as 'Enry's 'Ammer. I had four more fights and four wins under the banner of John Spencely, who worked with Cedric Kushner, and I was due to have a Title fight, but I injured my hand, and the fight was cancelled, after that there were no more fights arranged because my contract was just on a fight-to-fight basis.

I moved in with Amanda, the girl I had met in Corfu. She was living in Kingston Upon Thames, London. My boxing record was 18 wins and 1 loss, and I couldn't find a decent promoter. I was still training hard in case a fight was arranged. I was confused about the whole situation. I was in the prime of my life and couldn't get into any fights. In 1992 the middleweight division was strong and thriving. There were some talented boxers, including Nigel Benn, Chris Eubank, Erol 'Bomber' Graham, and Steve Collins. I wished

I had the physique to be a heavyweight; perhaps I would have had more opportunities as a boxer in that category.

When I first moved to Kingston Upon Thames, I went to a local amateur boxing gym; it was run by Freddy Barr, he had connections with the England squad, and he had good boxing knowledge. I liked Freddy, and he was a nice guy. He worked hard to keep the gym going using his own finances. I respected him. One day he watched me sparring and said, "You need to change your boxing style if you want a long career as a professional boxer." I was shocked. I thought, who is this guy telling me what to do? I had only known him for a few weeks, and he was telling me to change my style. At the time, I was a bit upset by his remark and didn't respond. I was pissed off and left the gym in a bad mood. I spent the evening thinking about what Freddy had said. I took out all my diaries and read my old entries. I used to analyse my fights and judge myself between 1 and 10. I'd keep all the notes in my diaries so that I could learn from my mistakes. I was always my worst critic. I wanted perfection and to be the best, it's difficult to be a perfectionist in the sport of boxing, but I tried extremely hard. The next day I apologised to Freddy for pouting over his advice to change my boxing style. I was young and arrogant, but I thought Freddy might have a point. I was willing to learn. Instead of working on my front foot, I used my back foot more, becoming more skilful and becoming a counterpunch boxer instead of using brute force to beat opponents.

A few weeks later, I was at the Henry Cooper gym in Old Kent Road training when I met Howard Rainey, and it was nearly a year since I had my last fight. I was at a low point. I was lost, unsure of my future. I wished then that I had my dad to help me find my way again. I needed a mentor, someone to tell me what to do, someone to point me in the right direction. Howard and I started chatting about boxing, and I told him that I didn't have a trainer. He said, "Why don't you come here and train with me for a few weeks to see how we get on?" I agreed. Howard had some great fighters, including Colin McMillan, who was a British, Commonwealth, and WBO World Featherweight Boxing Champion, and Paul 'Scrap Iron' Ryan, who was a British and Commonwealth Boxing Champion. And Terry Dunstan, a British and European Cruiserweight Boxing Champion who also fought for the IBF World Title. Howard was a staunch Yorkshire man, down to earth, physically a big man, and easy to get along with. I liked him straight away.

Howard had dealt with Micky Duff previously and suggested that a meeting should be arranged between us. I knew of Micky Duff, and he was a big boxing promoter. He had many huge names on his books. I thought meeting him would be my big break. Howard and I met Micky in a posh office near Soho in London, where he was straight to the point. There were no niceties, no bullshit. I didn't really like him, but he was Mr. Boxing, and I was fucked. There were no other options. He told me that he could get me into a few fights and said, “Let’s see what happens.” He was cold and indifferent. Financially, the offers on the table were scandalous, and I was going backward. I would be earning the same money that I earned when I started out as a professional boxer with Frank Warren. Perhaps I thought that my record of 19 wins and 1 loss was worth more than it actually was. It was shit money with Micky Duff or nothing. Here I was four years down the line, training my balls off as a professional boxer and offered a pittance to be a warrior in the ring. The words of the head boxing coach of the English youth team all those years ago on my way back from boxing in Sardinia came echoing through my brain, ‘Don’t turn pro until you are twenty-one. Get as much amateur experience as you can.’ Looking back, I turned professional far too young, but I don’t blame anyone. It was my decision, and circumstances at the time dictated my fate. I just had to deal with it.

My first fight under Micky Duff was at the NEC Birmingham. I was on the undercard of Frank Bruno vs Carl Williams. As I was warming up and about to enter the arena, Frank Bruno saw me and said, “Is my music too loud for you?” He was focusing on his fight, which was coming up after my fight, and he was worried about me. He was caring enough to think of others during his nerve-wracking time before his fight, he was a good man, and I was shocked at his thoughtful manner in this often selfish world of boxing. The NEC was packed. There were about 10,000 boxing fans there, the audience was waiting for the Frank Bruno fight, which was on after my fight, and I wanted to put on a good boxing show, this was my chance to show my skills to a huge crowd, and shine, I was sure I could impress them.

My opponent was Graham Burton, a Brendan Ingle fighter, and he was a young boxer from Sheffield. He was one of the first boxers whom I fought in the ring like a wrestler and not a boxer. At one stage of the fight, he picked me up in a bear hug, carried me across the ring, and slam-dunked me on the floor. I had knocked him down a few times, but he was one of those boxers who just wanted to survive and didn't want to exchange any punches. He kept hugging and holding me, it was hold, grab, and run. It reminded me of a hilarious boxing match scene in a comedy film starring Jerry Lewis in Sailor Beware. I didn't think it was funny at the time. I could also hear Brendan Ingle shouting to Graham from his corner, "Get behind the referee!" I didn't understand this behaviour at all, and it made me look bad. In fact, it made us both look bad, and I was angry. It was embarrassing for me to look so incompetent in front of all those thousands of people. It was like I was performing in a bad pantomime. It was my big break to show my boxing fans my skills, but instead, I felt like a laughingstock.

If you have a fighter who is hell-bent on just getting through a contest without fighting like a boxer, it's difficult for you to show off your boxing skills. I know that Graham wanted to survive and did what he was told to do by his trainer, but this was out of order. Perhaps Graham really did want to fight me but wasn't allowed for whatever reason. Boxers are meant to be brave, and I thought that his behaviour had let the side down. Professional boxers are paid to be fighters, and that's what the public wants to see, a battle between two warriors who each desperately want to win. If one is playing tricks and not up for the challenge, it can make the other boxer look unprofessional. At the end of the fight, I won on points, and I was so infuriated by his performance that I went to Graham's changing room afterwards and said, "What the fuck was that all about?" Graham said, "I just had to do whatever I could to get through." I walked away, shaking my head and saying, "That's not boxing." Fighting under Frank Bruno was my big break, and I felt that Brendan Ingle and his boxer had fucked it up for me. I have spoken to Graham since then on Facebook. He's a nice guy, and I know he regrets listening to his trainer on the night of our fight.

I also sparred with a few boxers in preparation for their title fights, one of the boxers I sparred with was Chris Pyatt. He was a WBO World Middleweight Boxing Champion. Jimmy Tibbs was his trainer, but he wasn't there during our sparring sessions. It was Dean Powell. We sparred at

Thomas A Becket Gym on Old Kent Road for a few days, and I was pleased with the way I sparred Chris. I felt in control and confident. My self-belief had kicked in, and I thought I could beat this guy if I were to face him in a fight. This was probably the first time that I genuinely believed that I could achieve something in the boxing world. I'm not sure if it were the experience that gave me the boost or if I was maturing. Everyone has their day in boxing. I was enjoying training with Howard and being around good quality fighters. I was training with world-class boxers who made me stretch myself, and I wanted to be at their level. As I always say, I am persistent and keep pushing myself, never giving up, I had a dream, and I wanted that dream to come true. I was determined to succeed and become a boxing Champion. I had sacrificed my youth for the sport, but I gave it gladly; I loved boxing.

Whenever I fought or sparred with any top fighter, I always raised my game and rose to the challenge. I was sick of being skint. I wasn't earning big money for each fight, and I needed to up my standards to get quality well, paid fights. Howard arranged some sparring at The Match Room Gym in Romford with Freddie King, who was the head coach of Match Room Boxing. One of the fighters who trained at the gym was Steve Collins. I didn't know that much about him because he had spent a lot of time training and fighting in America. Steve was Irish and a middleweight boxer.

Originally it had been arranged that I would spar with Gary Delaney at the Match Room gym in Romford, but for some reason, Gary couldn't make it, Gary was a light heavyweight boxer at the time, so Freddy King offered me some sparring with Steve Collins instead. I was asked to do four three-minute rounds, and after the third round, Steve said, "That's enough today. We'll see how good you are tomorrow." On the way to Kingston on the train with Howard, I asked him, "How did I do?" He said, "You bashed him up, Corny." I knew I had, but it was nice to hear it come from my trainer. That evening I was eager to face Steve again. I knew this time that he would try and bash me up in retaliation for the beating I gave him the day before.

The following day Howard and I arrived at the Match Room gym to continue where I had left off. I was looking forward to bashing him up again but was cautious because I knew Steve would be prepared. I'd travelled 90 minutes for the privilege of sparring with Steve. I had changed into my boxing gear. I was prepared, and I was shadow boxing and warming up in readiness for the session. I waited for thirty minutes for Steve to arrive when Freddy King said, "It doesn't look like he's coming." Five months from that date, Steve Collins won the WBO Middleweight World Boxing title by beating Chris Pyatt. At that time, I was a fringe fighter. I was well-known and respected in the boxing fraternity but wasn't a household name. I hadn't managed to break through the mainstream and receive the coverage that I deserved.

I had been living with Amanda in Kingston for two years and used to go home to Middlesbrough regularly. I was always a home bird; Middlesbrough was a magnet that had an invisible force that always pulled me towards it, but I knew in my heart that the best opportunities were in London at this time. Shaun's birthday was coming up, and he asked me to go home to celebrate with him on a lad's night out. I had no fights due and thought it would be a great opportunity to catch up with my old friends. There were a few mates who went out one evening, including Young Marty Turner, Kenny Johns, and Shaun. We had a few beers locally in various pubs in Eston; it was refreshing to be amongst friends who knew me well. I could relax around them and be myself. Local people congratulated me on my career and asked me many questions, especially the question, "When will you get a shot at the British Title?" Many people shook my hand and wished me well. It felt lovely that my hard work was appreciated. We took a taxi into Middlesbrough town centre and were dropped off at one of the liveliest bars in the Boro, Corner House. There was a long queue to get in. The head doorman was Dennis Lowe, who was my old amateur boxing opponent back in 1987. Dennis saw me and shouted, "John, how many people are with you?" I shouted back, "Four!" He said, "Follow me." We skipped the line and headed straight into the busy bar, Dennis, and I had a few minutes to talk about old times, and then he disappeared back to his station at the front door of the bar.

We were all knocking the drinks back and having a laugh. It was a great atmosphere in the bar. After an hour or two, we decided to go to another bar/club, Chicago Rock. Shaun and Kenny went to the toilet whilst young Marty and I sat down, drinking our pints of lager. My back was facing the dance floor, and young Marty was facing me near an emergency exit. Young Marty suddenly looked over my shoulder, shouting at some lads who were threatening and spitting at him. He said, "What's your problem?" Before I had a chance to turn around to see what was happening, about five lads just barraged us with punches, we were in shock. We were unprepared and pissed. I didn't know why they wanted a fight, but they must have recognised us as boxers and needed to prove their fighting skills to their friends. Young Marty and I punched our way through them. We were trained to use our fists. Young Marty was a good boxer too, but we were drunk and unready, which was a disadvantage to us in this situation. We did our best to try and defend ourselves against the unprovoked attack. I hurled one of the scumbags to the floor and pulverised him. I repeatedly punched him in the face and was stopped when I felt a heavy blow to my head. I lost consciousness for a few seconds, and when I came around, all the so-called hard men cowards who fought in packs ran off out of an emergency exit. All the violence happened quickly. Within seconds, all the adrenalin kicked into my body, and I sobered up immediately. I was angry and wanted to find them. I was furious, I was enjoying a night out with my friends back in my hometown, and then a few arseholes ruined our evening. We didn't discover who the twats were, but I believe in Karma, and I hope they got their just rewards in life. I can't stand bullies. The next day I woke up with sharp pains in my head and touched my scalp to find shards of brown glass from a Budweiser bottle embedded in my skull. I was lucky that the damage wasn't severe enough to warrant hospitalisation, but the violent act of stupidity and recklessness could have led to tragic consequences. As a boxer, there are always idiots out there who want to fight you to show how hard they are. I tried to avoid confrontation because I knew I could really hurt someone if I was pushed into a corner.

In 1993 I was training every day, but there were no fights arranged for me. I was four months without a contest. Chris Pyatt had been sparring with Chris Eubank and put his name forward to Ronnie Davies, who was Chris' trainer. Sparring was arranged with Chris Eubank at his gym in Brighton. I was 12 stone, and Eubank was about 13 stone. I was a middleweight, and he was a super middleweight. I hadn't met Chris before the sparring session, and as I walked up the stairs into his gym, I saw him doing a strange form of shadow boxing alone in the ring. The movements were quick, short, and quite different from the way shadow boxing is done. He had his own unique method, which I hadn't seen before. I wasn't nervous about the sparring session with Chris. I was looking forward to it, Chris was at the top of his game, and I wanted to test myself to see how well I could do. Chris looked at me and then his trainer, Ronnie Davies, and said, "He's too small." I just looked at him and said, "We'll see."

As we were about to spar, I noticed that Chris was wearing small boxing gloves. I said, "They are not 16 oz gloves." He replied, "They are." I looked at Ronnie and shook my head, and was about to get out of the ring when Ronnie told Eubank to get his proper gloves on. I don't like mind games or being taken for a fool. I was annoyed that he was a stone heavier than me and was trying it in on by wearing 12 oz gloves, thinking I was a naïve mug.

Eubank sparred hard, but I gave as good as I got. As soon as the sparring finished, he said, "Yeah, yeah, I want you to stay." I wanted the job. I wanted to get valuable experience. I was getting paid good money for three rounds of sparring. Eubank would video our sparring sessions for him to analyse my moves, but he would never allow me to watch the videos. He wanted to keep the valuable films to himself. I'd learnt many good boxing techniques in the States, and these moves would wind him up. There was a move, in particular, that would piss him off: Eubank had a high guard; putting each glove up to the side of each temple, I would bring my right hand onto his right hand quickly and push his hand down and whack him with a left hook, and vice versa. I don't think a sparring partner had ever done this to him before. I couldn't do it too much because he watched the videos and learnt how to counter. I also knew that I needed to keep something back just in case we ever fought in the ring. I never gave away everything. There wasn't YouTube back then, and there was no way of analysing an opponent before a fight, apart from looking at videos of previous fights, and sometimes these weren't available. More often than not, you would face an opponent with no previous knowledge of their boxing style and have to suss them out pretty quickly in a fight.

Eubank was an aggressive fighter with a hard chin, probably the hardest chin I had encountered. I had been sparring with Eubank for five days when I received a phone call from Micky Duff. He asked me if I wanted a fight at Wembley. I needed to work, and of course, I needed the money, too. I felt sharp and prepared due to sparring daily with Chris Eubank. The fight was against Horace Fleary. It was an eight-round contest. I won the fight by a unanimous decision and ended up with a small cut over my right eye, which prevented me from continuing to spar with Eubank. It was unfortunate that I had to stop sparring with him because I learned so much and was enjoying the challenge. I did return a few more times to Eubank's gym to spar with him, and we had mutual respect for each other as boxers.

Working with Micky Duff was like history repeating itself. I was in the same situation as I was with Frank Warren, I couldn't get hold of Micky Duff, and I was so frustrated that there were no fights organised for me. I was twenty-four years old and training like a madman eager to make my mark in the boxing world, and I felt like time was running out. There is a small window of opportunity for a fighter. I needed to box big names in order to become recognised and earn large purses. I believed that I was good enough to face top fighters, I had done my apprenticeship, and I was ready to graduate and become a top fighter myself. I was a dedicated boxer who wasn't getting the rewards that I thought I deserved.

Out of the blue, Mick Duff actually called me. I was surprised when he asked me if I wanted a fight against James Cook, who currently held the title of British Super Middleweight Boxing Champion and was a former European Super Middleweight Boxing Champion. I was wary about accepting the fight but thought I had nothing to lose, and I was a middleweight fighter. I had never fought as a Super Middleweight before; Micky convinced me to take the fight, which would be held in just over five weeks' time.

I met Micky at his office to discuss the purse for the contest. Here is an example of a young boxer getting ripped off financially: Micky offered me £4,000 for the fight, and he would take 25% commission, and the trainer would receive 10% commission (which I had no quibble with because he actually worked for his money). After other deductions such as gym fees and income tax, I would be left with under £2,000 for putting my life on the line and boxing in a British Championship Title fight against a dangerous opponent. I had to accept whatever Micky Duff offered. I was held to ransom, and I'd been out of work for six months. I had no income, and I was desperate. I knew it would be a big ask for me to become a Super Middleweight boxer. I had only five weeks to gain weight and prepare myself to box in the biggest fight of my life to date.

Howard knew James Cook well and believed I could beat him in the contest. I didn't watch fighters before a contest, but perhaps I should have so that I could analyse their boxing techniques, strengths, and weaknesses. I trained hard, ate well, and my sprints improved. I didn't like the sprinting side of training, I wasn't good at it, but I always gave 100% in the effort. I used to run with Colin Macmillan and Terry Dunstan, who were both fast on the track, they were my inspiration, and if I could keep up with them, that meant I was in good shape. The longest contest I had ever fought before this fight was eight three-minute rounds, and this fight was twelve three-minute rounds. I knew that I needed to be in top condition mentally and physically. I think having a fit mind is so important for a boxer; sometimes, if my head wasn't in the right place, I would lose the fight before getting in the ring. I didn't research my opponents before a fight because I would have made them into superheroes in my head, and I thought I'll never beat them. They are way too good, and I often allowed my brain to work overtime instead of thinking rationally. I preferred high-class boxing fighters, they stretched me, and I rose to their level. James Cook had previously boxed some great fighters, including Michael Watson, Errol 'Bomber' Graham, Errol Christie, and Brian Schumacher.

Left to Right: Cornelius Carr, Colin Macmillon, Howard Rainey, Terry Dunstan

I feared losing like most boxers, but some boxers are Journeymen. They are professional boxers who fight prospects under no pressure to sell tickets or to win or to lose. They are simply there to make money, and keep having fights. The best way to become a successful journeyman is to lose on points, and not get stopped or have a TKO. If a boxer is stopped or knocked out, he automatically receives a twenty-eight-day ban from attending training, sparring and fighting. Journeymen try to fight regularly and can earn a decent living. Generally, they have full-time jobs, not necessarily linked to boxing, and would fight to earn extra income. Some journeymen are exceptionally talented boxers but choose to lose so they can get regular work. If they win, promoters may not use them again; promoters want their prospects to win. Prospects need journeymen to build their professional boxing records and gain valuable experience, and they are the lifeblood of professional boxing. Out of my thirty-eight professional fights, eight of my opponents were classed as journeymen, although I was unaware of what they were at the time. As a young professional boxer, I was naive. I didn't understand the business of boxing. I'm not saying that fights were fixed because some journeymen won their fights. Every professional boxer would have faced a journeyman at some point in their career.

My head guard broke during a sparring session, and Arthur, one of the coaches, gave me his old head guard to wear. I loved that head guard. It felt comfortable. It had been lived in, it was a bit tatty and worn, but it was lightweight and fitted me perfectly. I kept nagging Arthur about keeping his old head guard. He said, "If you win the fight, you can keep the head guard." Those words were such an incentive to me. It seems daft that a forty-year-old head guard was a carrot for me to win the fight, but somehow winning that old guard meant more to me than the money Micky Duff offered.

The fight was held at York Hall, Bethnal Green, on 11th March 1994, a few weeks before my 25th birthday. York Hall was built in 1929 and was renowned for its Turkish Baths, it's now known as York Hall Leisure Centre after a face-lift in 2004, and it offers a larger, more versatile leisure space than the time when I boxed there, boxing contests are still held there. York Hall has featured in movies and television programmes due to its iconic boxing history; I love that venue; it has a special place in my heart.

My weight was 11 stone 11 pounds, I had a big breakfast before the weigh in because I knew I was a bit light; the fight limit was 12 stone, normally both boxers attend the weigh in before a fight, but I didn't see James at the weigh in which happened on the afternoon of the fight. All the media thought that this fight would be too much of a jump for me, The Boxing News said that I would get stopped in a late round, I was determined to prove all the media wrong.

On the evening of the fight the hall was full, the venue is a historic boxing mecca, I'd had four fights at York Hall previously and won them all and was hoping this fight wouldn't be any different. Because I was the challenger, I came out first, as I walked to the ring, with my hood up and head down I heard the crowd chanting, "Ooh Ah Cantona, Ooh Ah Cantona." I thought bloody hell Eric Cantona is in watching me, that's good. James Cook entered the ring with Micky Duff, who was a manager for both of us, but I didn't see Micky before the fight. I found that to be a bit weird. It would have been nice of him to have wished me good luck. I was the underdog yet again. I knew The Boxing News and Micky Duff amongst others hadn't given me a chance, they didn't have any faith in me. James had a huge reaction from the crowd as he walked in, he was a popular talented boxer. I was shocked at his size, he was six foot two, and I'm five foot nine and a half (don't forget the half inch, every half inch counts).

The first seven rounds of boxing were cautious and uneventful, we were both counter punchers, and neither one of us wanted to take the lead, hardly any punches were thrown, neither boxer was willing to take a risk. After round seven I went back to my corner where Howard told me to start throwing punches, and win the fight, he said, "Do you want to win this fucking fight or what?" It dawned on me that I shouldn't waste any more time being cautious, I had nothing to lose, but I also knew James had a wicked right uppercut which was dangerous.

Cornelius Carr in the Ring with James Cook Fighting For The Super Middleweight British Title 1994

In the eighth round the fight I came to life, I went for it, throwing punches and trying to make a show of the contest. In round ten I caught James with a left hook, and he went down on his arse, the crowd went berserk when the champ hit the floor, I thought round eight had pushed me in front, and by round eleven I thought I was in front. Micky slithered over to my corner and put his thumb up to me, he knew I was winning, and he switched corners, from James' to mine. Just before the final round Howard told me to be careful, and to keep my hands high, and to keep doing what I was doing.

Just before the bell rang for round twelve to begin, I got up from my stool and looked at Arthur saying, "That head guard's mine!" He smiled and said, "It's yours if you win the fight." During the twelfth round Howard said to Micky, "What are doing in this corner?" Micky replied. "I manage him, don't I?"

The final bell rang, and I instinctively stuck my arm out to the referee as a sign that I had won, he grabbed my arm and held it up high, I had won! There are no judges for a British title fight, the referee decides who wins, I was the new British Super Middleweight Boxing Champion. I was overwhelmed with joy; the years of hard work and dedication had paid off. Marty had always said that I would be a British Champion one day, and this was the day. I went over to James' Corner, hugged him and said, "You are a top fighter, James." He disappeared shortly afterwards with his team.

Arthur was the first to hug me, and whispered in my ear, "The head guard's yours." Howard and my team were ecstatic, it was a memorable night. The moment they presented me with the Lonsdale Belt was precious, it was the proudest moment of my life, the little boy, John Carr with his oversized wellies had achieved something no other boy from Middlesbrough had ever achieved before or since. I stood up on the second rope of the boxing ring and punched the air, as I looked out at the crowd, I noticed a familiar face, he was smiling at me, he had a trilby hat on, I stared in disbelief, he looked like my dad. I wanted to run over and hug him and never let him go, but the wonderful vision quickly disappeared, the brief sight of my dad brought me so much joy, I knew it was him. It was comforting to know that he had seen my achievement, his smile at that moment meant the world to me. I kept searching the faces of the crowd, trying to find him again, but everyone was a blur.

Cornelius Wearing The Lonsdale Belt

When I left the ring, I was grabbed by Keith Bristol, a former light heavyweight boxer; he was swinging me around in a bear hug and shouting, "You did it!" There were many Middlesbrough supporters there who had travelled all the way to London to watch my fight. I was thankful to every single one of them for being there that night. I looked up at the balcony where all the Boro boys were, and I stuck my arms in the air as a symbol of victory. Saluting to them, they chanted, "Ooh Ah Corny Carr, ooh ah Corny Carr." I realised then that Eric Cantona wasn't there. They had been shouting for me.

After the fight, the changing room was packed, full of my friends, including Amanda, Damien, Ollie, Shaun, young Marty, and of course, Big Marty. They were all congratulating me. The changing room was buzzing with excitement when a guy approached me and asked if he could have a quiet word. He said, "Do you know Morrissey?" I said, "Morrissey, the singer from The Smith's?" He nodded his head and told me Morrissey was outside waiting to meet me, and I asked him to bring Morrissey into the changing room to see me, as this was my night, and this was my moment. I didn't want to leave the crowd of people. I was revelling in my success amongst my friends. The guy left the changing room, and someone popped open a bottle of champagne. Then the guy appeared again, and standing behind him was Morrissey with a photographer. Morrissey congratulated me, put his arm around me, and the photographer quickly snapped a photo of us. I thought it was weird meeting Morrissey. The introduction to him and his departure had happened so quickly.

Cornelius with Morrissey After He Won The British Super Middleweight Title At York Hall

I changed into my tracksuit with the Lonsdale Belt around my waist, hidden by a tracksuit top. I made an excuse to leave the packed changing room and headed for the exit. I needed some time alone to absorb the huge achievement and get some fresh air. I walked onto the main high street and started jogging in the night air with the streetlights of Bethnal Green shining on me, and then I had an overwhelming desire to sprint as fast as I could, the feeling to run just came over me, gradually the jog became a full-on sprint. I was running faster than I had ever run before, and then I started crying. It was a huge release; I needed to expel all the emotions within me. I ran a few hundred yards and thought, what am I doing? I must have looked like a madman. I stopped, pulled myself together, and looked up at the stars, thinking about my dad. I blew him a kiss, then lovingly touched the belt and walked back to the changing room.

I took my Lonsdale Belt back to Middlesbrough to show my friends and family. I was brimming with pride. It used to be called the 'Lord Lonsdale Challenge Belt' and is commonly known as Lonsdale Belt. It's the oldest Championship belt in British Professional Boxing. The first belt was awarded on 8th November 1909 to Freddy Walsh after winning the British Lightweight Title. Henry Cooper was the first and only boxer to win three Lonsdale Belts during his seventeen-year career. A boxer needs to win three title fights to permanently keep the belt.

Whilst I was home, Middlesbrough Football Club asked if I would like to make an appearance at the stadium during halftime at a football match to display my Lonsdale Belt. I felt nervous, Riverside stadium was full, and as I went out to face the crowd, the announcer said, "We have a special guest who has won the Super Middleweight Boxing Title, and he's from Middlesbrough. He is Cornelius Carr!" I wasn't sure of how the football supporters were going to react to me, but to my surprise, I had a rapturous warm welcome. I was in my hometown, showing off my Lonsdale Belt, and I felt honoured, and proud of my achievement.

Three weeks after the title fight, I had a phone call from one of Morrissey's representatives asking if it would be possible for Morrissey to meet me. The meeting occurred at one of my training sites, the Battersea running track. Morrissey and I met up, and I shook his hand, and he congratulated me again on my win. He had just finished recording a song, 'Boxers', and wanted to make a video to promote the new song. He asked me if I would be interested in starring in the video. I was excited at the thought and told Morrissey that I was interested in filming the video, I thought it would be good fun, and it might help me to further my career.

After we met at Battersea, Morrissey's people called me to discuss the details of the film shoot. The video would be filmed in a few weeks at York Hall, Bethnal Green, the historic venue where I had many of my fights and had just won my British title fight. Morrissey's team asked me to bring a few boxing colleagues with me who would also get involved in the filming.

On the day of the filming, we arrived at York Hall and met Morrissey and all his team, including the young actor who played my opponent. The video and song were about a boxer being defeated in his hometown, and I would play the part of the challenger. The actor who played my opponent had never boxed before; he was petrified. I think he was worried that I would batter him. I put him at ease and told him not to worry, saying that we would choreograph the boxing moves safely and he wouldn't get hurt.

We sat down before the shoot to discuss the technicalities of the filming. I did the boxing choreography and other parts of the video, choreographing the fight scenes, skipping in the ring, and shadowboxing. Morrissey made a cameo appearance in the video. We completed filming the scenes in one day, and I hoped the song and the video would be successful. I thought the filming went well, and the song sounded fantastic. Morrissey's team organised a big marketing campaign to promote the single 'Boxers', which was released in January 1995. They also went on a tour of the same name. The single reached number 23 on the UK Singles Chart, despite not featuring on an album at the time of its release. I was proud to feature on the cover of the CD and on a huge backdrop during Morrissey's 'Boxers' tour. I was stopped and asked for my autograph a few times whilst out and about in London, I assumed it was for my boxing fame, but it was due to my appearance on the video 'Boxers.' I wanted to be recognised for the years of my hard toil in boxing, and I had done a few hours of work for a video, and I was getting more attention for that. Morrissey still has a cult following and is still performing, and recently he is scheduled to perform as a resident in Las Vegas, USA.

Morrissey has a huge fan base, and he is adored worldwide. A few years after I worked with Morrissey, he appeared in 1995 on the Jules Holland Show. Jules asked him who his favourite boxer was. I felt privileged when he said, 'Cornelius Carr'. He mentioned me, saying that I was his favourite boxer. He rarely gives interviews, and for him to mention me was truly kind of him. After I filmed the video, Morrissey wrote me a handwritten letter, thanking me for working with him, which I thought was a nice gesture. Sadly, I lost the letter. I have moved homes many times, and I am annoyed with myself that I can't find it, it was something I treasured.

My boxing training continued. I was preparing for my next fight, which was against Slugger O'Toole, a Brendan Ingle fighter, this was a contest to defend The British Title. Micky Duff asked me to meet him at his office in Soho, London, to discuss the terms and fees of the fight. Micky had a large glamorous office and sat behind a huge oak desk that was covered in boxing memorabilia. He looked like a typical boxing promoter, power-dressed and sharp looking. He was booted and suited and had a receding hairline and a large bulbous head with a flat nose. Micky was a former welterweight boxer. I had never had a conversation other than business with Micky, I suppose I was just the little guy, and small talk was wasting his time, he just wanted to get to the point. I remembered that he hadn't congratulated me on winning the British Super Middleweight Title on the night of the contest. I didn't see him after the fight, I thought this was bizarre. After all, he was my manager, and I was paying him. Micky did open doors for me, and gave me the opportunity to fight James Cook, but I believe Micky didn't expect me to win, and that's why he gave me the opportunity.

He warmed me up by informing me that the fight would be held in Middlesbrough and would be covered by the BBC. I thought, bloody marvellous news; something good was coming my way for once. I had only ever boxed once before in my hometown of Middlesbrough as a professional boxer, and the idea of defending my British Title at home was exciting. Then I asked him about the purse and how much money would be offered on the table. Micky offered me £8,000 for defending the title, which I thought was too low. I said, "Give me £10,000, and you forfeit your 25% fees, and I'll pay Howard." He looked at me and laughed. I thought it was reasonable. Slugger O'Toole was a good fighter. He would attract a good audience, and Micky would make money on media deals, sponsorship, and ticket sales. What is a couple of grand to Micky Duff? He was a multi-millionaire. I felt devalued. I was putting my life on the line and was offered £4,500 after deducting all costs. He told me to go away and think about it. I thought about it for a few seconds and turned the offer down. I knew my decision not to accept the offer would end my relationship with Micky Duff. In hindsight, perhaps I should have accepted the offer. It would have given me good publicity, and who knows where the opportunity might have led to, especially as the BBC was filming the fight. I could have taken advantage of the publicity if only I could have swallowed my pride. I am a stubborn bastard, I can be my own worst enemy, I won't back down, and pride sometimes stands in my way. I am a loyal person, but if I feel someone is fucking me over, I just walk away.

I left Micky's office feeling like shit. What had just happened? I wasn't going to defend the British Super Middleweight Title, and I felt bad about that. Super Middleweight was a strong division, and there were some talented boxers in that weight category. I knew other boxers who were British Champions and earned far more than me. I felt it was a kick in the teeth to be offered peanuts for being a warrior. All said and done. I had to pick myself up, dust myself off, and start all over again.

After the breakup with Micky Duff, Amanda and I went on holiday to Lanzarote, where we met a lovely couple, Mark Rogers (known as Chippy) and Sizzle, his girlfriend. Mark was from Swansea and worked in London as a paparazzi – a freelance photographer. Mark was one of those guys who was easy to get on with. After a few hours with him, it was like I had known him all my life. Sizzle was a lovely girl. They made a nice couple. We would meet up at the swimming pool every day. I treated myself and had a couple of drinks. As a boxer, I still had to keep in shape. I used to run whilst on holiday every day. I loved running in the warm sunshine.

One day all four of us visited the Waterpark, which was ten miles away. We had a fabulous day there, enjoying the waterslides. I thought it would be a good idea to get my daily run and start running back to the hotel about thirty minutes before they set off; the others would catch me up in the hire car. There was a scenic route back to the hotel along a winding beach road, and I enjoyed feeling the warm sunshine on my body and smelling the sea air as I ran. I carried a small bottle of water which I drank almost immediately. After about forty minutes of running, I was sweating profusely, feeling thirsty and exhausted. I kept looking out for the car, hoping it would arrive soon. I stopped running after about seven miles and sat under the shade of a tree to wait for them. I was feeling light-headed and was probably dehydrated. I wasn't feeling too good. With relief, I saw the car coming towards me at last and felt glad to see them, and I waved to make sure they saw me. I flopped into the car and felt the cool blasts of air from the air-conditioning on my overheated body. They looked worried when they first saw me. I must have looked ill. I caught a glimpse of myself in the rear-view mirror of the car and was shocked at my appearance, I was pale, and my eyes were red and bloodshot. Luckily, they had brought some cold drinks with them, and I sipped the drinks and placed the cool bottles against the side of my head. The trouble with me is I don't think things through, I am impulsive, and a situation like that is dangerous. I dread to think what could have happened to me if I had been left for a longer period of time.

At home, Howard still trained me, but I didn't have a promoter. My record was twenty-three wins and one loss. I was a former British Boxing Champion with no fights lined up yet again. I had put myself in this position, and I thought I had really fucked up this time. I had to go cap in hand back to Frank Warren and see what he could offer me.

Frank offered me £4,000 per fight, and there would be a possibility of getting a Title fight, but there were no promises. My first fight under Frank was at Cardiff Ice Rink against Colin Manners, a muscular, aggressive boxer, and he was the type of fighter I liked to fight. He moved forward so that I could counterpunch him. I had returned to Middleweight. I always thought it was the correct weight for me. I had won the fight on points. It was eight three-minute rounds, it was a comfortable win, and I felt I had a good workout.

The second fight with Frank was against Chris Richards, and the third fight was against Barry Thorogood. I won both fights, stopping Chris in the third round. My fight with Barry was held at Cardiff Ice Rink again. Barry was a Welsh Champion. After the weigh-in and having my medical examination, I decided to get some fresh air and do some shadow boxing in the local park. I was warming up when my foot caught in a small pothole, and I badly twisted my right foot. The pain dropped me, and I sat on the floor, holding my ankle. I was in agony, it was around 5pm, and the boxing show's doors opened at 7pm. I hobbled back to the hotel in severe pain. I saw Howard, who said, "Do you want me to pull you out?" I didn't want to lose out on the fees for the fight. If I didn't box, I wouldn't get paid a penny.

Howard put ice on my ankle and strapped it up the best he could. I put on my boxing boots. I could just about cope with the pain. Howard said, "If you moan once about your foot when you're in the ring, I'll pull you out. If I hear one more word about your foot, the fight is off. Deal?" I agreed.

During the first round, I went over on my bad ankle, I nearly screamed in agony, but I tried to blank the pain. I carried on fighting, and the contest was stopped in round five. I had won my third fight. As I walked back to the changing room, the adrenalin was wearing off. The pain was kicking in. I dreaded taking my boxing boots off. I knew my right foot was swollen. I took off my right boot slowly. The pain was excruciating. The side of my foot was black and blue. I took a few painkillers to relieve the pain. Barry came into my dressing room to shake my hand. He said, "Well done, and you're a good fighter." I started to walk away when Barry noticed me limping, asking, "What happened to you?" I told him what had happened and that I had been fighting through the pain. As he headed to the changing room door, he turned around and said, "Bloody Hell, if I had known that, I would have stamped on your foot." We both laughed. My ankle took a while to heal, and I gradually began training again, I still have problems with my ankle, and I have permanent weakness in my right foot.

Round Ten - Ambition

In 1995 Chris Eubank and Steve Collins had two fights, and Steve won the first fight. Later that year, a return fight was arranged in Cork, Ireland. I had been sparring with Eubank for just over a year, and I was interested in watching him fight. Rumour had it that Chris Eubank was worried about Steve Collins and his hypnosis theory. Steve was apparently hypnotised to become more confident and aggressive in the ring, and this news had apparently affected Chris Eubank.

I had been sparring with Chris Eubank before his second fight with Steve Collins, and I only sparred with him twice instead of the arranged ten days; the reduced number of sparring days was due to Chris being unwell. On the Monday before the big fight, which was held on the following Saturday, I was in Brighton sparring with Chris. He tried to bully me around the ring, trying to knock me out, I hit him with the hardest shot I had ever thrown in my life, and I was shocked that he took it; he had a granite chin. I said sorry to him for the shot, but I wasn't really. I was surprised when Chris turned and said to me at the end of the round, "Don't ever say sorry to me because I would do it to you." At the end of our sparring session, a British Boxing Board official turned up to check Chris's weight in preparation for the oncoming fight. This was a time when the Boxing Board of Control was really trying to clamp down on boxers dropping too much weight just before a fight. Chris didn't seem at all happy about the weigh-in, but he accepted that it had to be done. Chris stepped on the scales and looked up at the ceiling, saying, "Don't tell me my weight." I thought this was strange as most boxers would be desperate to find out how much they weighed, particularly before a fight. I thought he obviously had his own method of making the weight, but I still found it bizarre that Chris didn't want to find out what he weighed; most boxers are obsessed with their weight.

A few of us went to my friend Chippy's house to watch the second Steve Collins vs. Chris Eubank fight. I watched Steve Collins bully Eubank in the ring, and Steve won the fight on points. As I watched the fight, I was thinking to myself; I fancy fighting Collins or Eubank. I had sparred with both Collins and Eubank and genuinely believed that I could beat both of them. It wasn't big-headed. I was just confident in my boxing ability at that time. I'd already asked Eubank if he would fight me when we were sparring together. He came into the changing rooms and let his guard down for a while, which was rare for Chris. We were chatting about boxing when I asked Chris if he would be interested in having a boxing match with me. Chris was fighting once a month for SKY TV for large amounts of money, rumoured to be £1,000,000 for every fight. Chris responded to my question, "Why should I fight you?" I was shocked by his question, I said. "I'm British Champion. I think it would be a good fight." Chris said, "I'm not fighting you when I can fight easier opponents." Even though I didn't like the way that Eubank behaved, sometimes I respected him as a fighter. He was a hard, strong boxer with a chin of iron. I told my friends as we watched the fight that I fancied fighting Collins or Eubank, they thought I was crazy, but I meant it.

Frank Warren was my promoter, and it was the same old story, no fights coming up, I couldn't speak to him, and there was always a barrier of secretaries protecting Frank from speaking to me. I was getting frustrated, and I was on the verge of walking away from boxing; I didn't seem to be getting anywhere, and I was training hard with little income. I attended a boxing dinner with Amanda, and Frank Warren was sitting at the top table with other big names in the boxing world. It was the end of the evening when Amanda told me to go and talk to Frank Warren. It was my opportunity to speak to him face to face. Frank seemed shocked to see me, he shook my hand gently, and I asked him to arrange a fight with Nigel Benn. He said, "No, Nigel won't fight you!" He surprised me when he then said, "How about Steve Collins?" I was excited, saying, "When?" I walked back to my table and thought the fight would never happen.

That weekend I was pissed off. I didn't feel like training. In my head, I was retiring. I was walking away. I was disillusioned by the whole boxing fraternity. On Monday morning, I was in my pyjamas, drinking a coffee and debating whether I should start looking for a job away from the boxing world. I had a habit of looking at sports on Ceefax (which was a sort of TV news bulletin screen) just to check what was happening in the sporting news. I was stunned to see the caption, 'Steve Collins has got his next opponent.' I clicked on the caption to view the full story, thinking Frank Warren has let me down again. I wonder whom he has arranged the fight with? The full news story caption was 'Steve Collins to fight the former British Super Middleweight Champion, Cornelius Carr.' I jumped over the chair with my hands in the air screaming, "I've got the fight!" I couldn't believe it; that was the way I found out that I was fighting a World Champion boxer via a TV screen.

I called Howard, my trainer who was like me, in the dark. I also called Frank Warren, but he was 'in a meeting' yet again, I spoke to Frank's secretary to try and get some clarification about the fight, but she couldn't confirm anything. She said, "Please hold the line, and I'll see if I can help you." She came back after a few minutes and spoke. "Yes, you have the fight with Steve Collins." The only detail I had that day was that I had the biggest fight of my life in front of me, and I had just under five weeks to face Steve Collins in the ring, who was at that time a formidable opponent. My intensive training regime commenced that day. Time wasn't on my side. In order to fight someone like Steve Collins, I really needed an eight-to-ten-week training programme so that I was well prepared. I think Steve had plenty of time to prepare for the fight, he was already in his training camp, and he had also just fought Chris Eubank. Therefore he was in prime condition.

It's strange how things work out; a few weeks before I was told about my fight with Collins, I was telling my friends that I fancied fighting Collins or Eubank, and now it was a reality. I was up for it. I believed I had the potential to win the fight. I trained hard in preparation, and Howard was by my side, creating various new training programmes, and pushing me to the next level. This fight was a huge leap. It was like playing in the second division and then jumping up to playing in the premier league, and this fight was my biggest opportunity thus far.

A friend of a friend was a hypnotist, and I thought perhaps hypnotism would help me. I had suffered from nervous tension, and I was unable to rest. Normally, I was laid back and calm, but the fight was playing on my mind. Before any of my fights, I got anxious, and this, for me, was a massive fight, and I wanted to be in control. I wanted to be calm and collected. I knew Steve Collins had tried hypnotism, and it appeared to have worked for him; he beat Eubank in his last two fights. I didn't really believe it would work on me, but I thought I'd try it and see what would happen.

The hypnotist came to the flat to see me, and we chatted for a while. I had only met him socially before. He was a nice lad, and he immediately put me at ease. He asked me to lie down on the sofa and spoke softly to me, asking me to chill out and unwind. I listened to his mellow slow voice, which relaxed me, and after a few minutes, my whole body felt weightless. I was totally relaxed; I didn't feel as if I were hypnotised like you see people reacting on TV and in a trance. They would be doing crazy things. I just felt wonderful, peaceful, and confident. He came to see me two or three times every week, asking me to visualise the fight step by step. We would repeat the visualisation at every session. I think it helped me to prepare. I was sleeping better, I became more confident, and I had self-belief; I was positive. Boxing is all about self-belief, I was David fighting Goliath in his backyard, and I needed to have inner strength. My body was ready for the fight, and my mind had to be in top condition too.

I had been training for just over a week after I found out from Ceefax that I was fighting Steve Collins. I didn't know what the purse was or any other details regarding the contest. Frank Warren asked me to meet him at the Dorchester Hotel, London, to finalise fees, etc. The meeting lasted about ten minutes, if that, and Frank told me the deal. I said, "Why are we talking in dollars, Frank? We are in England?" He replied. "This is the way we do business." I thought it was strange because all my other fights were paid in pound sterling. Part of the deal, if I took the fight with Steve Collins, was signing a six-fight contract that stipulated the amount of money I would receive for each fight.

Cornelius and Marty Turner Preparing To Face Steve Collins 1995

Middleweight and super middleweight divisions were the hottest divisions apart from the heavy weights at that time in the mid-nineties. I was shocked at the low amounts of money offered to me; all the fees were low in comparison to other top super middleweight boxers. This was a big fight, and I knew Steve Collins would be well paid, I understood he was the Champion, and he had beaten Chris Eubank on two occasions, and his last fight was only one month ago. My hands were tied. Frank said, "Do you want the fight or not? I can get another boxer who will jump in your place now for less money." What could I do? I had to sign the contract. I just wanted a fair deal. Many boxers get fucked over, and I was one of them. I needed Warren more than Warren needed me. I knew I wasn't a name, but I was hoping this fight would enhance my public profile, boosting me into becoming a household name. I was thankful for the opportunity, but I felt I'd earned that position; it was bitter-sweet for me; I was signed up for a great contest but thought I was undervalued. It wasn't all about the money. It was about being paid a fair purse. It was about respect. I understood that Frank thought boxers like me were fair game. We were hungry and willing to accept any scraps thrown at us. I had to think positively and believe that this was my moment. After sparring with Steve, I thought I had the ability to beat him.

Two weeks prior to the fight, a press conference was held in Dublin organised by Frank Warren. When I arrived at the hotel where the conference was held, I was informed that Steve Collins wouldn't be attending the press conference because he was at a training camp somewhere preparing for the fight, and Frank Warren hadn't turned up either, God knows where he was. I was gutted. I couldn't believe that neither of the main people had the decency to turn. The whole charade was pointless, I had flown from England especially to be there and give up a day's training to promote the fight.

Steve was earning the bulk of the money for the contest but decided not to attend the press conference; Steve did his interview on a loudspeaker phone and predicted that I wouldn't last four rounds. After Steve had completed his negative monologue, the media asked for my opinion. I said, "I'm going to surprise a lot of people in this fight, including your lot." Everyone laughed. Their reaction made me more determined to win, and they were all taking the piss out of me. I was the underdog yet again, they all thought I was a lamb to the slaughter. Adam Smith was a presenter for Sky at the time and is now head of Sky sports, and he interviewed me along with other fighters who were on the bill of my fight. He was the only person from the media who were supportive. The press conference only lasted about an hour, and I flew home straight afterwards. As soon as I arrived home, I put on my boxing gear and did ten rounds of shadow boxing in the park. I was fucking fuming about the way I'd been treated; it was a complete lack of respect, Collins and Warren didn't bother to turn up, and the press was mainly all Steve Collins fans. The situation just made me more determined.

I was in the best condition I had ever been in. I was training like a madman. I was sparring, running, and lifting weights; I was ready. I had been sticking to a strict diet. My friend Amiah from Middlesbrough would stay for a week before the fight to cook for me. He was a great cook and looked after my diet. Amiah was a lovely guy who would do anything for me. I really appreciated his support. I was staying at Howard's flat in Lambeth, which was closer to the gym. I didn't want to sit in traffic for hours every going back and forth to the gym.

One week before the fight Sky TV did an interview with me at St Pancras gym, the first gym where I had started my professional boxing career with Ernie Fossey as my trainer. I was pleased that Sky had taken an interest in me, and I enjoyed all the attention, and it was another step closer to becoming recognised as a celebrity boxer. I was thinking a lot about the fight and how I would prepare my entrance and walk to the ring, I wanted my entrance to be dramatic, and I thought about the noise of the crowd as I approached the ring. I was the bad guy, and the crowd wanted Steve Collins to whip my arse. I thought of a way to drown out the negativity. I bought a large pair of headphones and a Walkman tape recorder to play dance music. I had chosen Golden Eye, sung by Tina Turner from the Bond Film, 'Golden Eye' with Pierce Brosnan as James Bond. I'm not sure why I chose that song. It wasn't as upbeat as it should have been for the contest, and I hadn't put that much thought into the entrance music.

My team flew to Dublin on the Monday afternoon before the fight, which was on a Saturday. The team was Howard, Arthur, Stevie Williams, and the hypnotist. I needed the hypnotist with me. He gave me the ability to believe in myself, gave me confidence, and he was a huge support. He was my security blanket.

In Dublin, there were posters of the fight everywhere; Irish people love boxing. It's almost their national sport. Apart from rugby, this fight was a massive event. The Irish public was supportive, people who wished us well. I was surprised when a taxi driver I met wanted me to win the fight. I thought it was strange. He looked after me all week, driving me around Dublin to training sessions, etc.

On Tuesday morning, I continued with my training regime: I ran three miles with sprint intervals, shadow boxing, and then I went to a gym. At the gym, I did a few rounds on the pads, a few rounds on a bag, skipping, punching, and light weights. I worked on head movements, rope slipping, stretching exercises, and side-stepping. This was just to maintain my physical fitness, I knew I couldn't go toe to toe with Steve, so my goal was to beat him on skill and outbox him. I was so keen that I didn't want to stop training, and Howard had to force me to stop. I felt so good, and I thought I was ready to fight. After I had my evening meal, I'd go for a walk with the team. It was during this time that we would discuss how we would approach the fight. It was freezing cold. I was wrapped up like an Eskimo, but the cold made me feel alive. I had so much energy I was bursting to get into the ring.

The hypnotist would come to my hotel room around 9 pm every evening. He relaxed me and prepared me mentally for the fight, and he made me visualise the whole fight scene so that when the fight happened, I was prepared for whatever Steve threw at me. I didn't sleep very well during the few days before the fight. I'd wake up early hours of the morning thinking about everything. I would remember what the hypnotist had said to me, and that calmed me down, and I'd drift back to sleep. I just wanted to get the fight over with. It was playing on my mind. I felt anxious. I had to snap out of it, and this was my job. I was a professional boxer, a gladiator. I was brave and needed to focus. I was hungry for the prize. I had trained all my life, since the age of eleven for this moment, I was about to fight one of the most high-ranking super middleweight boxers in the world, and I wanted to win despite the odds being against me. The fight was marketed as Steve Collins' 'homecoming.'

On Thursday, a day before the weigh-in, I trained lightly, conserving all my energy for the fight. My weight was 11 stone and 13 pounds. The weight for a super middleweight title fight should be 12 stone (76 kg) or under. I was pleased that I was on target. I felt strong, but I was nervous. They were good nerves, though.

On the day of the weigh-in, my weight was perfect, and I ate some scrambled eggs for breakfast and drank half a glass of water. I still had to make sure my weight was correct. The weigh-in was held at a shopping mall in Dublin, and it was a big event, and the mall was packed with people who came to watch the weigh-in. The weigh-in was scheduled for 6 pm, and I was anxiously waiting in a cordoned-off area, ready to get on the scales. It was five past six, and I was getting agitated because there was a delay. I am a punctual person, and I expect other people to keep good time keeping, too. I thought it was unprofessional to be late for such an important event. Ernie Fossey, my old trainer and the main matchmaker for Frank Warren, popped his head around the cordoned area and started to make pleasantries with me. I knew how false Ernie was. I'd worked with him for years. I told Ernie abruptly, "I'm getting on the scales now. It's gone 6 pm," Ernie came over and whispered in my ear, "Steve Collins isn't here yet," I replied, "I don't give a fuck. I'm getting on those scales now!" I got up and walked out to where the scales were; I faced a barrage of boos from the large crowd, but it didn't bother me. I just wanted to get on the scales and fuck off. I could see all the judges, press, and spectators looking at me. I turned to the officials and said, "It's 10 past 6. I'm getting on the scales now!"

Because I had been forceful and forthright, they immediately announced me to the audience, and I took off my gown and jumped on the scales. They told me that I was two ounces over the weight limit. I turned to Marty and said, "Get a towel to cover my arse. I'm taking my boxer shorts off." Marty held the towel to cover my arse whilst I took off my boxer shorts; I got on the scales again, and this time, the announcer said I was 12 stone exactly. As I took one step back from the scales, Steve Collins appeared and angrily shouted in my face, touching my nose with his nose and his breath stank. Marty was pushed back by Collins and dropped the towel that protected my manhood. I was bollocked naked, arguing with Steve. It was all macho shit, I know it was his game plan to psyche me out of the fight, but it didn't work. I didn't know what all the fuss was about, but I wasn't going to be bullied or intimidated and shouted back at him, even though I was in the nude. I think Steve was annoyed because he hadn't made the weight and wanted to keep me waiting until he was ready, Steve was in his sweat suit, trying to work off some weight, and that's what the delay was about. Steve had been there all along. Ernie had lied yet again. Steve was in sweat gear and looked as though he'd been skipping off any excess weight. This was the first time I had seen Steve face to face since I had sparred with him a year or so previously. I was expecting a media circus at the weigh-in, and the Oscar-winning performance Steve had given was appreciated by the crowd, who were booing, clapping, and cheering, enjoying every moment of the pantomime. Marty and Howard broke up the shouting match, and I fucked off. Before I left, I asked Marty to keep an eye on Steve's weight to ensure that he made the 12-stone limit. I know all the tricks. Ernie had a good one. His boxer would be on the scales. He'd get really close and crowd over the top of the scales and slyly put his hand to the side of the boxer and lift up the boxer's hand. How much does a hand weigh? It could mean the boxer weighing in is a few pounds lighter. Fortunately, today no one can be around a fighter near the scales at a weigh-in.

When I had escaped the mayhem and madness of the weigh-in, I appreciated the silence of the taxi ride on the way home, and my ear drums were still recovering from the loud noise of the media circus. I remember the gentle sound of the light rain hitting the window of the taxi and the squeaky rhythm of the windscreen wipers sweeping the ripples of rainwater away. It was comforting and made me feel normal and calm again. I had just experienced a surreal moment, being completely naked in a shopping mall and then verbally attacked by Steve, and now I was driving through the Dublin streets in the dark winter night listening to Christie Moore on the radio singing folk songs. The music lightened my mood. We had a designated taxi driver who shuttled us around Dublin for the duration of the team visit; he took us to the gym, to the hotel, etc. He was a happy, funny guy who didn't stop talking, and he was a nice guy who loved to talk about boxing. The taxi driver listened to our conversation about the saga of the weigh-in. He was excited because he had inside knowledge about the boxers, and he was going to attend the fight with his son on the following day. We all ended up laughing about me being naked on the scales and the whole shopping mall seeing my hairy arse. I just kept thinking about food. I couldn't wait to have something good to eat. I was starving.

As soon as I got back to my room, I ordered room service, ate a delicious pasta meal that evening, and carried on grazing on a big bowl of chicken, vegetables, and pasta throughout the night. The hypnotist did his session on me again. I felt really relaxed and was prepared to face Steve the following day. I couldn't do any more preparation work. All the hard work had been done. I was twenty-five years old, in the prime of my life, and in the best condition of my life. This was my opportunity to show the world my boxing talent, and I was ready to put my thumbprint on the world of boxing. I reminisced about the past and how far I had come since Marty discovered me fighting on Grisedale Crescent in 1980 and made me go to the Boxing Club. It was 24th November 1995, and I was lying in bed reliving moments from my life that meant so much to me; when my dad came to my first ever fight and poured the Newcastle Brown Ale into my trophy, when Ginny the pig had escaped, pushing my mam through the snow in her wheelchair, and going on holiday to Salou with our Sue and our mam. My mind was overflowing with images, words, smells, and feelings from the past. I wished my dad were there to talk to me, support me, comfort me, and give me some fatherly advice. I did speak to him. I often spoke to him, and I hoped he could hear me. I told him that I wanted to make him proud of me and that I loved him. I was lucky I had some great people around me who genuinely cared about me, Howard, Marty, Steve Williams, and the hypnotist. Memories are important. It's strange how we can only remember certain things. We can have selective memory and sometimes recall silly things which are often meaningless. That night I didn't stop thinking, I was just a boy from Grangetown with a dream, and here I was in a Dublin hotel room on the eve of the biggest fight of my life. I relived those happy, precious moments until my mind eventually had enough and switched off, and I fell asleep.

I managed to have seven hours of sleep and felt refreshed the following morning. I walked down to the dining room on my own. I was looking forward to a slap-up breakfast. I desired food so much. It was like when I couldn't have something, I craved it even more. As a boxer sticking to a strict diet is important. Being the correct weight is a huge factor. I loved my food but had to be careful what I ate. Within a few minutes, my team joined me for breakfast, and the dining room was filling up quickly with boxing fans who wished me well for the fight which was taking place that evening. I surprised myself. I wasn't as nervous as I thought I'd be. I was in a good mood, having a craic with the guys. I was more nervous about attending the weigh-in than I was about the fight. I think it was the fact that I had seen Steve in the flesh at the weigh-in. I had built him up to be a superhero, and the media hype had given him super-human status, but now I thought he was just a man whom I wasn't scared of.

That day I spent my time walking, shadowboxing, resting, and mentally preparing myself for the battle ahead. My fight was scheduled for 9.30 that evening at The Point, which was a large venue owned by Bono from the Irish band U2. The previous night Morrissey had performed there to a sell-out crowd, and someone told me he had stayed in Dublin to watch my fight, but I didn't see him.

I arrived at the venue at 8 pm, there were fights on, so I couldn't get close enough to complete my usual rituals, but I found a seat in the auditorium to look at the ring and check out the entrance points, this was important to me, I had to know where I was going to do my fight walk to the ring. The stadium was half full, but the seats were slowly filling up with boxing fans. They were a rowdy crowd. I knew that Steve would have thousands of fans, and I probably had a few hundred, but that didn't bother me.

I had a fleeting thought about the time I had boxed Jamie Nicholson in his backyard. This was a similar scenario, but obviously, on a much higher level, I was the underdog, and most people didn't expect me to win. I returned to the changing room to rest before my contest started. I found a sofa where I could stretch out for a few minutes before I started to get ready. As I lay there, a Sky camera crew turned up, and they didn't speak to me. They just filmed to see what was going on behind the scenes. I just lay there with my baseball cap on, calm as a cucumber. I didn't see Frank Warren, who was my promoter, before the fight, which was surprising as it was a world title fight. I wonder if Steve Collins saw him because he was his promoter too. My face didn't fit in the boxing world, and I didn't lick arse and suck up to the big boys. Maybe I should have played the game, but it wasn't in my nature. I was young and feisty, I was born in Grangetown, and I was a straight-talking Yorkshire man, as Shirley Bassey sang in one of our Mam's favourite songs, 'I am what I am.'

I was happy that Big Marty was by my side at this important time in my boxing career. Howard told me to get ready, and then a member of Steve Collins' team and a boxing official watched me getting my hands wrapped. When I was happy with both hands wrapped comfortably, the official asked the representative from Steve Collins' team, "Are you happy with the hand wrapping?" He nodded, and the official signed both hands. As I was getting my hands wrapped, I felt a little nervous. The realisation of the fight ahead had kicked in. I warmed up, doing some stretching and shadowboxing. I needed to get my boxing gloves on, which were 10 oz gloves. The official brought my boxing gloves to me and inspected my hand wraps again to ensure his signature was in place and the wraps hadn't been tampered with, and then Howard put my gloves on.

Five minutes before my entrance Howard and Arthur decided to go to the ringside to wait for me and prepare my corner. I wore a black hooded silk gown. It was magnificent. It was bespoke, with my name emblazoned on the back. I thought I looked like the girl in the Scottish Widows advert. I admired myself in the mirror, and I had black silk shorts with 'Cornelius' in red letters on a white background on the waistband of the shorts. They were Middlesbrough colours. I also had a small Middlesbrough badge on the leg of the shorts. I hoped Boro would bring me luck. I felt like the dog's bollocks in all my gear. I was ready for the battle to commence. I was like a gladiator in armour going out to fight the lion in the lion's den. A guy from Sky TV came in and said, "Five minutes Carr," then he said after a while, "Two minutes Carr!" I could hear the crowd chanting 'Collins, Collins, Steve O!" I turned to Marty and said, "I need a piss Mart," He was shocked and said loudly, "You have got to be fucking joking!" I said, "Nope." Marty quickly ushered me to the toilet cubicle, where he lifted my gown and placed it over my shoulder. Just before Marty pulled my shorts down, the Sky guy shouted, "We are ready, Carr!" I was panicking. Marty said, "Fuck 'em!" He pulled my shorts down and the body protector and then pulled down my underpants, and we just looked at each other. I had my boxing gloves on, so I couldn't hold my cock. I arched my back and pushed my cock out, and I said, "Marty, you're going to have to hold it; I don't want to piss on my shorts." Marty said, "The things I do for you!" He grabbed my cock, turning his head away not to look. I think my cock had shrunk. My cock was more frightened of Steve Collins than I was, it was shrivelled up, and Marty tried his best to handle it with care. I only managed to squirt out a few drops of piss, to Marty's annoyance. The Sky man was getting impatient, banging on the cubicle door and shouting, "Carr, we need you now!" Marty made me decent as quickly as possible, and we both giggled. I looked at him and said, “Let’s go and have a fight, Mart!”

The Sky man counted down ten seconds as Marty and I stood behind the doors that opened into the auditorium, waiting for our cue to enter the arena. Before the doors opened, I could hear the crowd chanting loudly for Steve Collins. I knew I was going to get a raw reception from the audience. I asked Marty for the headphones and the Walkman, Marty put them on, and I was ready to face the masses. I was about to face the biggest challenge of my life. I was calm and ready for action.

The doors opened widely. I walked in front with Marty following me. My entrance music, ‘Golden Eye,’ played as I came out to face the crowd. The entrance music I had chosen wasn’t as loud as I thought it would be, but I had my headphones on anyway. The film crew was filming me, and the camera lights were bright and shining in my eyes. I could still hear the roar of the rowdy audience even though I was listening to AC/DC loudly on my Walkman. There were two beefy security guards on either side of me, escorting me to the ring. As I got to the apron of the ring, and before I went under the ropes to enter the ring, I stood there for a few seconds, facing the crowd and enjoying the moment. I slowly waved my fist in the air, signifying to them that I was ready for the fight. I turned around in a full circle for everyone in the arena to see me. As I went into the ring, the Walkman stopped playing my music, but I pretended I was still listening to it. The lights went down, and Steve Collins made his grand entrance. His entrance music was Irish music, which was blasted out loudly, and the crowd went berserk, but I kept on pretending I couldn't hear anything apart from the music in my headphones. I nodded my head as if I were enjoying music.

As soon as Steve Collins entered the ring, he came straight over to me and screamed in my face. I screamed back at him. He was playing intimidating games, but I wasn't scared of him. I wanted this fight more than ever. Someone broke up the show, and we both went to our corners. In his corner, I was surprised to see Ernie Fossey, my old trainer. He also had with him the legendary American trainer Freddy Roach and Steve's hypnotist. The referee was South American. He spoke in broken English, called Steve and me to the middle of the ring, asked us to touch gloves, and said he wanted a clean fight. Just before the bell rang to start the contest, Steve did his trademark boxing gesture, bending forward and smashing his hands together whilst staring at me, I thought anyone could do that, and I copied him, mocking him. I don't think he liked it.

The bell rang, and Steve came racing towards me, throwing basic one-twos. In Steve's head, he thought he could bully me out of the fight by the fourth round. He had predicted this at the press conference in Dublin. He was a strong man, the strongest opponent I'd ever boxed. He was solid, a hard object to move. Steve was naturally bigger than me, he probably was around 13 stone in the ring, and I was about 12 stone 4 pounds. (I wasn't a super middleweight, really, I felt better boxing in the middleweight division). Steve kept coming forward, and at one point during the second, he literally pushed me outside of the ropes onto the apron. I think my reactions during the first few rounds were over-cautious. I respected him and allowed him to take the first three or four rounds, giving him the upper hand.

Just before the fifth round, Howard gave me a pep talk in my corner, "You've got to let those punches go, catch him as he comes in, make him miss, and counter." All my team was encouraging me, they believed in me, but I needed to believe in myself. In round five, I made no more allowances out of respect. This was my moment. I wanted to show Steve what I was capable of. I sprung up off my stool with a different mindset. I had nothing to lose; I had to go for it. I thought I had won the next four or five rounds, my punches were clean, crisp, and accurate, and Steve was stumbling, missing me. I could tell he was tired; I was tired too. The fight was untidy. He was grabbing and holding, preventing me from getting into my boxing flow. I felt I was throwing cleaner punches, and I was more technical. Steve was strong and relentless. I couldn't get a foothold in the fight. All the mauling and grabbing was tiring me. By the time we got to the final few rounds, my energy was fading, and so was Steve's. He was holding on to me, and the ref kept telling him to break away. Steve's tactics were working, and he slowed me down.

Cornelius Challenging Steve Collins at the Point Dublin 1995 for the WBO Super Middleweight Title

At the end of the fight, I saw Glenn McCrory, who had commentated on the fight. I looked at him as if to say what do you think? He shook his head, I was disappointed because I had dug deep and given everything I had, but the judges had given the fight to Steve. It was close, and Steve had the benefit of boxing in his hometown and was the existing World Champion. I'm not making excuses. Steve was a great Champion and a hard man. At the time, he was a top boxer. The opportunity had been there for the taking that night, and I failed to take the opportunities that were given to me. I was disappointed that Sky didn't interview me after the fight. I wanted to talk about the fight and that I was ready to take on another tough middleweight contender, but I didn't have that opportunity to promote myself. The Irish crowd was very responsive to me after the fight. A few Irish boxing fans told me that they thought I had won the fight, but I still get people telling me that they thought I had won to this day. I know it was close, and if I had won, who knows where my path would have taken me. I met Steve and his wife at The Savoy a few years ago, and it was great seeing him. I remember him telling his wife, "This is the man who nearly took our house." We both laughed.

I was in my dressing room after the fight when someone came in and said there was a press conference taking place and that I should be there. I quickly put on a tracksuit top and made my way to the gathering. When I got there, the press conference was already taking place, and in the middle of the long table was my promoter Frank Warren and on either side of him were Steve Collins and Nigel Benn. I realised quickly that my fight was a prelude to Collins fighting Benn. My fight had been a promotional opportunity for Warren. They sat me at the end of the table and discussed the Collins vs. Benn contest, no one from the press asked me any questions about the fight I had just fought and worked so hard for. I just sat there like a spare part, and after a few minutes, I thought,' What the fuck am I doing here?' And walked out in disgust.

After I had showered and packed my gear up, I just wanted to go home and relax, but I had many Middlesbrough supporters to meet and thank. I appreciated them for making an effort to come to Dublin to watch my fight. There were many friends there that night, including Damien and his brother Frank. A few of my closest friends took me to a local nightclub; I must have looked a mess with two black eyes, and I was dressed casually, wearing a tracksuit. The doorman looked at me and said, “You can’t go in looking like that, mate,” Damien proudly defended me, saying, “He’s just fought, Steve Collins!” After Damien said that the doorman said he had watched the fight but hadn’t recognised me, he congratulated me, saying I had put up a good fight. He let me in and introduced me to the owner of the club. I didn’t have to put my hands in my pockets that evening, and the Irish people are very generous. I didn’t stay there long, and I had a pint of Guinness with a dash of lemonade. I left the club. I enjoyed seeing everybody. I felt exhausted and just wanted to chill out. It had been a gruelling few weeks up until now. I had trained hard and fought a tough fight, and I was glad it was all over.

After the Collins fight, I had a break from training for a few weeks. Even though I had lost against Collins, I was proud of my performance. I returned to Middlesbrough and received a warm welcome; I was congratulated by my friends and many people in the boxing community. All the lads at Marty’s boxing club, Grangetown ABC, were pleased to see me. It felt comforting being at the old gym, reminding me of where my journey began all those years ago. I wondered what the reception would have been like if I had won the Collins fight. Again I was a 'nearly man.' I started back training again, running up Cally Bank, but I was gutted because I couldn't reach the top. I'd lost a little motivation. Most of my training was done alone. I had to be self-motivated. Deep inside, I still had a burning desire to be a Champion. I wasn't prepared to give up yet. I'd been living the high life over the past few weeks, and I was out of condition. I met up with Shaun and young Marty and wallowed in normality for a while.

I was offered a fight on the undercard of Nigel Benn vs. Sugar Boy Milinga. I fought an African named Danny Guma, who was a tough fighter. I felt as if I was going backwards in my career. This was an eight-round fight, and to top it off, they told me I was a 'floater.' I didn't know what this meant, but just the sound of it pissed me off. I realised that a floater was someone who had to be ready to get into the ring at the drop of a hat. They said I would be boxing before the World title fight was on, so I got prepared and warmed up. Then they turned around and said I would be fighting after the main event. This situation was fucking my head up, I had just fought Steve Collins, and here I was being used as a 'floater,' like a turd floating in the toilet water on the boxing circuit. I wasn't pleased with my performance, but I won unanimously. I had an off night, and I wasn't mentally in the right place.

Round Eleven - Susan

A few months after the Guma fight, I was at home in Kingston, London, when I had a phone call from my friend Shaun in Middlesbrough asking me if I had heard from my sister Susan. I said I hadn't heard from her for a while, and then he told me that there was a rumour that Sue was on her way to London to see me. I told Shaun that my sister didn't know where I lived, she hadn't been to my home before, but she did have my address and phone number. As soon as I finished the conversation with Shaun, I rang Susan on her landline, but there was no reply. I left a message for her answerphone. The last time I spoke to Susan was about my mam. Sue was finding it hard looking after my mam with two small children. Sue had been a carer her whole life, and caring for my mam was a huge responsibility for her. We both decided that my mam needed specialist care which would be provided in a local nursing home, my mam settled in quickly at home and seemed incredibly happy there, receiving the care that she needed, and a huge weight had been lifted from Sue.

Susan had two small children at the time, Paul, who was about 5 years old, and Georgina was about a year old. I'd forgotten about the Sue conversation with Shaun when at about 8 pm on a cold rainy winter's night, about two weeks before Christmas, I heard a car horn beeping outside. I looked out of the window, and there was a black cab with the engine running with the headlights on outside my flat. I went outside and walked towards the headlights of the taxi and watched in surprise as our Sue got out of the passenger side of the cab with baby Georgina in her arms. She ran around the car, moving away from me, then she stood behind me, laughing in an odd manner. I thought it was really bizarre. The taxi driver said, “That’s £30, mate”. Then Paul got out of the cab, and I said to him in shock, “What are you doing here? How did you get here?” He said, “Car.” Sue shouted, “The car is outside The Ritz!” I was trying to rationalize the situation, I couldn’t believe this was happening, the taxi driver kept asking for his money, I wasn’t listening to him, I just kept looking at Sue and the kids, and trying to make sense of it all. Eventually, I went upstairs to the flat and got some money to pay the driver.

I took Sue and the children into the living room of the flat and made them a cup of tea, Sue was behaving strangely, and I couldn’t understand why. She seemed as if she had taken some kind of drug; she was manic, she wouldn’t sit down, was animated and loud, and she was very excitable. I asked her where her car was again, trying to get some sense out of her, and she laughed, dangling the car keys in front of me, and said, “It’s outside The Ritz.” I laughed, too, thinking this was a joke. I said, “Fuck off. Come on, Sue, where’s the car?” She grinned and spoke slowly, “Outside The Ritz!”

I left Sue and the kids with Amanda and took the train to central London to get Sue’s car. When I found Sue’s car, it was parked partly on a pedestrian crossing near The Ritz, and I was shocked that the vehicle hadn't been clamped or towed away. I quickly drove it away and headed home, and my head was all over the place. I had so many questions which required answers. Why did she drive from Middlesbrough to London with two small children, unsure of where she was heading, without letting me know? It's nearly a three-hundred- mile journey from Middlesbrough to London.

I arrived home at about 11 pm, and the children were in bed. I wanted to speak to Sue to get a better understanding of the situation and why she had driven to London. Sue had calmed down by the time I returned home, and we spent that evening watching TV. She behaved as if nothing had happened. I was frustrated and couldn't understand her behaviour. She was acting crazy, completely out of character. I tried to have a conversation with Sue, but she wouldn't discuss anything with me. Before I went to bed, I looked at Sue, who was engrossed in a TV programme, and said, "Are you Ok?" She looked up at me with a blank look on her face, as if she didn't recognise me. She didn't say a word and then turned around and carried on watching TV. I felt many emotions, from anger to fear, I didn't know what would happen the following day, and I didn't get much sleep that night worrying about Sue.

When I woke up the following morning, I wasn't sure what to expect. I was hoping I could speak to Sue and get some answers. Sue was in the living room. Amanda had taken the children out for the day so that I could speak to Sue alone. I tried to have a conversation with her, but she was difficult to communicate with. She appeared to be lost in her own world. She would dance around the room, then try and walk out of the flat. She said she heard voices and was hallucinating. I was scared. I wasn't sure what to do. I thought she had taken drugs. I told her that she needed to go home and that I would drive her back to Grangetown, but she was adamant she wasn't going anywhere.

Looking back at the situation, I should have taken her to a doctor immediately or called an ambulance to find out what was wrong with her. I'm not sure why I didn't do anything. I thought that her behaviour would improve, especially if she took drugs. I thought I could talk to her and make her better. During all this mayhem, I was due to go training in preparation for my next fight; I had a phone call asking if I wanted a fight in the next few weeks, but due to the circumstances, I had to refuse it, my head was messed up, the last thing I needed was a boxing match.

I kept coaxing Sue to go home, and eventually, she agreed, I put the children in her car, and after some persuasion, Sue also got into the car. I was driving up the M1 and bombarding Sue with questions. I was trying to understand her actions. She got angry and opened the car door, I was doing 70 mph, and she was trying to take her seatbelt off and jump out of the speeding car. I quickly put my arm across her and, with all my strength, held her back.

I swerved the car and braked hard, pulling over into the hard shoulder. I screamed at her at the top of my voice. The children were crying. She had put us all in danger. I couldn't believe her actions. I was angry at her. A truck blasted its horn and swerved to avoid us.

I placed my head on the steering wheel of the parked car, trying to gain composure, and after spending a few minutes parked on the hard shoulder calming down, I drove to the next Services, where we had a cup of coffee and a quiet chat. Sue had calmed down a bit but still didn't realise that her crazy behaviour could have killed us all. As I drove all the way back to Middlesbrough, we were all silent. The children had fallen asleep, and Sue and I didn't speak to one another. I suppose we were both engrossed in our own thoughts.

On arrival at Sue's house, she refused to get out of the car. She wouldn't go indoors. I went inside her house and faced a huge rottweiler, which had been stuck inside the house for a day or two. Obviously, there was a hell of a mess, shit and piss everywhere, and chewed-up pieces of furniture. I took the dog out and started cleaning up the mess, Sue sat in the car whilst I tried to sort the house and the children out. Every now and then, I'd go to the car and coax her to go inside the house, and every time she refused.

Eventually, after hours of encouragement, she got out of the car and went inside the house, but she was still behaving strangely, dancing around the place euphorically. I tried to care for the children as best as I could, as Sue was in her own world and in no fit state to look after herself, let alone the children. I decided to call St Luke's hospital in Middlesbrough. I knew it was a psychiatric hospital, and I thought maybe they could help her. Somebody had to help her. I was struggling to cope. I called St Luke's, and they told me I needed a referral from Sue's GP for them to start the admission process. I knew getting Sue to a doctor was going to be difficult. She was adamant there was nothing wrong with her.

I rang her GP and made an emergency appointment for that day. At the surgery, Sue wouldn't allow me to go in with her, she went in to see the G.P. alone, and I waited outside for a few minutes. After a while, I thought I needed to speak to the doctor about Sue, so I knocked on the doctor's door and went in, I introduced myself as Susan's brother and told him what had happened, and I said, "I am worried about Sue's mental state, I need your help." The doctor asked me to remain silent as he asked Sue some questions. To my amazement, Sue was acting normally; she was able to mask her behaviour. The doctor said, "What's been going on, Susan?" Sue was calm and controlled, answering all the questions. The doctor said, "I can't see anything wrong." I was angry and said, "You try living with her for one day and tell me there's nothing wrong." The doctor replied, "I'm sorry, there is nothing I can do." I looked at Sue, who had a smirk on her face. As soon as we left the doctor's office, I felt lost and alone, not knowing whom to turn to next. Sue turned to me and said, "See, I told you there's nothing wrong with me. You are the one who's nuts." I can look at the situation from Sue's perspective now. She was unaware that she was ill, and her behaviour was perfectly normal in her mind, but I was looking at her from the outside and could see clearly that she was poorly. It was obvious to me that she was suffering from a mental health illness.

When we returned to Sue's house, she had transformed into a maniac again, she had masked it for a few minutes to fool the doctor, and now she was worse than ever. She was excitable. She was shouting and laughing and dancing to loud music. I couldn't control her. I experienced days of this behaviour and was desperate for help. I told my friend Shaun about my situation, and he advised me to call St Luke's again and tell them that I was afraid for my sister's safety. I called the hospital to speak to someone in charge. I received the same reaction as before from a receptionist, a doctor's referral was required, etc., then eventually, after I refused to end the phone call, I spoke to a sister at St Luke's, and I told her I was desperate. I informed her that we had seen Sue's GP, who didn't help and begged her to take a look at Sue. My last plea was, "I think she may harm herself." The sister reluctantly said, "Bring her down." I said, "Now?" She said, "Bring her here now."

I went into the kitchen and asked Sue to sit down, I told her to trust me and believe in me, and that I would never hurt her, I told her that we needed to go to the hospital, and she said, "The general hospital?" I replied, "No, St Luke's." Sue laughed, "What? You want to put me in the nuthouse?" I tried to explain to Sue that the staff at St Luke's could help her and said softly, "If you go to St Luke's and they say there's nothing wrong with you, I will accept it, and I won't say another word on the matter." Sue agreed to go, probably thinking she could bluff them as she did with the doctor before.

At the hospital, we walked to the main entrance, where we were greeted by a nurse, and then we were shown into a small room whilst we waited for a sister to arrive. We both sat there quietly, and I didn't know what to say to Sue. I was praying that the hospital staff would help us and would be able to see through Sue's masking. When the sister arrived, I was asked to leave the room; as I left the room, I heard the sister speaking to Sue in a soft, controlled tone. I was just hoping that they could see that Sue was ill and needed help. After a few minutes, they both came out of the little room, and the sister said to me, "Sue will be staying with us tonight." Sue looked at me angrily, saying, "You got what you wanted." I felt guilty but knew in my heart that she was in the right place. I went to walk alongside them and follow them to wherever the sister was taking Sue, but the sister stopped me and said, "You go home now. We'll take care of her." I watched them silently walk down the corridor together and noticed Sue's shoe was hanging off, it was slapping up and down as she walked, and that memory has stayed with me. Both the nurse nor Sue didn't look back, and they just kept walking. I got back to the car and cried like a baby. I felt guilt, relief, and sadness all at once and a feeling of thankfulness that she was in the right place and that she would receive the right help to make her better.

I stayed in Middlesbrough over the Christmas period and visited Sue at the hospital every day. The first time I saw her after she has admitted was heart-breaking. She was heavily sedated and had been sectioned because she kept trying to leave the hospital. She just wanted to go home. Sue kept threatening that she would leave the care and safety of the hospital. Sue was nasty to me, blaming me for her hospitalisation, but I was thick-skinned. I knew it was the illness talking and not my loving sister. Sue and I were awfully close, she was like a mother to me, always supportive and protective, and I had to watch her suffer and couldn't help her. I felt like the helpless ten-year-old boy who couldn't stop my father from giving her the belt. I tried to help with Sue's children for a few weeks and then arranged for their care by other family members before I returned to London.

It took months for Sue to recover from that episode, and she is still fighting her illness. She was diagnosed with bipolar disorder. I love Sue so much, and we have a special bond as siblings. She played a big role in my upbringing and had enormous pressures placed on her shoulders from a young age. Mental illness can affect anyone at any time, the person suffering often finds it difficult to express the pain and trauma they are enduring or feel that they are behaving perfectly normal, and everyone else is behaving abnormally. I believe it's so important to try and talk to someone and get the help that's out there. No one should suffer alone. It has been a strenuous journey for Sue, but she has the support of her loving family and friends.

It was a wrench leaving Sue to return to London, but I had to get back to work and start training again, trying to resume my career. I hadn't fought for ten months. I wasn't in a good place. I was worried about Sue. She was constantly on my mind, I tried to speak to her on the phone every day, but on bad days she wouldn't talk to me. I accepted that was part of her illness and gave her time to heal.

Round Twelve – The Last Round

Warren's office rang and told me that there was a possibility of a title fight for the WBO Middleweight Title against an American middleweight boxer named Lonny Bradley. Warren said the fight would be held in Middlesbrough, and I was really happy about that. It was an exciting thought boxing for the WBO Middleweight Title in my hometown. I was training like crazy to make the weight; I was coming down from Super Middleweight to Middleweight. I was expecting this fight to happen soon. As far as I knew, everything was in place. All that was required to seal the deal was an actual date for the fight.

I was getting anxious that a date wasn't given for the fight. At the time, I briefly had an agent. I didn't believe in agents, they were just another person wanting a slice of my purse, but at this point in my career, I thought I needed a go-between to negotiate a better deal. I asked him to contact the WBO to enquire about the title defence fight which Warren had organised with me and Lonny Bradley. The agent discovered that Lonny Bradley's next defence fight was not against me but against a Canadian boxer named Otis Grant. I was pissed off. That fight was off, I was twenty-six years old with fire in my belly, but Warren kept pissing on the fire. I knew that Warren didn't like me. I was a Northern lad who didn't sugar coat or lick arse, I was straight talking, and some Southerners don't like that.

I went off the rails for a while, drinking and partying. I hadn't trained for weeks, and I felt lost and deflated. I was seriously considering leaving the boxing world behind again. I felt that I hadn't achieved anything, I was ambitious and dedicated to my sport, but I hadn't received any recognition for the blood, sweat, and tears that I had given over the years. I loved my job, fighting in the ring and training hard. I was proud to be a professional fighter, but fighters have masters, and I felt that boxers were just puppets; people like Warren and Micky Duff had complete control. They could play with your strings and make you or break you.

As a young fighter, it's not just your boxing skills that count. It's your ability to communicate and have business sense. It's so important to ensure you have the right people around to support you. For a boxer, it's advantageous to come from a boxing family and have people around you who have the knowledge, experience, and skills to deal with promoters, etc., who could also watch your back. At the time, it was advantageous to live in London, where all the best gyms and sparring were based. Today young boxers have more opportunities to branch out and fight and train throughout the UK, and there are great boxing hubs in Sheffield, Liverpool, and Manchester. I didn't have a game plan. I just drifted, unsure really of the route that I was going to take. I didn't use my head. I used my hands instead to try and be successful. You can be the best boxer in the world, but without a plan and the right people behind you, you're fucked. I just relied on opportunities that were thrown my way. I wasn't proactive. I was thinking about the money all time, and instead of using fights as stepping-stones, I saw the light too late. I was getting older, and the window of opportunity was closing.

I had been on a drinking weekend in Bournemouth with all my mates and enjoyed getting together with my old friend Damien. This conversation is an example of a boxer who needed management, protection, and support. Boxers can be easily manipulated. I had a phone call one evening from Ernie Fossey:

Ernie: Alright, Corny? How are you doing?

Cornelius: Yeah, all right.

Ernie: I've got a fight for you – Dean Francis.

Cornelius: Ernie, he's a super middleweight. A big super middleweight. I've been training for over six months to get to middleweight. I'm 11 stone 8 and feeling strong at this weight, and you want me to take a fight with under four weeks' notice to be a super middleweight.

Ernie: You'll be alright, Corn.

Cornelius: Ernie, I haven't had a fight for fifteen months. I know Dean Francis. He's a lively and dangerous opponent. This isn't the fight for me. I want to box at middleweight. That's where I feel the strongest. The reason I boxed Steve

Collins at Super middleweight was that it was a world title fight. Ernie, I don't want the fight!

Ernie: Well, if you don't take the fight, you won't be working for Frank anymore.

Dean Francis mainly boxed as a light, heavyweight boxer. He was strong and was a thick-set muscular boxer with a punch that was deadly. The following day I went training at the gym to discover that the fight between Dean Francis and me had been accepted; everything had been taken out of my hands.

I had four weeks' notice about the fight, I should never have accepted that the fight had been made, but I was afraid to reject the fight, even though I had rejected it initially. I knew that if I didn't accept the fight, Frank Warren wouldn't find me any more fights, and that would be the end of my boxing career. As I said before, Warren was God in the world of boxing at that time, and I had to accept anything he threw my way even though deep I knew it was a bad decision and a dangerous one.

I trained hard, but I lost the fight. I was stopped in the seventh round, and Dean nearly took my head off with some powerful left hooks. After that fight, my right arm shook for about five months. It worried me. The fight affected me badly. I didn't box again until eighteen months later. I should have trusted my first response and rejected the fight, and boxing can be a dangerous sport, so many boxers have been severely injured or killed in the ring. It was mentally hard to swallow that fight, it put a big dent in my confidence, and it was the end of my relationship with Frank Warren and Ernie Fossey, and it was also the end of my boxing relationship with my trainer Howard Rainey who moved to Sheffield after the Dean Francis fight. Promoter's use and abuse boxers, I didn't have any communication with Frank or Ernie after that horrendous fight, there was no aftercare, I was just another pleb, and there were plenty like me. I should have trusted my instinct and fought against those who made the decision for me to fight Dean. It was wrong. I was lucky to have survived that fight without permanent brain damage. I wish I would have stood my ground and stayed at middleweight, I was afraid to lose my promoter, Frank Warren, but it worked out that I did anyway. Imagine if I had ended up like Gerald McClellan. He was a super middleweight American boxer who was promoted by Don King and tragically had brain damage after a fight with Nigel Benn. Most people know the dangers of boxing, and as boxers, we take risks every time we step into the ring. It's like playing Russian roulette.

I was sorry to hear that Dean passed away a few years ago. It was a tragedy for someone so young to lose his battle against cancer. I almost threw in the towel after the Dean Francis fight, I'd been a professional boxer for ten years and had trained almost every day, dedicating my young life to boxing, but after that fight, I had lost my way. I wasn't sure where to turn. I questioned my career in boxing yet again. Where was I heading? I had stopped training for a few months, and there were no future fights planned. As I didn't have a promoter, I wasn't sure which path I was going to take.

I hadn't spoken to my friend Damien for a few months. He had moved back to Belfast. In fact, I didn't want to speak to anyone after fighting Dean. I think I was suffering mentally from the aftermath, and I felt ashamed that I had let myself and other people down because I had performed badly in the ring.

"You'll never guess where I am?" These were the first words Damien said to me when he rang me, and he was always winding me up. "Go on, where are you?" I said, pretending to yawn. Then Damien said, "I'm on a film set in Dublin." He told me he had been cast in a movie with Daniel Day-Lewis, and the movie was called 'The Boxer.' He was on set and had started filming. Damien went on to say, "Do you want to come over and help me with the boxing choreography in the movie?" I was quite nonchalant and said, "Yeah. Yeah. OK." I didn't believe him, and I thought this was one of his best wind-ups yet. He carried on saying, "A car will collect you at 10 am tomorrow morning to take you to the airport, you'll fly to Dublin, and you'll stay in the same hotel as me, and we can both go on set together." I agreed to go but was still unsure about the whole thing, thinking it was a wind-up. The phone call was brief, and I kept thinking, is this true or not? I tried calling Damien back to double-check if this was really happening, but I couldn't reach him.

At 9.30 am the following day, I hadn't packed, but my bag was on the bed ready, in case it was true. I was still unsure whether this was a joke or not, and then a huge top-of-the-range black BMW pulled up, I went outside, and I was greeted by a friendly booted, and suited driver, who asked me, "Are you, Mr. Carr?" I replied in shock, "Give me a minute." I ran indoors and quickly packed the bag on the bed. I grabbed my passport and was driven to Heathrow airport. I arrived at Dublin airport and saw a well-dressed man holding up a sign with my name on it. Everything was happening so quickly, I was then whisked off to The Burlington Hotel, where Damien stood grinning, with his hands on hips, and he handed me a key to our room. The hotel was stunning, and I was impressed. Damien said, "We need to meet Barry." I asked, "Barry?" "Yeah, Barry McGuigan, he'll be here soon. He wants to discuss the schedule." Barry McGuigan was one of my childhood heroes, he was an exceptional fighter, and I was about to meet him. I'm not one of these people who get starstruck, I take everything in my stride, but I looked forward to meeting Barry. Barry was down to earth, a nice guy. We got on well, and I was surprised that he knew all about me and my boxing career.

The next few weeks were spent on set, and we met some amazing people. Daniel Day-Lewis was polite and very professional. He was a method actor and took his role as a boxer seriously. I was shocked at his level of dedication to his art, he trained hard daily, sparring with Damien, and he learnt how real boxers prepared for fights. I thought he was good enough to box, there were rumours that he would have a proper amateur contest, but it never happened. I went out for a meal one evening with Damien, Daniel, his wife Rebecca (who is the daughter of the well-known American playwright Arthur Miller who was married to Marilyn Monroe), Barry, and a few others. I believed that Daniel was Irish because he remained in character throughout the evening, and whilst he was filming, I was amazed to learn that he was English. His Irish accent was flawless. We had a lovely evening; everyone was chatty and down to earth.

The movie was directed by a talented Irish film Director, Screenwriter, Producer, and Playwright, Jim Sheridan, who had directed many superb movies, including In the Name of the Father and My Left Foot, both movies starred Daniel Day-Lewis. Jim Sheridan has had numerous Academy Award nominations for his movies and is a master storyteller. It was a strange coincidence that Jim had sat ringside when I had boxed Steve Collins at The Point a few years previously. I was lucky that Jim offered me a cameo role in the film. I was overjoyed to be a part of the team. As an actor and as a boxing choreographer, I learned a lot from choreographing the Morrissey video, and that experience helped me enormously, and I passed on those skills for 'The Boxer' movie.

It was a fantastic opportunity for a young boxer like me to do a movie project like this, rubbing shoulders with celebrities and learning about filmmaking. I lapped it up and learnt a lot about the film industry. I met some talented individuals during the making of The Boxer. I worked on set all day, the days were long, and there was a lot of waiting around, and I spent some time in the trailer with Damien and a few other actors having a craic. One actor whom I met at the bar in The Burlington Hotel was Ken Stott, and he was such a lovely guy. He was down-to-earth and friendly. Damien, Ken, and I had a few drinks one evening; I didn't really know who Ken Stott was until I attended the Premiere of the movie and then realised what a superb actor he was. He played an important role as Ike Weir opposite Daniel Day-Lewis. During the times we socialised, he didn't brag or boast about his acting career. He was a genuine guy. He also loved boxing. It's amazing how much respect I had as a boxer amongst actors, they realised how tough it was to be a professional boxer, but it worked both ways. I respected them, too, and admired their dedication and hard work in their craft.

After four weeks, I left the set and headed back to London. About six months after working on 'The Boxer,' I had a phone call out of the blue from a guy I knew, Jonathan Feld, who was now working as a boxing promoter. I'd seen him at the gyms and knew that he loved boxing, he would often watch us boxers training, and I'd spend some time chatting with him. I told Jonathan that I'd meet him, and he suggested that I also link up with Chris Hall, who was a boxing trainer working out of my old gym where I first turned professional ten years earlier, St Pancras near Chalk Farm.

I liked Chris, and we hit it off from our first meeting. He agreed with me that I should be in the middleweight boxing category, he had some new innovative ideas about training regimes, and he was enthusiastic and supportive of me. Eighteen months had gone by since my fight with Dean Francis, and I was fighting again. My first fight under Jonathan was at Acton Sports Centre, a small venue in North London, and my opponent was Darren Covill. I stopped him in the third round; I felt a bit rusty, but I was happy to be back in the ring. I had two more fights, and they were against Danny Guma and Jimmy Vincent. I won both contests.

Jonathan treated me with respect and looked after me. Unlike any of the previous promoters, he believed in me and put me forward for three fights, one after the other. I could see that I was improving after each fight, I was feeling confident, and I was hungry again to win my fights. At the start of 1999, Jonathan mentioned that there could be a WBF World Title fight against a fighter, Simon Brown. He was a dangerous, strong opponent who had won various world titles. The match was to be held at Thornaby Pavilion in

Middlesbrough. I was excited about the thought of boxing in my hometown, but I was wary because I had been disappointed before. However, Jonathan was a man of his word, and I trusted him completely. The WBF is a lesser Championship title in comparison to other federations and associations; still, it wouldn't be an easy option. I knew I had to work hard, but it was a way in. I could fight with top boxers without working with the big promoters. Some great boxers who had won the WBF Title were Evander Holyfield, Joe Bugner, and Roy Jones Junior.

Five or six weeks before the fight, I had a phone call informing me that Simon Brown had failed his boxing medical due to eyesight problems, I was disappointed, but Jonathan reassured me that he would find someone else. Within twenty-four hours, I had another opponent Steve 'The Viking' Foster from Manchester, I didn't know much about Steve, but I knew he had campaigned at light middleweight, and he was a worthy opponent.

Sparring and training went really well with Chris, he pushed me hard, and I felt confident that I would win this fight. I was thrilled to be fighting in Middlesbrough. The fight was a sell-out, and I was proud to be on my home turf surrounded by friendly faces.

I was nervous all day before the fight. I'm not sure why maybe because I thought this was my last chance to be a world Champion boxer. I understood that this was a lightly regarded WBF Title fight, but for me, it what a big step, and my intention was to progress onto bigger and better titles. This was just a stepping-stone. At about 5 pm on the evening of the fight, I had a chat with myself. I gave myself a good talking-to. I asked myself why I was so nervous. I had trained hard, all the preparation was done, and after my little chat, the nerves disappeared, and I was eager to get to the venue.

I arrived at the venue early, and every ritual that I could think of was done in the ring. It felt good, but on the downside, I had to wait a long time before facing Steve Foster in the ring. It was crazy that I felt so desperate to do my rituals, and as the years progressed from the Denmark days, my rituals increased, I added little bits on, and the rituals would get longer and longer, starting the night before a fight. I would place all the boxing equipment I needed for the fight on my bed and then, one by one, place them in my sports bag. I would go to bed and think that I had forgotten to pack something, and I'd empty the bag and place everything on the bed again, ensuring that I hadn't forgotten anything. Before a fight, I had too much time and lots of energy. I kept mulling everything over in my mind. I couldn't relax unless I knew I was organised and prepared. I looked at the clock on the side of my bed. It was gone at midnight, and I thought, this time tomorrow, I'll know if I were a World Champion boxer or not, but I never went into a fight thinking that I would be defeated.

On the night of the fight, I was on last, and there were about eight fights before mine. I didn't enter the ring until about 10.30 pm. I had been waiting in the changing room for over an hour and thought I'd get some fresh air. I needed some space. I did some shadowboxing and stretching outside. I felt prepared for the fight; I felt that this was my night, my moment. I was going to shine and show everyone in my hometown what I could achieve in the ring. As I was shadowboxing in the car park, two young teenagers came over and asked me what I was doing. I told them, "I'm Cornelius Carr. I'm boxing tonight." They were excited and asked, "Can we come and watch you mate?" The young boys reminded me of the time when I watched boxing through the window of the British Legion, and their enthusiasm and eagerness put a smile on my face. I told them I couldn't get them seats, but as I walked away from them, I changed my mind and said, "Wait here and let me see what I can do." I asked one of the event organisers if I could get two passes for the event, and I went back outside and saw the boys sitting on a wall. Both lads watched me closely as I approached them. I grinned and dangled the lanyards with the passes in front of them. They were beaming and then sprung off the wall rushing towards me, and they were shocked that I had given them two free passes to the boxing show. They were jumping around with excitement as if they'd won the lottery. I wished that someone would have done something like that for me when I was a lad. I hoped my small deed would encourage them to participate in boxing or any sport that would give them a better life and deter them from hanging about the streets of Middlesbrough.

Waiting before a fight is one of the hardest things for any boxer. I used to listen to music and try to focus, and not allow anything to distract me. The fresh air and seeing those happy lads had done me a world of good. I went back inside and prepared for the fight. I did my own wraps, which were signed off by an official. I was gloved up and ready to go. As I entered the arena, there was a huge roaring reception from the hometown crowd. I focused on the job ahead, with my head down and hooded up, as I made my way towards the ring. I thought that title would be mine soon.

Over the first six rounds, I expected Steve Foster to be more aggressive, but I was shocked at the way he was boxing, I was the aggressor, and I was the one who kept moving forward and picking up points. I thought the fight was noneventful; Steve appeared to be laid back, and I thought any minute now he was going to surprise me and suddenly come alive, but it didn't happen. I was winning each round, I received a small cut above my left eye during round seven, but it was nothing to worry about.

I sat in my corner at the end of round eleven, and Chris, my trainer, said, "You are winning this fight comfortably. Keep your jab working, and don't do anything silly. You are three minutes away from winning this title." I went into the twelfth round focusing on winning and not getting caught with a lucky punch, Steve came at me with a mad flurry of punches for about twenty seconds, but I countered well with some good shots. The final bell went, and Steve and I hugged. We respected one another.

The ring was packed at the end of the fight. Marty was one of the first people to congratulate me. I said, "How do you think I did, Mart?" He said, "It's yours. You won that!" I always knew Marty would give me an honest viewpoint. He always did. From the moment I started boxing at the age of eleven, he was always truthful about my performances; after Marty's words, I knew in my head that I was a World Champion.

I remembered the words Peter Cairn said when he caught me smoking on the way to school, "Put that fag out, or you won't be a Champion." And here I was all those years later in Middlesbrough in front of the home crowd, waiting to hear the decision from the announcer, "And the WBF World Middleweight Champion, by a unanimous decision, is Cornelius Carr!" It had been a twelve-round fight, and I won the fight on points. I felt emotional and proud as they placed the belt around my waist.

I looked at my family and friends who supported me ringside, and my sister Sue smiled and waved me over to her, she had watched the fight with my mam, who was sitting next to her in her wheelchair, and my mam wore a Middlesbrough Football Club scarf which was wrapped around her neck. Sue had taken her out of the nursing home for the night to watch me fight. As I got out of the ring, there were crowds surrounding me and congratulating me, and I was trying to get to our mam through the masses of people. I eventually reached her, gave her a hug and a kiss, and proudly gave her the world title belt, which I had just fought twelve rounds for. She seemed a bit agitated and said, "About bloody time!" I wasn't sure what she meant. Was it because it took me thirteen years to win a world title, or was it because it was past midnight, and she wanted to go to bed? I think it was the latter, but she surprised me when she perked up after hearing there would be an after-party at the Marton Country Club, where I was staying. My mam suddenly sprung into life and was eager to get to the do, and she was always up for a party. It was a great night, I met old friends, and it meant so much to me to be celebrating amongst my people. We partied until the early hours.

Cornelius With Marty Turner Wearing The WBF Belt

Sister Susan, Mam And Nephew Paul On The Evening Cornelius Won The WBF Middleweight Title 1999

My dream as a boy was to become a British and World Boxing Champion, and I had achieved my goal, but I wanted more; I wanted to be a name, to be known and respected by the nation for all the hard work I had done. I know that fame and fortune are over-rated, and being happy and healthy is more important, but I just wanted recognition for my hard graft, the roads I had taken were long and winding. I looked back at my life and all the twists and turns that led me to this day. It had been a tough journey so far, my life hadn't been a bed of roses, but now I hoped that better times were to come, and I thought, bring it on.

I had some great publicity from the local and national press. I thought this was a new start. I'd have a couple of defence matches and then go for bigger titles. We had a problem getting financial sponsorship from television companies; TV Companies paid large amounts of money to cover boxing contests; that's where most of the money came from. Most big promoters have television backers, and they work for hand in glove. I wanted to fight bigger names, and I wanted to be a well-known boxer. I knew this would be difficult with a small promoter, but Jonathan was a good guy whom I believed in.

After the fight on 20th January 1999, I didn't fight again until 20th August 1999 against Jason Barker from Sheffield. It was a non-title eight-round fight which I won, and it was a fourth-round stoppage. I just needed to keep busy. If I didn't box regularly, I became rusty, I wanted to fight often, but I just didn't have the opportunity. Eleven days after the fight, my son Jake was born. I was pleased I had a boy and felt happy and blessed that he was a lovely healthy little baby. I was so proud that I was a dad. I enjoyed being busy and helping to look after the new baby, there were the usual sleepless nights, but I took my fatherly duties seriously.

Jonathan told me that there was a possible fight where I would have the opportunity to defend my title against a South African boxer named Dingaan Thobela (The Rose of Soweto). He was the first black superstar from South Africa. I hadn't heard of him but found out that he was a former Lightweight World Champion and regarded very highly in the boxing world. I always spoke to Big Marty about my boxing and told him about Dingaan Thobela. As soon as I mentioned his name, Marty said, "He's a good fighter. He's well known in South Africa".

I had been training at a David Lloyd Club in Raynes Park regularly and had a conversation with the manager about my career when I mentioned that I might have a title defence fight coming up and asked if he was interested in holding the fight at the Club. I didn't really intend for the fight to go ahead at the Club, but to my surprise, he seemed keen, and I soon arranged a meeting with him and Jonathan to discuss a possible show being held at the Club. After the meeting, it was decided that the fight would take place at the Club on Sunday, 31st October 1999. I think that this was the only time a World Title fight was held at a David Lloyd Club. I had been with Jonathan for just one year, and he had gotten me eight fights. My fourth fight was for the WBF title, and my sixth fight was to defend my title; for a small promoter, I thought he had worked hard for me and provided me with great opportunities.

I had eight weeks to train in preparation for the fight. I did some research on Dingaan and discovered that he had numerous World Title Defence fights. He was a very experienced boxer. Later I found out that Dingaan had taken our fight seriously and locked himself away for six weeks to train in a South African prison.

I trained hard for the fight and pushed myself to my limit. One day I went to Kingston running track for a self-fitness test to see how fit I was. It was four weeks prior to the fight. I warmed up by doing four laps of the four hundred metre track and then spent ten minutes stretching. It started raining heavily, but I still was determined to do the fitness test on my own, which consisted of twelve laps (each lap I ran represented to me one round in the boxing ring) of four hundred metres, with just forty-five seconds to recover between each lap. The first lap was easy, and it took me just under a minute to complete. This was encouraging for me; I did lap after lap, and my average time was still just over a minute for each lap. The last few laps were the hardest to complete, but I managed to get through them.

I timed myself for each lap, gave myself a time limit, and wrote down the time achieved on each lap. After I had finished the final lap, I lay on the wet floor, feeling physically and mentally exhausted. It was one of the most difficult fitness tests I had given myself, but I was proud of the outcome. I was feeling strong and confident. As I lay on the floor getting my breath back, another athlete came over to check if I was ok. I must have looked like I needed help. I reassured the guy that I was fine. The fitness test proved to me that I was ready to do the twelve rounds with Dingaan.

I needed a day to recover after the day at the track. Chris Hall, who was my trainer, helped me prepare for the fight. I trained five days a week, three times a day. Each morning I'd work out at the David Lloyd gym, lifting weights, shadow boxing, and doing technical boxing drills. There were often famous faces at the gym. One time I went in the jacuzzi with Max Clifford, the infamous PR guru sex offender, I knew who he was, but this was well before he went to prison. He seemed to be arrogant and full of himself, and I didn't take much notice of him.

In the afternoon, I would go to St Pancras boxing gym North London to spar and do some pad work. I would spend about ninety minutes at the boxing gym. Boxing training can be monotonous. It's a bit like 'Ground Hog Day,' just doing the same things over and over again. Years ago, I would have trained every single day. Now I was training for three days with one day off, and then another three days and one day off. I was happy with my fitness, and I was at the right weight. I weighed eleven stone ten after training, and I was about four pounds over the Middleweight limit; this meant I was on target.

One week prior to the fight, Dingaan arrived in London. Jonathan thought of a great marketing ploy to drum up support for the boxing match. We both appeared during halftime at Selhurst Park Stadium, the home of Crystal Palace Football Club, to promote the fight. We both pretended to square up to each other for the crowd. I think it was a success because the event was a sell-out. It stood out to me that Dingaan was being over friendly and wanted to be my buddy, always smiling, but I was wary of mind games, I knew he had been in this situation many times before, so I kept my distance from him and behaved professionally towards him.

On the evening after our appearance at the football club, I was asked to show my WBF World Title Belt at a nightclub in Kingston Upon Thames called Volts. I went along with a few friends, it was around 11.30 pm, and the club was packed. I spoke to the manager, who thought it was a great idea to put me up on one of the high podiums where the dancers performed. I wasn't sure it was a good idea, but I went along with it, thinking this was a great opportunity to sell the final few tickets for the fight. I assumed that I would stand on the podium, then the DJ would introduce me, and I would show everyone my World Championship Belt, the audience would applaud me, and the DJ would say a few words to promote the event.

That didn't happen. The DJ turned off the music and said, "We have a special guest with us tonight. It's Cornelius Carr, who is a World Champion boxer. Cornelius has a big fight coming up next week. He will defend his World title at the David Lloyd Club." After he made his announcement, I waved to the crowd and held up my belt above my head, and then the music came on. I can't remember what the song was, but it had a Techno beat, and I stood there unsure of what to do. All the people in the nightclub were looking up at me, I did some shadowboxing, thinking that would please them, but they kept looking at me, expecting more. I wasn't sure what they were anticipating, then I heard John Di Palma shouting, "Dance, start dancing!" I started dancing awkwardly to the music, which seemed to go on and on. I was running out of new moves. No one else was dancing. I just saw everyone staring at me. All eyes were on me. It was just me on the podium, uncomfortably dancing with a few thousand eyes on me. I was so embarrassed I felt my face going as bright as the disco lights; luckily, no one knew I was cringing inside. It was probably a few minutes of dancing awkwardly, but it seemed like I was on the podium for an eternity. When the music eventually stopped, they all applauded, and I darted off the podium as quick as I could and slunk off out of the door after I thanked the manager. All my friends laugh about my dancing to this day. It was probably one of the most embarrassing moments of my life.

The last week before my fight, I kept my weight down and didn't train too hard, preserving all my strength for the ring. I always felt comfortable fighting at middleweight and had an unbeaten track record in that category. Dingaan's team was greatly confident that Dingaan would beat me. Dingaan was a national hero in South Africa. He had many fights, and at the time I boxed him, his record was 46 fights with just five losses.

The day before the fight, we met at The Sheraton Hotel in Heathrow, where the weigh-in took place. The local press turned up, and I also had a handshake from the Mayor of Kingston, who wished me luck. It's funny when people say, 'good luck,' it's not really luck that comes into it. It's hard graft, dedication, and persistence. I had good luck cards from many dignitaries, including M.P. s. Everyone seemed to be coming out of the woodwork to wish me well. I felt good. I was in my prime and was in peak physical condition. The weigh-in was a polite one. It was nothing like the Steve Collins fight when Steve screamed in my face and tried his best to intimidate me. Dingaan was professional. He behaved like a gentleman in a gentleman's sport. He didn't give a performance. He was a quiet, dignified man.

That evening I booked into the Sheraton Hotel in Heathrow to prepare for the next day. I ate them out of the house and home. I had pasta, chicken, and ice cream, and then more pasta, chicken, and ice cream. After the weigh-in, I could eat whatever I wanted to. I didn't really feel hungry but knew I had to eat for energy. I drank loads of water, too, to rehydrate myself. My friend Damien had flown over from Belfast to spend the evening with me. It was great seeing him and having his support. We went for a walk around Heathrow, watching the continuous flow of aircraft, and chatted about old times. I was thirty years old and always dreamed of moments like this, from training in my wellington boots at Marty's gym to defending a World title. That night I had, I also had a supernatural encounter. I know I can see ghosts if that's what they were – I have seen my grandmother and my father, and now in my new home, I see fleeting images pass doorways, maybe of people who previously lived there. Some people are non-believers. I can understand their viewpoint, and people say there must be there's always a rational explanation for these encounters. I can't explain my sightings. For me, they were real and left a deep spiritual impact on me. I was lying in bed on the eve of the fight with every scenario of the contest tomorrow. I could think racing through my mind. There was a feeling at the bottom of the bed. It dipped as if someone had sat on the bed. I was afraid to look but knew I had to. In the darkness, a large shimmering figure sat there, there were no human-like features, but I instinctively knew it was my father. I wasn't scared. I spoke to it, "Dad is that you? Can you speak to me? I love you, Dad. Thank you for being with me tonight." The spectre shrunk away quickly, and I shed a few tears. I wish it could have spoken to me, but I was glad of the visit. I put the light on and looked around the room, but everything seemed normal, I was hoping it would reappear, but there was stillness in the room. I hadn't spoken to anyone about my spiritual encounters, apart from Bill in the States, when I had the beautiful encounter in the grimy loft room. I always thought people would think I was crazy or making it up. I think my ability to see a ghost is a blessing, another gift.

It was the day of the fight. I ate a huge full English breakfast, and then Damien and I went for a light jog and did a bit of shadow boxing. I was ready to fight. I was confident and eager to get to the venue. The fight wasn't until 9 pm that evening; waiting was the worst thing for me. I just wanted to get into the ring with Dingaan. I lay down and relaxed that afternoon and went through some scenarios in my head of how the fight would go and how I would react.

I arrived at the David Lloyd Club in Raynes Park at 6.30 pm. The car park was full, and there was a long queue of people waiting to enter the venue. I had to use the main doors to get in and had to pass the crowds of people who were waiting to enter the venue to watch the fight. They saw me and patted me on the back, wishing me well. Some people were calling me John. I knew they were from Middlesbrough, and some people were calling me Cornelius. It's as if I was two different people. I felt a bit nervous, but as soon as I walked into the venue, my nerves disappeared.

Jonathan had told me that Dingaan wanted a few female African Zulu warrior dancers to perform in the ring before the fight, so I thought, why not get a few of my friends to dress up like James Bond lookalikes and face the dancers with stony straight faces? Looking back, we should have had a dance-off. I think that would have been more entertaining.

Damien and I were upstairs in my makeshift dressing room, which was a large fitness studio. I put my training bag down and arranged my boxing gear, ready for the fight. I knew I had to do my usual rituals before a fight. I had to see the ring and touch the ropes and sometimes shadow box inside the ring before the audience arrived. This was a ritual I had done since I was a teenager in Denmark. I thought that the ritual would bring me luck. I used to think that if Middlesbrough lost playing football on a Saturday when I was due to box that evening, I would lose, and if they won, I would win. I recognise now that I have slight OCD. I have realised that I need to do certain rituals during my everyday life. I need to ensure that I lock doors properly and turn the lights off. I get worried that I haven't locked doors or switched lights off properly and will return to double-check that I have done what I was supposed to do. My OCD has got worse as I've gotten older. I am very predictable and very habitual.

I went downstairs with Damien to where the ring was situated. It was like a labyrinth of passages and stairs as I tried to find my way there. When we finally reached the ring, the boxing show had already started, and there were fighters boxing in the ring. There were a few fights before mine. My fight was towards the end of the show. This was a big fight for me, and I couldn't do my rituals. I felt anxious for a few seconds, but then accepted that I couldn't fulfil my rituals and went back upstairs to my dressing room to prepare myself for my fight. I have never spoken about these rituals to anyone before, apart from my partner, Jan, who says I'm a bit weird. I don't think I'm weird. I've just got my own funny ways.

After a few minutes of sitting in the dressing room with a few hours to kill before the fight, I noticed a softball in the corner of the room and said to Damien, "Let's have a game of football." I had so much energy, which I had to release. We were like teenagers chasing the ball and tackling each other, laughing and giggling, when my trainer Chris walked in, "What the hell is going on?" He couldn't believe I was risking an injury just before my fight. I hadn't thought about that. It was just a way to pass the time and have a bit of fun. Chris said, "You could have twisted your ankle!" I knew he was right, but I enjoyed the kickabout with Damien. It released the tension and pressure that I was feeling. I snapped back into fighter mode and prepared to defend my title. I was up for the fight and had warmed up, and was ready for action. I was in peak physical condition and oozed confidence.

For every fight, there is a walkout through the crowd and into the ring. Dingaan went out first as he was the challenger. I was to follow him coming out to 'Let Me Entertain You' by Robbie Williams. I had arranged for some of my friends to lead me out to the ring. I had my boxing robe on with the hood up over my head. I couldn't see where I was going and relied on my friends to lead me to the ring. It seemed like the walk-in was taking forever, we all ended up at the back of the auditorium, under the seating areas, and the cameras were waiting for me at the other side of the auditorium. John Di Palma, my friend, turned to me and said, "I think we've gone the wrong way." It was like a comedy sketch. I can see the funny side now, but at the time, I was panicking. It was the last thing I needed just before facing Dingaan. There were five of us wandering around the auditorium like lost sheep. I think I must be the only boxer to lose his way to the ring to defend his title.

Eventually, I arrived at the correct entrance, and my music played as I walked towards the ring shadow boxing. The noise was loud, and I kept saying to myself, 'take your time, don't rush in,' I knew Dingaan was a good fighter and a great counterpuncher. When I arrived at the ring, I walked up the steps and did a 360-degree turn on the spot punching the air, and the crowd went nuts. The sound was deafening. As I turned around, I spotted my old training partner sitting in the crowd, who was a former World Featherweight Champion, Colin McMillan. I always admired Colin, he was a gifted fighter, and I remember going to see him when he boxed Maurizio Steccka for the WBO Featherweight title, and he gave him a boxing lesson. Colin said to me after his fight, "You'll get the opportunity next." When Colin told me that, it stuck in my mind, it was lovely to see him at my fight, I nodded to him, and he nodded back. There were so many people there that night who meant so much to me and supported me throughout my boxing career. Many of my friends were there, including Stevie Carney, who flew from his home in Tenerife, and Shaun Lacey, so many people had made an effort to support me, and I was thankful.

I could see Dingaan in his corner with his three female Zulu warriors dancing around the ring, dressed in full African regalia, taking up all the space. They were doing a traditional African war dance. Damien was in my corner with Chris. Damien said, "Walk around them," because they were trying to take over the ring and intimidate us. My crew was dressed up like James Bond lookalikes, black suits, dickie bows, and sunglasses, and they watched the war dance with me in the ring. I knew we had to put on a show, but in my mind, I just wanted to have a go at Dingaan. His promoter had done some fighting talk previously, saying how Dingaan was going to knock me out by the sixth round, and that riled me up. I know it's all boxing bravado, and sometimes that's a good thing. It stirred up the fighting spirit and public interest in the fight, but I was genuinely pissed off.

The war dance ended after a few minutes, and my guys, who really didn't do much, walked out and sat ringside. Dingaan had South African supporters there, including the Springboks, the South African Rugby Union team, they had been playing in the UK as part of the Rugby Union World Cup the day before the fight.

All the entertainers left the ring, and the referee was just about to bring Dingaan and me together at the centre of the ring when Simon Block, a boxing board official, appeared in Dingaan's corner. I didn't know what all the fuss was about. I could see Dingaan getting annoyed and pulling unhappy faces. I turned my back on the situation and spoke to Chris, who was telling me to keep focused. I later discovered that Dingaan had not had his pre-fight medical exam, and the exam had to take place in the ring just before the fight. I couldn't believe that had happened. It took about thirty seconds for the doctor to give him the all-clear to fight. It was a crazy situation. I had been lost on the way to the ring, Zulus were eyeballing me, and Dingaan was having his medical in the ring, all within a few minutes, and the fight hadn't even started. Any of these things could have thrown me, but I was concentrating on beating Dingaan. I was mentally and physically ready.

The Fight

Round 1

After all the commotion of Dingaan's ringside medical and the Zulu war dance, the fight commenced. I felt comfortable. I was fit enough to go the full distance and felt confident that I would knock Dingaan out well before the twelfth round. I sat in my corner, and my cornermen prepared me for the fight. They smeared a small amount of Vaseline on my face, particularly my eyebrows, cheeks, nose, and ears. These were my opponent's target areas. The Vaseline would help when punches are thrown, making boxing gloves slip off the skin. The first round started tentatively. We both were feeling our range, and he surprised me by coming forward, but I liked that he was making a fight, and I returned the favour. We were both throwing good body shots at one another. I wanted to get as many body shots in as I could, I felt I was getting the upper hand. My jab was good. I caught him with some stinging punches. Dingaan seemed sharp. He was quick. It seemed we were in for a good fight.

Round 2

Dingaan boxed in flurries, punching fast. He was unpredictable. He was solid and dangerous. I had to be careful not to lose any concentration. I could be knocked out. He threw a good left hook to the body, which caught me off guard at the end of the second round, and I was in pain, but I did my best not to show that I was hurt. Chris, my trainer, saw the body shot I took, and when I returned to my corner after the round, he pulled my boxing shorts away from my stomach so that I could breathe easier, and that helped me. He said, "He hurt you there. Be cool, and don't show that you are hurt." I was lucky it was the last punch of the round, allowing me time to recover. Recovering from a head punch is quicker than recovering from a good body punch. I knew that the fight wasn't going to be easy. He was there to win.

Round 3

In the third round, I stamped my authority on the fight. I was using my left jab and left hooks to the head and body. I caught him with some solid right-hands. I kept pushing him away from me, making him step back as if to say I was the Champion. We were both getting into our stride. The fight was heating up.

Round 4

Dingaan was counterpunching well, but he spent a lot of time on the ropes. I was putting pressure on him. I felt confident that I was winning on points. I kept catching him with some good shots, Dingaan retaliated, and I caught some good shots from him too.

Round 5

The fifth round was close. It was Dingaan's best round in the fight. Dingaan was boxing in spurts. He just wasn't consistent, but he did show flashes of brilliance, but he lacked the ability to sustain the pressure on me. I could see he was tired from my constant body punching; he took a battering, and he was tough taking such punishment to his body. This was the first round that I realised how skilful Dingaan was. I was wary of him.

Round 6

The fight was heating up round by round. At the beginning of the sixth round, I threw four or five punch combinations to tell him that I meant business. I felt like I was getting on top, but I never dropped my guard. I knew he was a good fighter. I was at my peak physically, I had worked so hard for this fight, and I wasn't going to allow him to get a foothold in the fight.

Cornelius Carr Defending The WBF Title In London Fighting The Challenger Dingaan 'The Rose Of Soweto' Thobela 1999

Round 7

This was probably the quietest round of the fight so far. I was doing the cleaner work, and I could see that he wanted a breather, so I went along with it, thinking I'll take the rest too. In a twelve-round fight, it's important to take a rest when you can. I thought I had won the round. It wasn't an overly exciting round because I didn't want to burn myself out. Dingaan was a clever old pro, he was a two-time World Champion, and I knew he had a plan, and that was always in the back of my mind. He could come to life at any time during the fight, and I had to be ready.

Round 8

I was right about Dingaan's plan. He came to life in this round and hit me with some good punches, right-hand left hooks. I wasn't hurt, but surprised by his speed, he kept coming forward and throwing punches at me. He won that round, and I thought I needed to get back in the fight. I went back to my corner, and Chris, my trainer, said, "Don't let him get a grip on this fight. Keep focused and get your jab working."

Round 9

I knew that Dingaan came out with the mentality of stopping me in this round. He wanted to knock me out. It was the liveliest I had seen him in the fight at the start of the round. He had won the previous round and wanted to continue where he had left off and win this round too. The fight was turning out to be a cracking contest between us. We both wanted to win. We were both professional boxers, not using any dirty tricks or hug-and-hold tactics that I had experienced with other fighters. We were honest, clean boxers fighting toe to toe, and I think the crowd appreciated our gladiator spirit. This fight showed tenacity and bravery in the ring. The crowd was going mad, standing, shouting, and whistling. When I was a little boy, this was the kind of fight that I would dream about participating in, and here I was.

Round 10

We were getting close to the end of the fight, and I was feeling tired. I knew I had to find more energy and keep up the pressure on Dingaan. We both had success in the round, Dingaan with his flashing right-hand left hooks, and I had success with my body punching and left hooks to the head. It was difficult to say who won that round.

Round 11

This was probably the most exciting round of the fight. The crowd was going nuts, and Dingaan and I were going for it. We were like those wind-up boxer toys, going punch for punch. I thought I needed to dominate this round, and I gave it everything I had. Dingaan showed me that he was a true warrior. I couldn’t finish him off. He kept coming back no matter how much pain I gave him. I thought I had done enough to win the round.

Round twelve would be the finale. I had to keep my title.

The commentators of the fight were Steve Holdsworth and Jim Brady. Both commentators were very professional and gave a fair account of the fight. They both thought it was an exciting boxing match and believed that I had won most of the rounds. They kept saying that Dingaan was too old and that I 'had youth on my side.' I was only three years younger than Dingaan, I was thirty, and Dingaan was thirty-three years old. The pundits were saying that Dingaan was past his sell-by date, but he later proved he wasn't over the hill, he had a fight four months later, and he won the South African Middleweight Title against Soon Botes. A few months after that, he won the WBC World Super Middleweight Title against Glenn Catley. It felt like the pundits were undermining my ability by saying that Dingaan was not a strong challenger due to his age when I was just a little bit younger than him. I was always the underdog. It's not sour grapes. I suppose my face just didn't fit in the boxing world.

Frank Malone, now Kellie Malone, trashed my boxing and the event when he spoke to the commentators during the breaks between the rounds and said some unfair comments after the fight. I'm not sure why he was even there. All he ever did during the commentary was slag me off. I never liked him, and I know the feeling was mutual. I'm just being honest, I'm a straight person, and I think that's why my success was limited.

Round 12

I was exhausted and drained both physically and mentally; I felt the lovely cool water running from the top of my head and trickling down my bare back. It was refreshing to feel the coldness of the water on my steaming, sweaty skin. I was so hot from the heat of the ring lights, the humidity which emanated from the bodies of the 4,000 spectators in the arena, and of course, from boxing. I had fought solidly for eleven three-minute rounds. I sat on the stool numbly and listened to the words of my trainer Chris, "Keep doing what you are doing! Get some punches in! Be smart, don't get reckless. He'll come after you this round because you're in front." All the words he fired at me came loud and fast. I had one minute to recover before the last round of the fight began. I tried to relax and get as much oxygen into my lungs as possible, breathing slowly and deeply. Then the announcer said, "Seconds out, twelfth and final round." I heard the bell ring, signalling for the fight to resume, the referee brought us together, and we both stood up in the centre of the ring and touched gloves. The noise in the arena was overwhelming. I did my best to blank it out, focussing on the target in front of me. I faced my opponent, and the pace of the fighting was still fast, even though it was the twelfth round. I realised at that point that I had been in the ring with a highly skilled fighter, he was one of the first boxers that stood in front of me, and I struggled to hit him cleanly. All the years of dedication and hard work to the sport of boxing will be summed up in this round. I had to win, and I wouldn't allow my opponent to dominate any part of the round. If he threw one punch, I threw two. My opponent came at me like a lion, wanting to finish me off, but I countered well. I didn't want him to end the fight by knocking me out. When I was in the middle of the battle, I only picked up on certain voices, voices that were important to me, like my trainers' voice. Everyone else's voices just became like white noise. I heard Damien shouting from my corner, "Last thirty seconds! Dig in, Corny!" I bit down on my gumshield and dug in as best as I could. The last thirty seconds seemed to drag on forever, but I drew strength from somewhere deep within, I felt powerful energy spurring me on, and I finished the round strongly. The bell rang. I was relieved. The fight was over in more ways than one.

There was a standing ovation from the crowd. I went over to my corner and stood on the second rope acknowledging the crowd. Damien grabbed me and lifted me in the air as a celebratory gesture that I had won the fight. The doctor gave me a quick once-over to ensure that I was ok. I told him I felt fine. I still wasn't completely sure that I had won the fight, but all the men in my corner believed that I had won. Everyone gathered in the ring in preparation for the decision announcement. The ring was full of managers, trainers, promoters, friends, and boxing officials. I went over to Dingaan's corner, and we touched gloves. I told him that it was a tremendous fight. He didn't say anything. He just nodded his head. Dingaan appeared to be a quiet man. He rarely spoke. There was no hatred between us. I respected him for challenging me and giving me an amazing fight.

I went back to my corner, and Harry Holland, a boxing manager, promoter, and actor, said, “You won the fight, Corny. Every time he came at you, you had an answer for him.” I thanked Harry and shook his hand. I knew my body punching had slowed Dingaan down. He couldn’t come back at me strongly due to me repeatedly bombarding him with punches to his body.

I seemed to be waiting for quite a while for the judges to release the scorecards, which I found a bit strange. I hoped that there would be no funny business with the scoring and that the judges would do an honest job. After a few minutes of waiting, the announcer John McDonald came into the centre of the packed ring and said, “The judge’s scorecards are ready.” He proceeded to read out each judge’s score. The first judge Richie Davies scored 114/114. The crowd booed and gasped in surprise when they heard the score, (I later discovered that he had apparently made a mistake with his adding up, and there was a small article in The Boxing News about it two weeks later it stated that the score should have been 117/113), the crowd went quiet as the scores were read out, there was a haunting silence, and then the announcer continued, “Larry O’Connell scored 117/113”. I was winning, but what was the final score? We all were waiting anxiously to hear the final score, and it was like a dream. I couldn't absorb the information. The announcer was finding it difficult to understand the final scorecard and asked someone for help. He nodded as if to say, I get it now, and read out, "Terry O'Connor scored 117/114." The total scores didn't register with me at the time. I was caught up in the moment until the announcer went on to say, "And still, the WBF Middleweight Champion of the World is Cornelius Carr."

I was catapulted into the air by various people around me. I was in a haze. I felt elated. I was ecstatic. A representative of the WBF placed the belt around my waist, and I felt alive and thankful. I held my gloved hands in the air and looked out at the sea of faces, subconsciously, I was searching for him, and amongst the crowd, smiling was my dad wearing his trilby hat, and standing next to him smiling was my mam. I was distracted for a few seconds and turned away briefly, then looked back towards the place in the crowd where I had seen my parents. I couldn't see their beautiful smiling faces, just blurred images. I had suffered some knocks to the head that night and questioned the sighting, but I felt blessed that I had seen them, even though it was briefly. I wasn't sure why my mam was with my dad.

There were some brief interviews in the ring by various media sources, and then I tried to get back to the changing room. On the way to the changing room, I was stopped by so many people. I shook hands as everyone congratulated me. It was a nice feeling. I was shocked to see three old friends,

Stephen, Michael, and Gary Jellings, from Coniston Road in Grangetown. They were beaming and more excited than I was. They were so happy, and it was like they had won the World Title themselves. I think it took around twenty minutes to eventually get to the changing room. I just wanted to sit down and relax and absorb the moment. Chris took my wraps off and told me, “Don’t drink too much tonight. Your body has gone through a lot. Drink plenty of water.” He knew there was an after-party at a local restaurant later that evening and that I would have a few drinks to celebrate my win.

The shower room was a separate room. It was quiet. I was alone for the first time in a long time. I sat in the dark room with just my thoughts. I was thinking of my past fights, and one of those fights was prominent in my mind. It was the Northeast final against Karl Duke when I was seventeen. I’m not sure why that fight came to mind because I had many fights, and some were huge momentous occasions, but the fight against Karl represented to me a moment in time when I realised that I could become a Champion. Maybe if I had lost that fight, it could have altered my mindset, which was filled with self-belief. Would I have had the self-belief to continue in boxing if I had lost that fight? I was now thirty years old. I had been a professional boxer for thirteen years, and as I thought about my life, the ups and downs it brought me, and the loss of my dad and my mam’s and sister’s illnesses, my eyes filled with tears. I wasn’t crying. I was smiling. I was happy with who I was, where I was from, and the person I had become, and especially the way that my boxing journey had carved something incredibly special within me.

I couldn't wait to get in the shower and wash away the smell of the fight. I stood up, and the aches and pains of the gruelling twelve-round fight hit me like a sledgehammer. The hot water from the shower felt refreshing on my body. I washed all the Vaseline out of my hair, and the warm water sprayed onto my face and highlighted the slight swelling and bruising. My skin felt tight.

Amanda and I went to the after-party, where everyone waited to greet me, including Shaun, Kenny, and Shaun's sister Joanne. There were three important people missing from the party, and they were my mam, my sister, and Marty. I knew they couldn't make it. My mam was in a Nursing Home, Susan had to look after her young family, and Marty was working in Scotland. The room was packed with people, and the champagne was flowing, but I just had a pint of Guinness with a drop of lemonade. I had been there for about forty-five minutes when Amanda said. "I want to go home." I wanted to stay because it was a chance to wind down and see everyone, but I eventually gave in to her and agreed to leave the party early.

We arrived home, the house seemed so quiet compared to the noise of the arena, and then the after party, my ears were buzzing, and my hearing took time to adjust to the silence. Amanda's mother had babysat Jake that evening. I couldn't wait to hold him, he was only a few months old, and I pulled him out of his cot and cradled him. It felt amazing to be so close to that tiny little baby, who was completely unaware of the fight his dad had just been through. He slept the entire time I held him, then, after a while, I gently placed him back down in his little cot.

Amanda called me into the bedroom and said, "I don't know how to tell you this." And I was worried, "What is it? Just tell me." I was standing by the bed when she told me, "Your mam died today." I flopped down, sitting on the bed, trying to absorb the words that I had just been saying. I knew my mam had been poorly, but she was a fighter and always recovered from her bouts of illnesses. I couldn't believe that she had left me today of all days. I went from floating on air to feeling rock bottom in a second. "What time did she die?" Amanda didn't know the time of death when she lost her fight. "Why didn't anyone tell me before now?" I learned that Susan wanted to tell me because she needed comfort. Siblings need one another during a devasting time like this. We only had each other; she was our Mam. It was my Auntie Nina, my mam's sister, who told Susan not to tell me, which looking back, was definitely the right thing to do. I'm not sure if I could have performed well, or at all, knowing that my mam had died.

The fight had completely disappeared from my mind and was now filled with memories of my mam. I couldn't believe

I would never see her again or touch her. I wished I could have been there with her to say goodbye. I would have loved to have held her hand, comforted her, and spoken to her about all the good times that we shared as she lost her battle. I felt like I was in a dream as I lay down on the bed. I wanted to speak to my sister Susan. I needed to hear her voice. I wanted to know exactly what happened: Did our mam die alone? What time did she pass away? I had been fighting for a boxing title, and she had been fighting for her life. Was the ghostly visit last night my dad trying to tell me mam was going to join him? I wanted to leave London and go to Middlesbrough to be with my sister. I didn't sleep much that night and drove home to Middlesbrough the following morning to be with my family. The journey was long and emotional, and my body ached from head to toe. During the long journey home, I reminisced, thinking about my mam, dad, and my childhood. There was one consolation, though. She was now with my dad; they were together again for all eternity.

I stayed in Middlesbrough for a week to help Susan with the funeral arrangements etc. My mam had a lovely send-off, and later there was a spread laid on at a pub, The Albion in Southbank. My mam knew The Albion well. It was one of her local pubs over the years where she and her sisters Nina and Joan often drank. After the funeral, I wasn't in the mood to talk, but I tried my best to be sociable with everyone. I didn't feel like eating or drinking at the post-funeral gathering, and Sue didn't go. She couldn't face it. I spent some time being friendly to people, and it was traumatic for Susan and me. Even though our mam had been ill for many years, her passing was still a shock. When you lose the last parent, it's an end, it's a finalisation, a generation that has gone forever. It had been an emotional day, and I tried my best to be as sociable at the funeral party as possible even though I didn't really want to talk to anyone. As I came out of the toilet, someone said to me, "You've changed. You haven't got time for the likes of us." I replied, "I've just bloody buried my mother. What do you want me to do? Jump up and down?" Before I could say another word, John Trainer, my cousin, grabbed the man by the scruff of the neck and dragged him outside. I walked into the function room, and then about five minutes later, John walked back in and looked at me and nodded as if to say he won't be bothering you again. I was glad to see the day come to an end. I just wanted to be alone with my thoughts.

The following day I headed back to London. I was looking forward to seeing baby Jake. I wanted to try and get back to work to take my mind off the grief. I was feeling a bit lost. I knew it would take some time to recover from the loss of my mam. Jonathan rang and asked me if I was ready to get back to work. He said there might be a deal with the BBC. The money offered wasn't great, but the coverage of the deal meant that I could become a household name in the boxing world. The first fight was against a South African at

York Hall, Bethnal Green which would be held in a few weeks' time. It was another defence World Title fight.

My training was going well, I was still fit from the World Title fight, and I was looking forward to the opportunity to show my talent to the nation. A week before the fight, I was sparring with a Ghanaian boxer at a gym in Tottenham. We had planned on sparring for four rounds. During the final twenty seconds of the fourth round, I threw an overhand right which hit my sparring partner on the top of his head. It felt like hitting concrete. The pain immediately shot up my arm. I knew straight away that this was bad. I thought my hand was broken. I struggled to drive home, hoping that the injury wasn't as bad as I thought, but within two hours, the pain had increased and was unbearable. I went to Kingston hospital, and my hand was swollen and throbbing. I couldn't touch it. I went through the usual procedures at the hospital, and after the X-Ray results came back, I saw the doctor. He put the results on a screen and said, "The good thing is you haven't broken your hand, but the bad thing is you've knocked your knuckle out of joint." He pointed to the X-Ray on the lit screen and showed where the knuckle had been damaged, but I couldn't understand the image. The doctor said. "I don't know how much damage you have done. You will have to see a specialist." He asked me to make a fist, but I couldn't do it.

When I got home, I called Jonathan to give him the bad news about my hand. Jonathan asked if I wanted to see a specialist. I said yes, and an appointment was arranged for the following Monday afternoon. I saw the same specialist in Harley Street who looked after David Seaman and other sports stars who had suffered hand injuries. I was lucky to see him on short notice. He was very polite and looked at my hand. I told him that I had been to hospital and the X-Ray had shown that I hadn't broken my hand. I relayed the information that the doctor at the hospital had told me. He gave me a thorough examination and said, "I know exactly what you've done. You have ripped all your tendons along your metacarpal." I just wanted to know if I would be fit to box on Saturday, which was a few days away. I was worried. I asked him, "Could I have a cortisone injection to numb the pain during the fight," He went on to say, "Will the fight be worth your while financially?" I shook my head and said, "Not really." The doctor explained that having a cortisone injection just before the fight would numb my hand, but I wouldn't feel the pain and that I wouldn't be aware of any damage which would be inflicted on my hand. I wanted to fight, I had trained solidly for eight weeks, and this fight was my big break regarding exposure to a huge audience. I asked the doctor for his advice, and his words were, "You would have been better off breaking your hand, we would know where the problem was, but with your injury, it could take longer to heal."

The decision was made for me. I had to cancel the fight. I was devasted by the news that I couldn't fight. All my dreams were shattered. This accident was the final nail in the boxing coffin. I had been a professional boxer for a long time, and I realised that this was the beginning of the end of my boxing career, I had two more fights after the injury, but I had lost the spark and hunger that I once had. After I retired from boxing, I was lost for a while. I was doing various jobs which weren't boxing related. I was partying hard and rebelled against the sport for a long time. I used to go to a few of the Nightclubs in central London, String fellows, Browns, and Ministry of Sound. I often chatted with Peter Stringfellow, he was a northern lad too, and we always got on well. Because I had been a boxing champion, I had some perks in the Clubs, which allowed me to have free drinks, free admission, and a place in the V.I.P. area. During this partying period, I met a few interesting well-known characters. Some were from the gangster world, from the shady side; that way of life never interested me, and it's not something I wanted to get involved in. I had many opportunities to participate in the dark side of London business but always walked away. Some boxers get caught up with the wrong people after they retire. I had no intention of looking over my shoulder all the time. We are all fascinated with villains, intrigued about how they live their lives, and it wasn't a path I wanted to take. I had seen the results of gangster protection rackets and how they affected people, and I knew that life wasn't for me.

One evening I did meet someone who was a big name in the music industry. It was by chance that I was introduced to him in the V.I.P. area of a nightclub in London. I was talking to the owner of a club, who was also a good friend, and he told me he was busy and didn't have time to spend with me that evening and offered me the opportunity to sit with Tom Jones instead. I had a few drinks and was feeling merry. Nev said, "Do you want to sit with Tom Jones?" I've never been starstruck, and I always thought we are all human beings who must fart and shit like everybody else.

Over the years, I've met many famous people, and nine times out of ten, they are lovely, genuine human beings. It's the untalented wannabes that are normally up their own arseholes. Neville took me over to where Tom was sitting with his minder and a few other people. Tom had just finished a huge gig in London and was chilling out with a glass of champagne in his hand. Nev asked Tom if it was ok for me to sit at his table. He introduced me, and I told him that I was a former British and current World boxing Champion. Tom indicated for me to sit down next to him. I wonder if I had been a bricklayer or plumber, if I would have received the same respect, I doubt it. Tom asked me a few questions, and we started chatting about boxing, and one of the questions he asked was, "Who is your favourite fighter?" I said, "I like Roberto Duran." He chuckled and said, "Roberto doesn't like me because I'm good friends with Sugar Ray Leonard." I was impressed that he knew these iconic fighters whom I had admired since I was a kid. We talked for over an hour about boxing and nothing about music. Tom spoke of some great Welsh boxers and was impressed with Joe Calzaghe. I agreed with him that he was a great fighter. I enjoyed the conversation with him. He was a great guy who also had been given a gift, his amazing voice, which he shared with the world. Tom's minder interrupted us and pointed to his watch, saying that it was time to leave. He is now deservedly Sir Tom Jones, and it was a pleasure to have met him.

After the novelty of partying had worn off, I thought I would set up my own business and concentrate on making a living outside the boxing ring. From a young age, I committed my life to boxing and made many sacrifices, but it was all worth it. Although I never became a household name, boxing taught me that you must work hard, be persistent, and be brave, to be a man. I learned that nice guys get trodden on by ruthless bastards. I learned that I just had to be true to myself and be proud of whom I was, accepting my faults, including my stubborn nature. It took me years to realise that I had been given a gift that I used to the best of my ability. I realised that this gift should be passed on to others, and I started my own business training people, all kinds of people. It was rewarding to help others improve their fitness and boxing ability. I look back at my life and am grateful to the sport of boxing for providing me with a life fulfilled. I have met many amazing people along my life's journey, and I would like to take this opportunity to thank every single one of them, the good and the bad. They have all taught me how to be a decent human being. I hope my mam and dad are proud of me. I had a dream as a small boy in my shitty wellington boots when I visited Grangetown ABC due to the fatalistic encounter with my surrogate father, Marty Turner, whom I will be forever grateful. Marty was awarded the BCA in 2021, the British Citizen Award, for his services to the community. It was a big achievement for Marty and a well-deserved one. Without him, I wouldn't be where I am today. Thank you, Marty. I love you.

I somehow made my dream come true. I think anyone can fulfil their dreams if the desire is strong enough. Life is very short, and we should seize the day. My advice to anyone is to be happy in whatever you do and be kind to others. Find your gift and share it with the world.

Marty Turner Receiving the BCA Award In London On 30th September 2021

Cornelius Carr and Shawn Lacey at the Opening of the New Grangetown Boxing Club 2021 (Sited at the Old British Legion Club)

Printed in Great Britain
by Amazon

18030157R00200